WE ARE
INDIVISIBLE

WE ARE INDIVISIBLE

A Blueprint for Democracy After Trump

LEAH GREENBERG and EZRA LEVIN

ONE SIGNAL
PUBLISHERS

ATRIA

New York   London   Toronto   Sydney   New Delhi

**ONE SIGNAL
PUBLISHERS**

ATRIA

An Imprint of Simon & Schuster, Inc.
1230 Avenue of the Americas
New York, NY 10020

First One Signal Publishers/Atria Paperback edition May 2023

ONE SIGNAL PUBLISHERS / ATRIA PAPERBACK and colophon are
trademarks of Simon & Schuster, Inc.

For information about special discounts for bulk purchases,
please contact Simon & Schuster Special Sales at 1-866-506-1949
or business@simonandschuster.com.

The Simon & Schuster Speakers Bureau can bring authors
to your live event. For more information or to book an event,
contact the Simon & Schuster Speakers Bureau at 1-866-248-3049
or visit our website at www.simonspeakers.com.

Manufactured in the United States of America

1   3   5   7   9   10   8   6   4   2

Library of Congress Cataloging-in-Publication Data is available.

ISBN 978-1-9821-2997-2
ISBN 978-1-6680-2746-2 (pbk)
ISBN 978-1-9821-2998-9 (ebook)

*For the Indivisibles across the country
who took a Google Doc and turned it into a movement*

CONTENTS

Nineteen Indivisible Lessons   ix

Foreword by Marielena Hincapié   xi

Introduction   1

SECTION 1: What We're Up Against

Chapter 1: *The Problem: A Buckling and Rigged Democracy*   25

Chapter 2: *The Solution: Constituent Power*   59

SECTION 2: How We Win

Chapter 3: *How to Make Congress Listen*   93

Chapter 4: *How to Build Power Together*   151

Chapter 5: *How to Make Waves*   187

SECTION 3: A Blueprint for Democracy

Chapter 6: *A Day One Democracy Agenda*   233

Acknowledgments   309

Notes   313

NINETEEN INDIVISIBLE LESSONS

Indivisible Lesson #1:
Reelection, Reelection, Reelection
94

Indivisible Lesson #2:
Others Electeds Don't Care What You Think,
So Focus on Your Own
98

Indivisible Lesson #3:
People Have Opinions, Groups Have Power
103

Indivisible Lesson #4:
Get You Some Earned Media
108

Indivisible Lesson #5:
Pictures, or It Didn't Happen
113

Indivisible Lesson #6:
Don't Be Boring
123

Indivisible Lesson #7:
Beware of Fairy-Tale Tactics
131

Indivisible Lesson #8:
Partnerships, Partnerships, Partnerships (Partnerships)
140

Indivisible Lesson #9:
Don't Get Defensive About Your Privilege
156

Indivisible Lesson #10:
Follow Somebody Else
164

Indivisible Lesson #11:
Talk Is Cheap, So Ask for More
170

Indivisible Lesson #12:
Hold Your Friends Accountable
175

Indivisible Lesson #13:
Allyship Is a Process, Not an Identity
181

Indivisible Lesson #14:
The Virtuous Cycle of Advocacy and Elections
188

Indivisible Lesson #15:
Mobilizing Versus Organizing
197

Indivisible Lesson #16:
Fight to Win, Fight to Delay, Fight to Make It Hurt
205

Indivisible Lesson #17:
Primaries Are Good If We Make Them Good
213

Indivisible Lesson #18:
Electability Is a Mirage
217

Indivisible Lesson #19:
Vote Your Heart in the Primary;
Vote Your Head in the General Election
223

FOREWORD

When I was three, my family left Colombia, a country divided by civil war, and arrived in a new one that declared itself indivisible. So when my father, Arturo, was recruited to come to America to work in a textile factory, he and my mother, Teresa, like millions of immigrants and refugees before them, made the difficult decision to leave everything behind so that my siblings and I could have a better life.

My most formative memories are not of Medellín, Colombia, but of my new hometown, Central Falls, Rhode Island. One memory is indelible: standing up in second grade to recite words I didn't fully understand—"indivisible, with liberty and justice for all." I didn't speak much English then, but it served as an affirmation of why my parents had brought me here.

Growing up working-class, the youngest of ten kids, I became an interpreter for my parents and friends at schools, hospitals, and many government agencies. These experiences set me on a journey to become an attorney focused on issues of poverty, labor, and immigration. As executive director of the National Immigration Law Center, I have spent most of my career trying to help America live up to its promise of liberty and justice for all.

My work has long served to remedy fissures within our democracy that hid just under the surface. Donald Trump exploited those fissures, exposing Americans' cultural anxieties and economic insecurity by stoking fear of others, especially Black and brown immigrants, as a weapon to tear our country apart. Since that election night, I have thought about the word "indivisible." It holds new meaning for me. It should hold new meaning for us all. Our strength—and indivisibility—is not handed to us. We all must play a role in creating a country that lives up to its ideals.

This administration wasted no time enacting its xenophobic agenda, immediately issuing a series of executive orders aimed at instilling fear in immigrant communities. The first week was capped by the now-infamous Muslim ban prohibiting people from certain Muslim-majority countries from entering the United States. A relentless war against immigrants has been waged.

More than two years later the bonds we share across lines of difference have been tested. Whether by flooding the airports in support of Muslim immigrants, calling on Congress to protect Dreamers, fighting to preserve the Affordable Care Act, or showing up at the polls in November 2018, we have seen what we can do when we are indivisible. Our sacred democratic institutions, like the free press, free and fair elections, and the independence of our judiciary, endure only if we *believe* we are one nation.

Viewed from the top, American democracy is under aerial bombardment. But there's also the view from the bottom, where a democratic renewal is under way.

More ordinary Americans have shown up to defend each other and to stand up for American principles than at any other time during my life. America's better angels have sprung into action, rushed to airports across the country, marched, rallied, volunteered, donated, called their elected officials for the first time, held town halls, elected the most historically diverse House of Representatives, and elected state and local leaders who reflect our values.

And there to channel much of this grassroots power was the Indivisible movement born amid the resistance to Trump. Cofounders Leah Greenberg and Ezra Levin created a guide designed to make our representative democracy work for all of us by pointing the energy of millions of Americans toward Congress. When they first reached out to ask for my support of their new endeavor, I knew I was witnessing history in the making and that I had to do my part to help them and their growing membership.

Within weeks there were Indivisible chapters in every congressional district in the country, forcing members of Congress to listen to ordinary people's concerns. This is Indivisible's great contribution: they know that the fight for our democracy is not two years away at the voting booth. We must participate every day on the phone with our members of Congress, every week in district offices, and every month at town halls. This requires us not only to resist Trump but to build progressive power to create the America we want.

From the beginning, Indivisible's cofounders and national team understood that the attacks on immigrants were not actually about an antiquated immigration system that is broken by

design. They realized this administration's anti-immigrant policies are an assault on our democracy and an attempt to wrest
political power from the women and communities of color who
are increasingly participating in that democracy. They understand the invaluable role of standing in solidarity with impacted
communities and in working with grassroots leaders across the
nation to take action in Washington, D.C. Immigration is one
of the defining issues of our times. We are experiencing an existential crisis about what it means to be an American and who is
considered "worthy" of being an American. This is a fight for
the soul of our nation.

It's up to us to build a new America together. This fight
can be won only by reckoning with our past. When the Trump
administration began separating families at the U.S.-Mexican
border, thousands of Americans showed up again, this time for
the children ripped away from their parents. A refrain I heard
often at rallies was protestors declaring, "This isn't America."
But as many communities know, this is also America. We must
face the America that has failed to live up to its ideals in the
past. Family separation was U.S. policy when indigenous children were kidnapped, when Africans were enslaved, when Japanese Americans were interned, and still is today, when parents
in poverty have their children taken from them or when children lose their parents to mass incarceration. The suffragette
and abolitionist movements are American and so is segregation
and the separation of families. Our task now is to expect nothing less than a new America—to demand, every day, that our
policies live up to our aspirations.

That's why I hope every American who cares about democracy reads this book, a field guide, if you will, to restoring our faith in democracy. And I hope that, after finishing it, every American, looking out into our turbulent times, will ask, as Leah and Ezra and thousands of Indivisible members across the country are asking, "What more can I do?"

Marielena Hincapié
BOARD PRESIDENT, Indivisible Project
EXECUTIVE DIRECTOR, National Immigration Law Center
and NILC Immigrant Justice Fund

WE ARE
INDIVISIBLE

INTRODUCTION

WHY AN INDIVISIBLE BOOK?

We're writing this book because we believe American democracy is facing an existential threat, and we believe it can be saved.[1]

If you've picked up this book, you're probably worried about Donald Trump. And you should be! Trump has done previously unimaginable damage to our country. But Trump is not the source of the existential threat to our democracy. Trump is a symptom—a bulbous, bile-spewing symptom, but nonetheless just a symptom of a much more dangerous disease.

You might be skeptical. You might think Trump is a fluke, the product of Russian election tampering and James Comey's spectacularly bad judgment. And, sure, in the 2016 election, these factors helped tip the scales for Trump. But the only reason Putin or Comey mattered was because Donald Trump had already won a major party's nomination and was within striking

---

1. On a lighter note, we also know that saving democracy is a lot of fun, and we want more people doing it. Also, this is the first of many footnote asides, so buckle up. (If you're looking for citations, they're in the back of the book. There are lots of them because we're nerds.)

distance of the presidency. And in a healthy, functional democracy, there is just no way that someone like Trump—openly racist, brazenly misogynist, proudly ignorant, clearly unqualified to lead—gets anywhere close to that point.

If we had a society that valued the lives and dignity of all its people, Trump's campaign would have been over on his first day, when he attacked immigrants as rapists and drug-carrying criminals. Or when he attacked a pair of grieving Muslim Gold Star parents. Or when fourteen women accused him of sexual assault. That didn't happen. His support never collapsed. In fact, his bigoted appeals drew on deep currents of racism, sexism, and xenophobia that powered his rise.

If we had a healthy Republican Party, Trump would have never won the nomination. Or, when he did, his campaign would have faced defections from Republican elected officials appalled by his incendiary rhetoric, clear disrespect for democratic norms, and obvious unfitness to act as commander in chief. That didn't happen. Instead, once he was nominated, nearly every major Republican institution and officeholder lined up to elect Trump.

If we had a healthy political system, no one would have treated Clinton and Trump as comparable. Instead, Clinton was subjected to a barrage of wildly sexist coverage, Republicans lined up behind Trump, and the American public was treated to months of "both sides" back-and-forth media coverage. Clinton's email practices somehow ended up being framed as the equivalent of Trump's open racism, pathological lying, and authoritarian attacks on the press and his opponents.

If we had a functioning government with checks and balances, leaders of both parties would have reacted with bipartisan horror at the possibility of Russian interference in our elections and demanded answers. Trump would have been impeached after he fired FBI director James Comey, or in response to his ceaseless acts of flagrant corruption. That didn't happen. Instead, Republican members of Congress rallied to protect Trump from oversight or accountability.

In short, a healthy democracy would have fought off Trump the same way a healthy body fights off a virus. That didn't happen. The hard reality is that whatever part of our political system we've been counting on to protect us—the media, the political parties, the "elites," some sense of bipartisanship or national interest or common decency, some popular aversion to bigotry—all of it failed in 2016.

That means we can't just hope for the best in 2020. Getting Trump out of office is not going to fix the problems that allowed him to rise. Our political system is staggering from crisis to crisis, from one kind of dysfunction to the next, unable to address our society's problems. The Republican Party has been captured by an unholy alliance of white nationalists, Christian fundamentalists, and corporate interests—and they're systematically undermining democracy in order to consolidate their power. After Trump is gone—defeated, imprisoned, or both—these wounds will continue to fester. American democracy will not be healed unless we heal it.

But we're not writing a book because we're afraid. We're writing a book because we have hope that we can change this course. We're not hopeful in a warm and fuzzy Disney movie hero-inevitably-triumphs-over-evil kind of way. There's nothing inevitable about this story. It depends on overcoming entrenched, dangerous forces that are just fine with things as they are, thank you very much. Our hope is messier. It's the grit-your-teeth kind of hope rooted in experience, in a belief that, as bad as things are, there's still something we can do about it.

The "we" in the paragraph above includes *you*. It has to if we're going to win.

You're worried about American democracy. You know that it's under threat from Donald Trump and his enablers. Maybe you've marched, or called your member of Congress, or volunteered for a campaign. Maybe you've heard about this "Indivisible" movement or even been part of leading in your own community. Maybe you haven't done any of that. Maybe you don't yet know what to do or how to get involved. But you know something is very wrong with American politics and you want to be part of making it right.

We're with you, and this book explains how we can do this work together.

We believe the next few years will determine whether we have a truly inclusive democratic America, or something else—a continued descent into racist authoritarianism. We believe the only way to avoid that "something else" is to create a broad and lasting movement devoted to fixing our broken democratic norms and institutions. And we know we'll only win this fight if people all over the country understand the threats to our democracy, and how they can be part of saving it.

So we're writing this book to grow and strengthen a pro-democracy movement in America before it's too late. That movement is called Indivisible.

WHY SHOULD YOU CARE WHAT WE THINK?

We're not academics. We're not investigative journalists. We're not members of Congress. We're not running for president.[2] Our story is a bit weirder than that.

In 2016 we launched the Indivisible movement when we published a strategy for anti-Trump resistance, the *Indivisible Guide*.[3] To our amazement, thousands of locally led grassroots "Indivisible" groups formed and adopted our strategy. In red states, blue states, and purple states—in fact in every congressional district in the country—these new Indivisible groups began harnessing local power to stop Trump. By early 2017, Indivisible had become a nationwide phenomenon, the largest anti-Trump "resistance" operation in the country. As cofounders and co–executive directors of Indivisible, we've spent the past two years working directly with these grassroots leaders who joined the fight to stop Trump after his election in 2016. It's been a wild ride, and it's given us a unique vantage point into American politics and power in the late teens of the twenty-first century.

This was not a path we planned on taking. As of the 2016 election, we were a married couple steadily building our careers inside the Beltway. We were both former Capitol Hill staffers[4] turned do-gooder policy advocates, one of us working

---

2. Seriously.

3. It's available on our website, if you'd like to start at the beginning: indivisible .org/guide.

4. We started dating the weekend the Affordable Care Act passed the House in March 2010, when we were both House staffers for progressive members of Congress. Pretty solid weekend.

on poverty, one of us on human trafficking. But like so many folks around the country, the 2016 election threw us into the five stages of grief. We knew that an incoming Trump administration would threaten not just the issues we worked on but also everything else we cared about.

This put us out of step with some of our colleagues in polite professional circles of Washington, D.C. Immediately after the election, a lot of the political establishment seemed to be trying very hard to pretend that everything was normal. Policy wonks were hastily reworking the "transition memos" they'd prepared for the Clinton administration to deliver to Trump instead. Everyone was trying to track down the emails of the Trump staffers leading the transition so they could make contact. There was the usual speculation about who'd join the cabinet. Congressional Democratic leadership talked about it being their duty to find compromise with Trump.[5]

We knew we weren't alone in believing that this moment demanded not compromise but resistance. And as dark as the clouds on the horizon were, there was a silver lining: people around the country weren't just grieving. They were organizing. We were already starting to see it in the rapidly forming Women's March and a dozen new "resistance" Facebook groups in our own network of previously apolitical friends.

---

5. In fact, the same week in mid-November that a Trump lackey cited America's Japanese internment camps of World War II as a potential model for dealing with American Muslims, the incoming Democratic Senate minority leader Chuck Schumer explained to the *New York Times* that his plan was to find common ground with Trump on infrastructure. It seemed there was a looming bipartisan future in which there were would be no potholes on the roads to America's new internment camps.

They were pulling together protests. They were calling Congress. They were sharing homemade guides to resisting fascism and to evading surveillance. They were treating Trump like the threat he was, and they were looking for ways to stop him.

We wanted to help those people make their voices heard. Two policy wonks couldn't change what was happening in Washington, but maybe they could.

But how? As former congressional staffers, we didn't have many applicable skills, but we knew how Congress worked.[6] And we knew that local, organized pressure could have a powerful effect on Congress, because we'd seen it used against us by the Tea Party years before.[7] We could share that knowledge. We would write a quick, easy-to-share Google Doc laying out a strategy for how Americans could organize to block Trump's agenda. We could demystify Congress and show people how scaring the crap out of their own representatives was their most effective tool for resisting Trump.[8]

So, while home with family in Texas for Thanksgiving, we

---

6. If you ever wonder why so many congressional staffers become sellout lobbyists, this is mostly why: that's where the biggest demand is for their skill set. Also the money: they want the money.

7. The Tea Party was super-racist and sometimes violent, but the early iteration of the movement was smart about strategy and tactics. They focused on their own elected officials locally, and they relentlessly fought back against President Obama's agenda.

8. Our first draft literally opened with "The key to stopping Donald Trump is scaring the crap out of your member of Congress." (We meant it in a totally nonviolent-resistance sort of way.)

bailed on all our social plans and hammered out a draft guide.[9] We started passing it around to our friends and former congressional colleagues for thoughts. Some offered edits.[10] Some told us our careers in Washington would be over if we published it. Some did both. We tried very hard to get some of the people who worked on the initial draft to list themselves as coauthors, just so we'd have a little extra cover. Almost all declined. There were good reasons to be nervous about being attached to this publicly. The guide urged obstruction as a virtue; it flew in the face of everything "smart" establishment Democrats in D.C. were saying about working with the incoming Trump administration.

We had no idea how our bosses would react to it. We might end up being trolled by right-wingers and Breitbart. We might end up tanking our careers. We seriously considered just releasing it anonymously. But we also didn't want to create some sort of mystery around authorship; we wanted people focused on the strategy. So in the end we said "Screw it" and just went ahead and put our names on it. Only two former staffers agreed to do the same: Angel Padilla and Jeremy Haile.

After a few weeks of edits, we gave it a name: *Indivisible: A Practical Guide for Resisting the Trump Agenda*, and we tweeted out a link to the Google Doc to our handful of Twitter fol-

---

9. Leah: Much to the annoyance of Ezra's Texas family, who kept trying to get us to close our laptops and interact with them like normal people.

10. While we got edits from a half dozen or more people, nobody contributed more substantive and substantial edits than Matt Traldi, a longtime friend and labor organizer. Early strategy sessions for what would become Indivisible were always in our living room or Matt's. He would go on to be instrumental in building the Indivisible national operation, becoming chief operating officer.

lowers. It was twenty-three pages long and full of typos, and within a matter of hours it would completely upend our lives.[11]

At its heart, the *Indivisible Guide* was a short civics textbook with a snarky edge. It made one central claim: nothing that happens over the next four years will happen because of Trump; it'll happen because of what Congress does or doesn't do. And our members of Congress answer to us, which means we have power.

We recommended that readers form a local group of like-minded friends, neighbors, or random folks and pressure their own members of Congress, much like the Tea Party did. We were so bold as to suggest that readers call their local group "Indivisible," but we left it up to them. It was a basic plan: organize locally and pressure Republicans and Democrats alike. Make yourselves a constant presence in your elected representatives' lives. Show up at congressional district offices, pack their town halls, flood offices with calls, and never give an inch. It was simple, really.

Now, usually when you write a political manifesto and put it on the Internet, nothing happens. And that was pretty much what we were expecting. We hoped our friends would read it and share it with their families when they went home for Christmas. We thought that sometime in the next few months we might get an email from someone, somewhere in the country, saying they'd used the guide to ask a question at a town hall, and that would make us feel great.

---

11. Ezra: I'll never forget Liz Ramey, who would eventually join the Indivisible national staff, coming over to our house a couple of days later with a printed-out, marked-up copy helpfully pointing out all the typos we'd missed.

Instead, two unexpected things happened pretty much immediately after we posted it.[12]

First, the *Indivisible Guide* went viral. A flood of web traffic crashed the Google Doc. Journalists and celebrities were finding it and sharing it online. Robert Reich posted it to his Facebook page. George Takei tweeted it out. We were flooded with media interview requests. Our Twitter accounts exploded with new followers. Our bosses found out. (Fortunately for us, they were very nice about it.)

Second, and much more important, people around the country started putting the *Indivisible Guide* into action. We could tell because they were flooding our in-box by the thousands—with excitement, and thanks, and follow-up questions. We'd tapped into a massive surge of local organizing that was already beginning to take shape in towns and communities around the country. We hadn't aspired to create the playbook or the umbrella name that so many new grassroots leaders would adopt, but here we were.

We had to somehow deal with this barrage of incoming messages from people all over the country, and so we pulled in friends, coworkers, and every grieving campaign staffer we could find. In a matter of days, we had gathered dozens of people at our house and started organizing them into teams.[13]

---

12. Actually, the first thing that happened is we were overwhelmed with emails, many of which said something to the effect of "This guide is full of typos." Turns out if you want something copyedited, a good strategy is just to put it online and let strangers have at it.

13. We spread the volunteers across fifteen working groups, each with their own set of leaders, helpers, and approvers: Legal, Financial, Partnerships, Email

The web and design team created an online map of the United States and asked people to register if they wanted to create an Indivisible group. New group leaders had to commit to three things: resist Trump's agenda, uphold progressive values, and put the *Indivisible Guide* into action through local advocacy. In those early days, we got an email ping each time one registered: Indivisible Greenville, Indivisible Concord, Indivisible Front Range Resistance.[14] The first day we got about two hundred groups; within a few weeks we had thousands.

The Indivisible national team kept expanding. We drafted a former Obama campaign staffer, Julia Fox, who assembled a field team of volunteers assigned to cover each state and respond to the groups reaching out to us. We created a team of policy wonks who feverishly analyzed the latest news from Congress and turned their findings into activist-ready strategic updates. We created an enormous volunteer email team dedicated just to replying to the thousands of incoming questions and requests. Other teams were translating the *Indivisible Guide* into Spanish, organizing and filing stories coming in from around the

---

Response, Field, Story Collection, Volunteer Management, Data Management, Press, Social Media, Web, Design and Brand, Congressional District Targeting, Congressional Demystification, and Guide Updates/New Content. If this sounds like a chaotic mess to you, you should have seen our living room in early 2017.

14. We'd put a throwaway line in the "How to Form a Group" chapter recommending that people give their groups a name that made clear they were local, offering as the example "Springfield Indivisible Against Hate," and adding "You are also 100 percent welcome to pick up and run with the Indivisible name if you want, but we won't be hurt if you don't." People used the word.

country, and finding a lawyer to confirm that none of this was going to get us in any legal trouble. Anyone with press experience was helping us triage reporters and connect them to local groups. A guy who happened to have a Twitter account was put in charge of social media.[15]

We didn't sleep. We bought donuts and pizza for the volunteers now camped out at our house, but we were too scared and too amped to eat. Trump was taking office, and the world was terrifying. But something beautiful was coming together across the country, and we were right in the middle of it from our living room in D.C. By February 2017, there were Indivisible groups in every single congressional district in the country, from the bluest blue district to the reddest red.

And these newly formed Indivisible groups had a lot of follow-up questions. They needed ways to connect with other people interested in resisting Trump in their communities. They wanted to know what was happening in Congress, how to respond to the Muslim ban, how to cope with the flood of information coming at them, how they could be most strategic *right this minute*. They were reporting back as they took actions, sending us video clips and priceless stories that we turned around and pitched to national media. They were asking us how to *do stuff*, from renting meeting space to getting legal support to building their membership to raising money.

We had no idea who to connect them to. Whose job is it to help fuel a social movement?

---

15. He was removed shortly afterward when it turned out he wasn't actually very good at Twitter. He helped out in other ways. Thanks, Chad!

As it turned out, it was ours. We couldn't just put the *Indivisible Guide* and a few follow-up resources online and walk away. The future of our democracy was on the line. We had catapulted ourselves into the center of a nascent grassroots political movement and had an obligation to do everything we could to help it grow.

So we built up a national operation to support, coordinate, and uplift this burgeoning movement. We reluctantly and awkwardly sent out an email asking our growing email list for money to start an organization.[16] The response was overwhelmingly enthusiastic: donations poured in from across the country, often from the very folks who were also building their own Indivisible groups.[17] In early 2017, we quit our jobs and started hiring our first staff. For more than two years now, we've been the co–executive directors of Indivisible. Our mission has been simple: to support the local Indivisible groups all over the country that are working to stop Trump, and to build progressive power.

And we've seen that work up close. We've traveled the country, meeting with thousands of Indivisible members (af-

---

16. Casey Hogle, who had been volunteering for the nascent Indivisible effort since the guide launched, had been trying to convince us for weeks to do this. We were embarrassed to ask for money, but she was right. We needed resources to make the effort sustainable, and the best way to fuel a grassroots movement was with grassroots dollars. Casey would go on to become Indivisible's national development director.

17. This became particularly ironic a few months later when right-wing media tried to discredit us by saying that we were paying people to protest around the country. We could honestly say that the reverse was happening: the protestors were actually funding us.

fectionately called "Indivisibles") in hundreds of local Indivisible groups, from Oregon to Tennessee to Massachusetts. We've knocked on doors with Indivisibles in Wimberley, Texas; we've spoken to crowds of Indivisibles in Prescott, Arizona; we've held trainings for Indivisibles in Atlanta, Georgia; we've gotten drunk with the Indivisibles of New Jersey and Pennsylvania. In blue states, red states, and purple states, we've conspired with the local Indivisible leaders pushing the limits of what is politically possible in the Trump era.

We've seen what it looks like when people power lands in Washington, D.C. We've orchestrated pressure campaigns targeting Republican and Democratic members of Congress alike. We've been in closed-door meetings with congressional leadership, imploring them to listen to their grassroots base and fight back against Trump. We've been uninvited from these meetings in retaliation for our advocacy, and we've been welcomed back in recognition of the movement's power.

We've been there for the victories, defeats, and stalemates. We've seen where this local power has worked and where it hasn't, and the reasons why. We've worked with local Indivisible groups across the country to kill the repeal of the Affordable Care Act, stand in solidarity with the communities under threat from Trump's white supremacy and xenophobia, turn the Trump tax scam into a political liability, and build a historic wave election in 2018.

Through it all, we've learned, led, and been led by the local Indivisible leaders across the country. We've watched as they've grown from shell-shocked gatherings of friends and neighbors into political powerhouses. We've heard the stories of men and women moving from despair to action: finding their voices, building their power, and changing the political world.

We're not done yet. The movement is evolving. The challenge that lies before us is not just to stop Trump. It's to stop *Trumpism*—the forces that allowed Trump to rise and take power. It's to demand a democracy that finally, truly represents the people—all the people. We've seen where Indivisible and the anti-Trump resistance has been, and we have a sense of where it's going. That's our expertise.

WHAT'S IN THIS BOOK?

The book is part movement memoir, part civics how-to guide, and part blueprint for doing away with Trump and building a real representative democracy after he's gone. That's a lot, so we split it into three sections.

Section 1 is "What We're Up Against." Before we can talk about how we'll cure what ails our democracy, we've got to understand the disease itself. It's dangerous to treat Trump like a complete aberration or to put all the blame on him.[18] American democracy is in crisis not just because of Trump but because of real structural flaws in our system and a long-term campaign by powerful reactionary forces to undermine representative rule. Trump has benefited from this campaign, and he has accelerated it, but he did not invent it.

---

18. By all means, though, put a ton of blame on Trump. He's a sleazy walking blob of corruption and racism whose most grotesque acts are matched in scale only by his staggering incompetence. We're not fans.

In Chapter 1, we describe the forces that are causing our political system to come apart at the seams. We've got to face a hard truth: the representative democratic system that the Founding Fathers gave us is quite simply not built to handle ideologically polarized parties playing constitutional hardball. Every other country in the world with a presidential system of democracy like ours has eventually collapsed into gridlock, dysfunction, hyperpolarization, and escalating crisis.

Sound familiar?

This structural problem is being exacerbated by another hard truth: one of the parties has fallen off an ideological cliff. The Republican Party has been taken over by white nationalists, Christian fundamentalists, and corporate interests. And these reactionary elites are not stupid: they read the same demographic data we do. They understand the country is getting more diverse and more unequal. They know that, given the chance, this changing electorate will reject their reactionary policies. And so they have worked tirelessly for decades to sabotage our democracy and rig it in their favor. From packing the courts with ideologues to gerrymandering themselves into safe districts to gutting voting rights and disenfranchising voters—especially voters of color—to filibustering to death popular proposals, these elite reactionaries have done incalculable damage to American democratic institutions. And the frightening thing is that it's working.

So what do you do when a radical minority is systematically undermining democracy to entrench their power? The only solution for what ails our democracy is more democracy—and the only thing that gets us that is constituent power. Because while our political system is bruised and battered, it hasn't totally collapsed yet. We still have power—if we're prepared to use it.

Chapter 2 explains what this "constituent power" thing is and what we're going to need: mass civic engagement to pressure and replace our elected officials. It describes the role of constituent power in American political history and the historical precedents that make us believe this is possible, from the local civic engagement institutions of the nineteenth and twentieth centuries to, ironically enough, the Tea Party.

We all know by now that the Trump era has sparked an upsurge in American civic engagement. Indivisible and grassroots groups in communities all across the country, led largely by people who were never involved in politics before, are putting a modern spin on an age-old American tradition. It's been decades since the country has seen this sort of wide-scale, locally led, nationally networked civic engagement infrastructure. The multi-decade decline of civic engagement may have reached an inflection point. Indivisible is here for the upswing.

Which brings us to Section 2 of the book: "How We Win." It describes, well, how we win. It's a practical guide to building and harnessing constituent power. This section is rooted in our firsthand experience with Indivisible: leading and being led by local Indivisible groups that are building power and changing politics. This is partly our own narrative and partly based on interviews and surveys of hundreds of Indivisible leaders from across the country.

The first years of the Trump era have been packed with political intrigue: clashes between political parties, clashes within parties, and clashes between an aging Washington establishment and a burgeoning grassroots movement that was—and is!—fed up with fecklessness and failure. But Section 2 is more than storytelling: this section of the book is intended to be practical and actionable. To that end, throughout the narratives, we draw out key lessons for building power locally. We outline nineteen "Indivisible Lessons," to be precise,[19] from models for building local groups to tactics for getting earned media to strategies for holding friends and opponents accountable.

We split Section 2 into three action-oriented chapters: how to make Congress listen, how to build power together, and how to make waves.

Chapter 3 is where the real-world magic begins. We dive back into the world of the *Indivisible Guide* to explain how your elected officials think and how to use what they care about to make them listen to you.[20] We go over the practical principles of organizing locally to have an impact nationally. And then we put it into action, telling the story of the Indivisible movement's explosive growth and desperate effort to defeat Trump's top legislative priority of his first year in office: repealing the Affordable Care Act. From congressional town halls to die-

---

19. You might say there are an indivisible number of Indivisible lessons, but you'd be a nerd if you said that.

20. Spoiler: They wake up every morning thinking about reelection. That's basically it.

ins to late-night confrontations on the Senate floor, this was a legislative battle with many twists and turns—and a bunch of lessons about how to effectively apply constituent power.

In Chapter 4, we talk about building power the Indivisible way—and that means talking about privilege, responsibility, and partnership. We discuss what it means to get political and organize in the age of Trump and what standing in solidarity with the people under attack means—especially for those of us who bring real personal privilege and power to the fight. We draw out these lessons by telling the story of how Indivisible showed up after Trump launched his attack on immigrant youth and the Deferred Action for Childhood Arrivals (DACA) program.

In Chapter 5, we answer the question: What should you do when your electeds just won't listen? The answer is: Get busy replacing them. That's what Indivisible did in building the blue wave that gave Democrats control of the House in 2018. The sweeping progressive wins of the midterms didn't happen in a vacuum but were instead the result of painstaking political work carried out over two long years. This chapter tells the story of how the grassroots won, and what we'll need to do to build waves and retake power in the years to come.

But where are we going, and what do we do after the next blue wave? We answer that in Section 3, "A Blueprint for Democracy." Chapter 6 closes the book with a reform agenda for American democracy after Trump, a democracy that actually represents the people. That means breaking the gridlock in Washington, then moving on a bold agenda to reform our national institutions, from Congress to the Supreme Court to voting rights to the media. It's an agenda to make democracy inclusive and functional, rooted in the radical belief at the heart of Indivisible: in a representative democracy, your representative ought to represent you.

The best part is that every part of this agenda could be introduced on day one of the new Congress in 2021. A simple majority vote by Congress and signature from the (new) president is all that's necessary. No need for constitutional amendments or revolutionary overthrow. Just good old-fashioned legislation that could remake our political system to actually respond to the will of the people. And it all could be enacted in 2021. This isn't some far-off vision of utopia. This is a world we can build—and build faster than you might think.

WHAT'S NEXT?

This book is meant to stand on its own as an engaging take on the role of power in American politics and the potential future for our democracy. We hope it's a good read, but that's just the start. Indivisible is, most of all, defined by action. We want you in this movement, and that means doing more than just reading a book.

It doesn't matter if you have just an hour a month or an hour a day: you can be part of saving American democracy. There's valuable work you can do in this movement. We need you. Here are three immediate action items to take between reading this introduction and starting the rest of the book:

1. **Join up with Indivisible nationally.** Go to book.indivisible .org to be part of the nationwide Indivisible movement and join the conversation. Shoot us a tweet at @leahgreenb and @ezralevin if you want to get in touch directly.

2. **Join up with Indivisible locally.** Find your local Indivisible group and go to their next in-person meeting. Or if you want to start your own Indivisible group, great! There's a full-time Indivisible organizer covering your state who can help. Go to indivisible.org to find or start your own local Indivisible group.

3. **Join the fight for democracy.** We need people demanding that candidates and elected officials get behind the reforms to save democracy discussed in this book. Go to savedemocracy.org to get engaged in this fight.

We will not save American democracy if we rely on political elites to change the system out of the goodness of their hearts. Most of them have been doing just fine under the rigged rules. They like things the way they are, and they're going to fight like hell to keep them that way, regardless of political party.

That's where we come in. We're building something new together. Indivisible is an ongoing nationwide experiment. It's constantly growing and changing in response to the realities of the moment and the leadership of real people on the ground who own and build their local Indivisible groups. If you're reading this, you qualify to participate in this experiment. You can be an Indivisible leader, and in fact we need you to be.

Together we can make our representatives represent us,

and we can replace them when they fail to perform that basic function. Our goal is to build a more perfect union, a democracy that really represents the American people. It's not what we have now, but it's something we have the power to build. And the way we will build it is with local groups of constituent power in every community in the country. If we stand indivisible together, we will win. This books shows how.

SECTION 1:

What We're Up Against

1

The Problem:
A Buckling and Rigged Democracy

I don't want everybody to vote . . . As a matter
of fact, our leverage in the elections quite candidly
goes up as the voting populace goes down.
—PAUL WEYRICH, *cofounder of the Heritage Foundation
and architect of the modern conservative movement, 1980*

I had never realized that if you want a democracy,
you have to fight for it.
—OGIE STROGATZ, *California Indivisible group leader*

On November 8, 2016, we hosted the worst house party of
our lives.

The day started off well. We'd just come off a weekend canvassing for Hillary in Philadelphia with a dozen friends. We'd
voted at the elementary school across the street from our house
in Washington, D.C.[1]

---

1. Leah: When I voted, I picked up an extra "I Voted" sticker so that I could
   wear one and save one for posterity, in honor of the first female president.

Around 7:00 p.m., our friends—a collection of former Hill staffers, think tank policy wonks, and Obama administration officials—started to arrive at our house. We opened the champagne at 7:30 p.m. The mood was celebratory; the biggest concern was that Democrats might not take the Senate. Somewhere around 9:00 p.m., it became clear that this was not, in fact, the biggest problem we needed to worry about.

Things went downhill fast. Some guests recognized reality faster than others. Some people started crying, others started yelling, others started to quietly trickle out. The few who remained hit the bourbon hard, then fell into an intense argument about Hillary versus Bernie. At some point we gave up on our hosting duties, wished the remaining guests well in their increasingly heated debate, and went to bed.[2] As we fell asleep that night, we were scared, angry, confused, and shocked—basically just totally lost.

The coming days were surreal. The next morning, the streets of D.C. were eerily quiet. People were sitting on the metro and walking around downtown with tears openly streaming down their faces. Our community of D.C. progressive policy friends were stunned. Like, deer-in-the-headlights-that's-also-just-taken-a-brick-to-the-face stunned. This was supposed to be the crowd who knew stuff about policy and politics. But no one had answers and no one knew what was coming next.

And it wasn't just D.C. Nationwide, excitement for the first

---

2. The guests went on to have a thoughtful, constructive conversation that definitively resolved the question of whether Bernie would have been a stronger candidate in a way that left everyone with deep respect for each other. Just kidding! That's never happened. Stop arguing about 2016.

female president had given way to horror at the prospect of a Trump administration. Not everyone on our side of the aisle was shocked: plenty of people, especially people of color, had been warning that a Trump victory was all too possible. But everyone was devastated.

A sense of shock, horror, pain, shame, and loss were being felt in homes of future Indivisible leaders around the country. For Ivonne Wallace Fuentes of Roanoke, Virginia, it "seemed like reality had just broken in half in a really important way." In San Antonio, Texas, Trish Florence was "gobsmacked" on election night. Her two children are autistic, and when she told them the following morning, they both broke down in tears. At school, bullies chanted "Trump! Trump! Trump!" at her older son. In Arizona, Gabriella Cazares-Kelly and April Ignacio of the Tohono O'odham Nation were deeply concerned: the Tohono O'odham lands straddled the border, and with Trump's election, the threat that a wall would divide their community was suddenly imminent. Joyce Vansean of New Orleans "spent a lot of time crying and a lot of time trying to come to terms with what my country had just done." Those who moved quickly from grief to action found that they had company: in Tampa, Florida, a devastated Christine Hanna created a Facebook group for Tampa-area women the day after the election. By evening, she had a thousand members of what would eventually become Indivisible Action Tampa Bay.

The overwhelming feeling was one of fear. Fear of what the election of Donald Trump meant for the policy gains of the Obama administration. Fear of what this election meant for the people Trump had openly promised to harm: Muslims, Dreamers and other immigrants, refugees, and more. Fear of what this meant for the Supreme Court.

Fear, fundamentally, of what this meant for democracy itself.

We were right to be afraid, then and now. Trump is a uniquely grotesque human in a position of immense power, an aggressively ignorant buffoon whose authoritarian instincts and malice are only outweighed (when we're lucky) by his incompetence.

But while Trump's election was a shock to our democratic system, the system had already been weakened long before he arrived on the scene. That's why this chapter, this book—this whole Indivisible *movement*—is not about Donald Trump. It's about what allowed him to take power. It's about what came before Trump and what will remain after he is defeated or imprisoned or both.

It's not exactly provocative anymore to say that America's political system is broken or rigged. We're not here to convince you of that. You probably feel it in your bones. You probably know the system doesn't respond to the people's will. You know that big donors and corporations extract from the political system the way strip miners extract from a mountaintop. You probably know that the whole mess—from campaigns, to the courts, to officeholders, to ex-officeholder lobbyists—is a colossal revolving door of privilege and greed.

The point of this chapter isn't to convince you of this; it's to disentangle the various strands of dysfunction and shine a light on the forces behind the breakdown. This can all seem convoluted and overwhelming and impossible to grasp at first, but we think it can actually be understood as a relatively simple story with two parts: our democracy is buckling, and our democracy is rigged.

Part 1: Democracy buckling. American democracy just wasn't built for what we're dealing with now—and it's coming apart at the seams. The Founders didn't foresee two political parties like we have now, and for most of our history we didn't have them. Since the 1960s, the parties have grown ideologically distinct; they've polarized. That polarization, overlaid on top of our outdated democratic institutions, is a recipe for gridlock and dysfunction—and it's only going to get worse. Our democracy is buckling.

Part 2: Democracy rigged. Our democracy isn't just falling apart on its own; it's being intentionally rigged. An unholy alliance between wealthy plutocrats, practitioners of white identity politics, and religious ideologues has produced a reactionary conservative party—and they're systematically rigging the rules to keep themselves in power. They know that a truly representative democracy will reject their unpopular social and economic agenda. So they're doing their best to prevent that from happening. Our democracy is being rigged.

If we're ever going to fix the system and save our democracy, we need to understand how it came to be so broken and rigged in the first place. The following pages describe what we're up against.

PART 1: OUR DEMOCRACY IS BUCKLING

About three decades ago, Juan José Linz, a Yale political scientist and expert on totalitarianism and authoritarianism, wrote an essay called "The Perils of Presidentialism." The essay made a simple point: the presidential model of democracy, which divided power between the presidency and separately elected legislative branches, was inherently unstable. It naturally led to conflict between the president and the legislative branches, producing gridlock, brinkmanship, and escalating levels of dysfunction. Many countries had adopted presidential models in the early transition to representative democracy; overwhelmingly, they either reformed into parliamentary systems or devolved into violent conflict.[3]

This model was so unstable, in fact, that literally no country on the planet that tried it was able to sustain it for very long. There was, at the time of Linz's writing, only one exception: the United States.

What made us different? For our entire history, we had been running this outdated, beta version of democracy. So why hadn't our system crashed yet? Linz had thoughts on that too. The United States, he argued, had uniquely weird political parties.[4] Yes, there were Democrats and Republicans, but the parties were not ideologically polarized. There were conservative Democrats and liberal Republicans; there were liberal Democrats and conservative Republicans. These ideologically

---

3. Many of these countries were dominated by U.S. foreign policy interventions and—surprise!—adopted U.S.-style presidential systems. So you could say the United States has been a major exporter of political instability, but that's a topic for a different book.

4. We're taking some liberties with paraphrasing here. Linz did not literally call American political parties "uniquely weird."

all-over-the-map political parties could work out conflict and cut deals because they were each so incoherent. That lack of party polarization, Linz argued, was what allowed American democracy to keep chugging along.

But Linz wrote that decades ago. And things have changed.

A brief history of how we got here

Since the Civil War, there have been two major political parties on the ballot every year: Democrats and Republicans. But these were not the parties we know today. Each had been shaped by the battle lines of the Civil War, and as a result, each contained within it enormous racial, ideological, and regional variation. As the party of Lincoln, the Republicans attracted Black voters *and* rich white Northern businessmen but remained toxic to Southern whites. Democrats brought together a broad coalition of working-class immigrants in the North and a white cross-class base in the South. It was sort of a bizarro world version of modern American politics.

In the decades following the Civil War, if you were an elected official, the "D" or "R" next to your name didn't have much to do with your ideology. Both parties had reformers and populists and business interests and reactionaries. Both parties had pro–civil rights and segregationist factions. There were conservative Democrats and liberal Republicans, and vice versa. When you were in power, if you couldn't move your agenda with just members of your own party, you could usually do it by co-opting a faction of the other party. Each party's internal incoherence created room—and necessity—for bi-partisan legislating.[5]

In this golden age of bipartisan legislating, American democracy "worked"—or at least, it worked for some people. The kinds of compromises this system produced often depended on reaching agreements involving segregationist factions, which meant that even recent twentieth-century liberal policy advances routinely excluded people of color. Progressive-era reforms under Republican Teddy Roosevelt and Democrat Woodrow Wilson either offered little for people of color or actively reversed gains previously made. Wilson didn't just do nothing; he actively resegregated the federal workforce, defended the Ku Klux Klan, and told Black civil rights activists that "segregation is not humiliating, but a benefit, and ought to be so regarded by you gentlemen." Democrat Franklin Delano Roosevelt explicitly excluded farmworkers and service jobs from the original Social Security Act—a concession to segregationist Southern Democrats who didn't want Black and brown people benefiting from the new program.

The Great Depression and Roosevelt's New Deal populist policy agenda triggered a realignment within the parties on economics, with organized labor lining up behind the Democratic Party and business interests consolidating with the Republicans. But the racial divide within each party remained. The factions within the Democratic Party started

---

5. Don't throw down the book yet. Nobody associated with this book is aiming to "make America great again." We're under no illusions that post–Civil War America was some sort of paragon of political virtue, and so we're not pining for this mythical historical past. Read on.

to fracture after World War II as the civil rights movement forced the political system to grapple with segregation. In 1948, future vice president Hubert Humphrey fought to include civil rights in the Democratic Party platform, arguing that "the time has arrived for the Democratic Party to get out of the shadows of states' rights and to walk forthrightly into the bright sunshine of human rights." The argument won the day and also led directly to an immediate fissure in the party as Southern Democrats, or "Dixiecrats," staged a walkout from the convention.

In the mid-1960s, the internal tensions within the parties on race gave way to full-fledged transformation. Supported and pushed by a powerful Black-led, multiracial, and multifaith civil rights movement, Democratic president Lyndon Johnson passed a series of landmark civil rights bills with a bipartisan group of non-segregationist Democrats and liberal Republicans.[6] While Johnson was signing the Civil Rights Act of 1964, the Voting Rights Act of 1965, and the Fair Housing Act in 1968, segregationist Southern Democratic leaders like Strom Thurmond and his fellow Dixiecrats were jumping ship. They would not return.

The rise of a hard-right ideological force in the Republican Party offered Dixiecrats an appealing new home. Barry

---

6. It should go without saying that this was not a benevolent and unilateral decision on the part of Johnson or other elected leaders in the political system; it was the result of the power that had been built and applied to them by the civil rights movement, from pushing for inclusion through the Mississippi Freedom Democratic Party to forcing the Voting Rights Act onto the table through the Selma march.

Goldwater, the segregationist Republican candidate for president in 1964, lost in a landslide but nonetheless managed to flip much of the Deep South—an unthinkable feat for the party of Lincoln.[7] Johnson saw what was happening at the time: upon signing the 1964 Civil Rights Act, he told one of his aides, "I think we just delivered the South to the Republican Party for a long time to come." And indeed, President Richard Nixon's infamous "Southern strategy" revived Goldwater's efforts to bring anti–civil rights voters into the Republican Party while maintaining a strong alliance with corporate power.

This strategy neatly synced up with Republican courting of white evangelicals. Rapid movement on both civil rights and women's rights—including the 1973 *Roe v. Wade* decision protecting the right to abortion—were driving a backlash among white evangelicals that swiftly evolved into a powerful political force within the Republican Party.[8] Meanwhile, as Democrats bled conservative whites, they also continued to attract more and more voters of color.

So the 1960s were a major turning point for the Democratic and Republican parties—one that continues to define our politics today. Gradually, the Democrats became a party of multi-

---

7. Goldwater won nearly 70 percent of the vote in Alabama, which just a few years earlier had voted strongly against Republican Dwight Eisenhower for both election and reelection.

8. We're not doing justice to the rise of the Christian right here, because frankly, that history could fill a book (and already has filled many). The only note we'll make is that the Christian right has firmly lined up behind a twice-divorced charlatan who has allegedly paid hush money to at least one porn star with whom he had an affair. There's something more complicated than Jesus's teachings going into the hero worship here, so we'll just acknowledge that and keep it moving.

racial coalition builders with a center-left economic agenda,[9] while the Republicans became a largely white and culturally and fiscally conservative party. Slowly but surely, liberal Republicans and conservative Democrats retired, switched parties, or were defeated in primary elections. By the time Donald Trump won the presidency, the most liberal Republican in Congress was almost always more conservative than the most conservative Democrat.

These are the political parties we have today, one conservative and one left of center.[10] There's some real ideological variation within the parties, but on the whole the two parties are more internally homogenous than ever before in modern American history. We call these political parties "polarized."

So that thing that the political scientist Linz argued shored up the stability of America's presidential democracy? Unpolarized parties? Yeah, we don't have that anymore.

Polarization + American political institutions = trouble
Now, polarized parties aren't inherently bad. In fact, another synonym for "polarized" might be "coherent." And there are good

---

9. Not that the Democratic Party is unified on its economic agenda. It's outside the scope of this book, but there's a battle playing out within the party between anti-monopolist economic populists and the pro–big business Wall Street wing of the party. If you want an overview, Matt Stoller, firmly an anti-monopolist partisan, tracks this development in an *Atlantic* piece, "How Democrats Killed Their Populist Soul." And if you actually want to read a book on it, pick up Thomas Frank's (of *What's the Matter with Kansas?* fame) *Listen, Liberal: or, What Ever Happened to the Party of the People?*, published months before Trump's election.

10. Foreshadowing part two of this story, while the Republican Party has gradually become a full-on conservative party, the Democratic Party has not become a full-on progressive party. More on that to come.

reasons why a representative democracy should have coherent parties. It gives you a choice between real alternatives. In a functioning system, you ought to be able to choose the party or candidate you support based on their agenda, and if they win, they ought to be able to enact that agenda and be judged on the results.

That's not what happened under the early twentieth-century system of ideologically wacky parties. You could vote for a populist Democrat in the Midwest and accidentally empower the archconservative segregationist Democrats of the South. You could vote for Republicans based on their civil rights record and end up with a bunch of anti-union attacks. The legislation passed in Washington was often only loosely related to the results of the last election. But at the same time, these weird internal contradictions within each of the two parties were fundamental to forging common ground over much of the twentieth century. It just might not have been the common ground you voted for.[11]

Today, as a voter, you've got a better idea of exactly what you're getting when you pull the lever for a Democrat or a Republican. Sure, there's a yawning ideological gap between a progressive Democratic congresswoman like Alexandria Ocasio-Cortez from New York and the Democratic Speaker of the House Nancy Pelosi.[12] But policy-wise they have more in common with each other than they do with Republicans in Congress.

This is all pretty normal. And in most other industrialized

---

11. And, just to reiterate, if you weren't a white guy, it was pretty much never the common ground you voted for.

12. Early plug here for why it's important to fight for your side in primary elections. Primaries are where a party debates which wing wins. More on this in Chapter 6.

nations, party polarization is a functional part of democracy. Nobody asks why the progressive Social Democratic Party in Finland can't find common ground with the ideologically opposed right-wing Finns Party. That's not what they're supposed to do! In most of the rest of the democratized world, what political parties are supposed to do is run on a policy platform, get elected, implement the platform, and then face the voters, who can choose to either keep them in power or not.

What's bad and destabilizing is not polarized political parties themselves. It's when you combine those parties with an outdated presidential system like we've got in America. The democratic system the Founders gave us is just not set up to deal with this. The Founders didn't envision ideologically driven party politics. They thought the size and diversity of the country would make it more difficult to organize into big warring ideological factions. They thought it would incentivize compromise and dealmaking rather than zero-sum brinksmanship.

They thought we'd keep chugging along.

They were wrong. Today, if you want to pass your agenda, you need the presidency, the Senate, and the House. If you don't have all of those, the ideologically driven opponents in the other party will veto your agenda. And even if you *have* control of those three bodies, the opposition party has an *enormous* number of ways to stop the president's party from getting stuff done; it's baked into the rules. The system is loaded with veto points and procedural roadblocks that allow a determined minority to block the will of the majority.

For generations, politicians of both parties had a gentleman's[13] agreement to exercise restraint in using those vetoes. But as the parties have become more polarized, the traditional restraints have been thrown out the window. Political scientists call this "constitutional hardball," and it's a really big problem.[14]

Modern American national politics is now defined by dysfunction and gridlock. We spend most of our time operating with a divided government where the minority party has no incentive to cooperate and the majority party is almost never in a position to enact its policies. The multiple veto points built into our system were intended to protect against a tyranny of the majority. They've led to a tyranny of the minority instead.

The modern pioneer of this scorched-earth approach is Republican Senate majority leader Mitch McConnell.[15] He understands the game and isn't afraid to explain it openly. In 2010, less than a couple of years into Barack Obama's presidency, McConnell told a journalist, "The single most important thing we want to achieve is for President Obama to be a one-term president." He did his best to deliver on that by pulling out all

---

13. It should escape no one's notice that the period of "bipartisan restraint" was a period when the majority of Americans—women and people of color— were barely represented in the halls of power. It's a lot easier to compromise when only rich white guys are in the room.

14. We talk about the book *How Democracies Die* by a pair of Harvard political scientists in Chapter 6, and the concept of constitutional hardball features prominently in their international and historical analysis of how democracies, well, die. It's scary stuff.

15. McConnell is a modern practitioner but he didn't invent the style. Republican House Speaker Newt Gingrich employed similar ideologically driven oppositional tactics against President Clinton more than a decade before McConnell used them against President Obama.

the stops to tank Obama's legislative agenda,[16] blocking him from appointing federal judges and undermining his administrative actions. McConnell couldn't stop everything, but he stopped a hell of a lot.

There's a terrible logic at work here. If a president gets elected and can't get anything done, voters usually punish that president's party in the next election. Voters don't care about excuses; they care about results. So if you're in the opposition and you vehemently disagree with the other party on basically everything—and you know that blocking their agenda hurts them, not you—you stop compromising and start playing hardball. It's not nice, but it is politically effective.

The losers in all this are everyday Americans and our faith in government. From legislative showdowns to government shutdowns, the level of dysfunction is rising, our social and economic problems are getting worse, and our democracy isn't producing any solutions. Americans' faith in democracy is at a record low, and why shouldn't it be? All we've seen for years is gridlock or marginal tweaks in the face of economic devastation and a growing climate crisis. And there's no way out in sight. No wonder people are increasingly turning to the kind of outsider politicians who promise to shake up the system: the system is broken and needs to be shaken up!

Now, a democracy where it's nearly impossible to move legislation is bad for everyone. But it's uniquely bad for progressives. We actually want to change things. We urgently need to change

---

16. Prediction: When scholars write about this period in future decades, they are going to put Mitch McConnell at the white-hot center of the crisis of American democracy.

things. Our societal problems—climate change, health care, gun violence, economic and racial inequality—are getting worse every day. Our political system is not equipped to deliver solutions— in fact, it's equipped to block them. And every election, the gap between what our politicians promise and what they're able to deliver widens—and faith in our system gets a little weaker.

Think about what this means for rising generations. The two of us are in our early thirties as we write this, putting us on the older end of the millennial cohort. In our adult lives, there has been literally a single six-month window—from mid-2009 to the beginning of 2010—where the federal government successfully passed *any* major progressive legislation. In that brief, fleeting period, Democrats were able to deliver change because they controlled not just the presidency, not just the House, not just the Senate, but *sixty seats* in the Senate. That's it—that's the one period of progress. And even then it was wildly insufficient to meet the scope of the economic and political crisis of 2009, which punched us millennials in our generational face.[17]

Is it any wonder that survey after survey shows that millennials are starting to lose faith in democracy? What will the next generation think? Why should they believe that government can be a force for good, or that their vote matters?

So, yes, our democracy is buckling. And it's pretty common for people bemoaning gridlock and dysfunction to blame both parties for being too extreme and causing the decline of country. But this is not a "Both sides are equally to blame" story. And that brings us to Part 2 of this story.

---

17. The metaphor got a little out of hand here, but just go with it.

PART 2: OUR DEMOCRACY IS BEING RIGGED

As the two parties diverged over the past few decades, the Republican Party wasn't simply becoming more ideologically polarized; it was also becoming reactionary and hostile to twentieth-century social and economic reforms. Republican leaders understand that their reactionary ideas and appeals to white supremacy are increasingly unpopular in an increasingly diverse and unequal society. Faced with that fact, they could moderate their social and economic policy positions, or they could seek to systematically make democracy less responsive to the will of the people. They've pursued the latter strategy.

That's a big allegation, we know. Frankly, it sounds almost like a tinfoil-hat-wearing kind of accusation, right? Something about a vast right-wing conspiracy? If only that were the case. The fact is, this reactionary conservative assault is well-documented. So let's review the evidence.

The GOP gets shoved off an ideological cliff

One thing that's not really up for debate among reasonable people is that the modern Republican Party has fallen off an ideological cliff.[18] The GOP has been captured by its extreme right wing, fueled by an unholy alliance between corporate power, Christian fundamentalism, and white nationalism. In

---

18. As former Democratic congressional staffers, we never had a particularly positive view of congressional Republicans. But seeing what has happened in the lead-up to Trump and in the early Trump years has shocked even us. We never would have accused the GOP of sinking to the depths they have during the Trump era.

both policy and temperament, elected Republicans have moved dramatically to the right, embracing new levels of radicalism on nearly every issue: health care, climate change, immigration, race, economics, foreign policy, and the basic functioning of our democratic institutions.

This isn't our opinion: it's what the data says. A survey of voting records of all House members found that while there's been a moderate shift leftward for Democrats, Republicans have *vaulted* to the right. We see similar effects when comparing the records of Republican presidents (dramatically more conservative in recent years) and Democratic presidents (often advancing the same or even more conservative policy ideas than their predecessors).

A pair of traditionally moderate political scientists, Thomas E. Mann and Norm Ornstein, explained in 2012, "We have been studying Washington politics and Congress for more than 40 years, and never have we seen them this dysfunctional . . . [W]e have no choice but to acknowledge that the core of the problem lies with the Republican Party." They updated their analysis a year after Trump's election, concluding that the Republican Party is the "root cause of today's political instability."

At the center of the GOP's evolution over the past several decades are a few guys you may have heard of: Charles and the now-deceased David Koch—aka "the Koch brothers."[19] As

---

19. There are actually two more Koch brothers, Bill and Frederick. The two pairs of brothers spent years in "bare-knuckle legal brawls," and at one point Charles purportedly tried to blackmail Frederick out of his shares of the family business. Yes, this all seems like a bad soap opera. Daniel Schulman's 2014 book *Sons of Wichita: How the Koch Brothers Became America's Most Powerful and Private Dynasty* goes into all the melodramatic details if you want them.

documented in Jane Mayer's eye-opening book *Dark Money: The Hidden History of the Billionaires Behind the Rise of the Radical Right*, the Koch brothers have led a secretive, decades-long, coordinated campaign to reshape America in line with their radical reactionary agenda.

The Koch brothers inherited quite a bit of money from their father, Fred, who made a fortune building oil refineries in, among other places, Stalin's Russia and Germany during the rise of the Third Reich. Charles and David took their inheritance and turned it into a sprawling oil empire, making themselves billionaires many times over.

If you guessed these oil-tycoon inheritors would have shockingly conservative politics, you'd be right![20] The most jaw-dropping distillation of their political philosophy comes from a rare moment when the Kochs publicly announced their goals: when David Koch ran for vice president on the Libertarian ticket in 1980. The platform he ran on included, among other initiatives:

- Eliminating Social Security, Medicaid, and Medicare
- Abolishing the FBI, the CIA, the FEC, the FDA, the EPA, and the U.S. Postal Service
- Eliminating campaign finance laws

---

20. The business practices of Koch Industries itself are beyond the scope of our book, but suffice it to say that the anti-worker, anti-environment, anti-government proclivities of one of the most destructive companies in the country are about as bad as you'd expect. If this whets your appetite, Mayer's book will sate it, but for a shorter read you can check out Tim Dickinson's 2014 *Rolling Stone* article "Inside the Koch Brothers' Toxic Empire."

- Eliminating child labor laws and the minimum wage
- Eliminating individual and corporate income taxes

To call this agenda extreme is an understatement. The Kochs' aim was not just to roll back Lyndon Johnson's Great Society and Franklin Roosevelt's New Deal but Teddy Roosevelt's and Woodrow Wilson's progressive-era reforms as well. In short, they wanted to drag America back to the nineteenth century—to usher in a new Gilded Age of laissez-faire government in which a cadre of robber barons could rule without restraint.[21]

This is now, and was then, a truly radical vision of the world—a fundamentally different conception of American society, in which the government's only role is to protect private property and fight off the inevitable mobs of starving, pitchfork-wielding masses.

Given the extremeness of this agenda, it may not surprise you that the Libertarian ticket won only about 1 percent of the vote in 1980. But the outcome was an unpleasant surprise to David, his brother, and others who wholeheartedly supported their *Lord of the Flies* agenda. And they weren't the kind of people who took defeat sitting down.

The Koch brothers appear to have learned two things from their 1980 electoral wipeout: first, their agenda was not exactly popular; and second, if they wanted to win, they would have to not just elect politicians but change the political game.

So they took their operation underground and turned their

---

21. Think the bad timeline in *Back to the Future II* where Biff is president. In fact—can't make this up!—the *Back to the Future* screenwriter has said that Biff was based on Donald Trump. Swear to God. Look it up.

focus from extremist third parties to the Republican Party it-self. They never ran for office again. Instead, they built an ex-traordinarily powerful network, bringing together a coalition of conservative donors to fund think tanks, advocacy groups, messaging firms, academic institutions, and individual politi-cians. Instead of running candidates who would trumpet their brand of conservatism in all its glory, they sought to change the very political environment in which all politicians operated. In the span of just a few years, they had become a relentless orga-nizing center of gravity for the forces of extreme conservatism.

Their philanthropic efforts were disguised by lofty nods to civic engagement and the pursuit of knowledge. They funded conservative academic institutions and think tanks with blandly patriotic names (e.g., the James Madison Institute) that hid their true political purposes. These institutions set out to build a narrative that reinforced their power and view of the world, spreading radical ideas into the mainstream discussion: "cut-ting taxes raises revenue,"[22] "more guns means less crime,"[23] "Social Security is a Ponzi scheme."[24]

And while as comic-book-style villains, the Kochs make easy targets, they weren't alone. Their efforts were complemented by, and often coordinated with, a menagerie of wealthy reac-

---

22. A real argument that's been used to support massive tax cuts for rich peo-ple and corporations under Reagan, George W. Bush, and Trump—all of whose schemes (shocker!) lost revenue.

23. A real argument made in a real book cited by real politicians who kill gun-regulation legislation.

24. The contention of former Republican Speaker of the House Paul Ryan, along with many other non-fringe, establishment-conservative figures.

tionaries: casino tycoon Sheldon Adelson; public-education enemy Betsy DeVos; John Menard Jr. of Midwestern home-improvement store fame; Richard Mellon Scaife of Mellon family fame; and the Coors family, among others.[25]

In a generation, the right-wing landscape had been transformed. A combination of think tanks, political operatives like the Club for Growth, and donors enforced adherence to extreme conservative orthodoxy. An under-the-radar Koch-funded effort called REDMAP (the "Redistricting Majority Project") transformed the political map by flipping key state legislatures and gerrymandering districts to maximize the number of Republican seats. The American Legislative Exchange Council (ALEC) pumped out model pro-business, anti-environment, anti-immigrant legislation that conservative legislatures copied and pasted into law across the country. A thriving right-wing media ecosystem has further bolstered radical-conservative positions.

Democrats didn't respond by moving aggressively in the other direction; instead they moved toward Republicans in search of consensus. President Carter governed as a conservative Democrat, trumpeting fiscal conservatism and deregulation. More than a decade later, the next Democratic president, Bill Clinton, proudly embraced ideologically muddy "third way" politics—announcing that "the era of big government is over." President Obama's landmark policy victory, the Affordable Care Act, had its roots in the health care proposals of the conservative Heritage Foundation.

---

25. Jane Mayer's *Dark Money* covers all of this in an exhaustive survey of the pantheon of modern reactionary plutocrats engaged in a flank attack on democracy. We can't recommend it highly enough if you enjoy horror stories.

In short, as the Republican Party became extreme and re-actionary, national Democratic Party leaders have searched, often in vain, for increasingly scarce and increasingly conservative middle ground. Almost forty years after the Kochs' first run at electoral politics, the Republican Party is more tactically and ideologically extreme—and more powerful—than ever. They've shifted the entire political debate far to the right. And they are winning.

A wildly successful divide-and-conquer strategy

Of course, conservative ideologues and billionaires in America have a fundamental problem: there aren't that many of them. And no matter how many think tanks you fund or campaign ads you buy, "Let's Bring Back the Gilded Age" is never going to be a popular platform for winning elections. The public likes Social Security, Medicare, public schools, and, you know, child labor laws. People get upset when you try to take those things away. They might even vote you out of office if you do it. After all, most people benefit from broad-based social-safety-net protections, and few people benefit from massive giveaways to the rich.

But fortunately for conservative reactionaries, our country is divided not only along economic lines. It's also divided along demographic and cultural lines, and shaped by a historic legacy of white supremacy. And this presents a big opportunity for those seeking to maintain political and economic power in an increasingly diverse and unequal society. They've just got to exploit those divisions.

This basic strategy—divide and conquer—continues to

drive the modern Republican Party's policy making and messaging. The message goes something like this:

> *Government cares about helping "other" people—not you.*
> *Those other people are Black or immigrants or poor or gay or*
> *godless. They are not part of us. So you shouldn't trust gov-*
> *ernment, you shouldn't want it in your life, and you certainly*
> *shouldn't want your taxes raised to support what it does.*

Famed Republican political strategist and former chair of
the Republican National Committee Lee Atwater explained the
strategy more crudely in a 1981 interview:

> *You start out in 1954 by saying "N****r, n****r, n****r." By*
> *1968 you can't say "N****r." That hurts you. It backfires. So*
> *you say stuff like forced busing, states' rights and all that stuff*
> *and you're getting so abstract.*

This is called "dog whistle politics." And when Republicans
talk about forced busing, law and order, welfare queens, Willie
Horton, panic over gay marriage, "illegals" getting health care,
the Ground Zero mosque, Obama Phones, bathroom bills,
sanctuary cities, and migrant caravans, this is what they're actually talking about. These coded appeals—often centered on
race, but also routinely adapted for gender and sexuality, ability, religion, and more—are everywhere, once you start looking for them. Acknowledged or not, they're at the very center
of our politics.

And each of those appeals has at its core that basic message: *government exists to help "other" people, not you.*

There's a reason this narrative shows up everywhere: it's been *working*. After all, if you're convinced that public schools or unemployment benefits or food stamps mostly help some undeserving "other" group of people, you're less likely to support the taxes needed to cover those entitlements. And if you think government doesn't care about you, then you're not going to have any faith in its ability to protect workers' rights, regulate corporations, or reform the health care system. The distrust this narrative breeds suits billionaires and corporate interests just fine, because it means they get to keep humming along with low taxes and no government interference. And when things go bad, there's an easy enemy to blame: those "others" who are sucking up all the resources and endangering your family.

Trump's innovation in 2016 was simple: he threw out the dog whistle and used a bullhorn instead. While the Republican establishment squirmed, the Republican primary voters heard him loud and clear—and they loved it. In a crowded field of conventional Republican candidates, Trump cast himself as the avatar of pure, unfiltered white rage. In announcing his campaign in 2015, he proclaimed:

When Mexico sends its people, they're not sending their best. They're not sending you. They're not sending you. They're sending people that have lots of problems, and they're bringing those problems with us. They're bringing drugs. They're bringing crime. They're rapists. And some, I assume, are good people.

This clarity of message gave him enough of an edge to win the Republican nomination. And his victory meant that suddenly the elites who had been strategically using racism to get tax cuts had to deal with a new phenomenon: a president who genuinely believed the racist tripe they'd been feeding voters this whole time. Trump had started saying the quiet parts out loud, but the underlying strategy was the same: divide and conquer the people so that the rich can get richer.

For a textbook example of how this works, let's take the single legislative accomplishment of the Trump administration: the 2017 multitrillion-dollar tax cut for millionaires and corporations. You probably haven't heard much about this recently, because Republicans stopped talking about it within a few months of passing the legislation. They didn't run their campaigns on the tax cut—again, their only legislative accomplishment—in 2018. Instead, they ran on xenophobia and racism. As the headline of one *New York Times* article on Trump's closing argument in the lead-up to the 2018 midterms read, "As Midterm Vote Nears, Trump Reprises a Favorite Message: Fear Immigrants." The leader of the Republican Party was actively running away from the Republicans' signature legislative achievement. It's an old playbook: downplay your plutocratic policies and play up your racism and xenophobia. Divide, conquer, and distract. Rinse and repeat.

Taking the "representative" out of representative democracy

In 2018, Republicans elected thirty-one new members to the House of Representatives. Thirty were men, and all thirty-one were white. In the entire country, precisely one Black Republican was elected to federal office that year. This is stark. And the Republican Party leaders aren't stupid. They can see that the country is growing increasingly diverse and increasingly unequal even as the Republican Party increasingly becomes the party of white men and corporate interests.

Republican elites know America's near-term destiny is to become a majority-minority country. They know that growing economic inequality is creating a lot more have-nots than haves. They know that an increasingly diverse and unequal electorate is a threat to their unpopular policy agenda. They see the writing on the wall.

In 1960, non-Hispanic whites made up 85 percent of the U.S. population—about the same proportion as they did a hundred years earlier. Today, whites make up about 60 percent of the population. And this proportion is dropping.[26]

In 1960, there were fewer than 10 million immigrants in America, representing about 5 percent of the population. Today, 45 million immigrants represent nearly 14 percent of the population. And this proportion is growing.

In 1960, America's richest 1 percent took home about 10 percent of the income and owned about 30 percent of the wealth. Today, the top 1 percent take home more than 20 percent of the income and own about 40 percent of the wealth. And this gap is expanding.[27]

---

26. For the first time in American history, between 2015 and 2016 the total number of white people—not just the percentage of the population, but the actual number—declined. This will continue.

27. It's worth noting that—surprise!—these trends aren't race neutral, either. The racial wealth gap is huge and growing in America, with median Black wealth declining over time as median white wealth surges.

These trends present a real long-term strategic problem for the modern Republican Party. They understand that their agenda of unchecked corporate greed, open racism, attacks on women's and LGBTQ rights, opposition to gun violence prevention, and inaction on climate change is not going to get more popular over time. Not when the American electorate is getting more diverse every year and inequality continues to skyrocket.

And that brings us to the next, crucial part of the GOP's strategy: rigging the democratic system so this changing electorate's voice will not be heard.

If you're looking for a succinct description of the vicious political logic behind the GOP's antidemocratic efforts, look no further than Carol Anderson's explanation of voter suppression in *One Person, No Vote: How Voter Suppression Is Destroying Our Democracy*:

> *Pushed by both the impending demographic collapse of the Republican Party, whose overwhelmingly white constituency is becoming an ever smaller share of the electorate, and the GOP's extremist inability to craft policies that speak to an increasingly diverse nation, the Republicans opted to disenfranchise rather than reform. The GOP, therefore, enacted a range of undemocratic and desperate measures to block the access of African American, Latino, and other minority voters to the ballot box. Using a series of voter suppression tactics, the GOP harassed, obstructed, frustrated, and purged American citizens from having a say in their own democracy.*

The devices the Republicans used are variations on a theme going back more than 150 years.[28]

If you're a GOP strategist, the strategy is simple and devastating: when you get power, you rig the rules to stay in power. You gerrymander—i.e., redraw—the maps so that in the next election, your candidates run in ideologically "safe" districts. You disenfranchise voters from communities that don't support you, especially voters of color and young people. You stack the courts with judges who'll back your moves and strike down your opponents' policies. You roll back campaign finance restrictions so your corporate friends have free rein to spend. You attack your opponent's power bases—organized labor, communities of color, immigrant advocates, women. You block all attempts to expand the electorate to diverse voters.

If you change enough of the rules, you've got a good shot at staying in power, whether your ideas are popular or not.

This is the road conservative reactionaries chose decades ago. Republican electeds functionally abandoned their support for voting rights as part of the broader Southern strategy shift in the 1970s. By 1980, Paul Weyrich, cofounder of the conservative Heritage Foundation and described by admirers as the "Lenin of social conservatism," was explaining his opposition

---

28. This is on the first page of Anderson's book and serves more or less as a preview of the rest—a history, from the post–Civil War period onward, that includes voter purges, proactive voter suppression, legal sleight of hand, gerrymandering, and intentionally exclusionary institutional reforms intended to keep people of color from voting.

succinctly: "I don't want everybody to vote . . . As a matter of fact, our leverage in the elections quite candidly goes up as the voting populace goes down." Weyrich's words echo across gatherings of GOP officials today as they exchange strategies to lock people—especially Black and brown voters—out of the system. And sometimes GOP elites just slip up and say it out loud, like in 2018, when Senator Cindy Hyde-Smith of Mississippi made a comment calling voter suppression to dampen progressive turnout "a great idea."

These attacks on democracy don't just occur at the federal level—and in fact the ugliest fights often take place in the states. Between the 2010 and 2018 elections, the Brennan Center for Justice reports, *twenty-five states* enacted reforms making it harder to vote, including voter ID laws, cuts to early voting opportunities, and higher barriers to registration. Whether it's blocking the restoration of voting rights to the formerly incarcerated, making it harder for Native Americans on tribal lands to vote, purging Black voters from the rolls at the state level, or blocking reauthorization of the Voting Rights Act, modern elected Republicans do whatever they can to shape the electorate and lock out voters who might oppose them—especially communities of color and young people.

In the lead-up to the 2018 midterms, Republican-led states aggressively pursued antidemocratic reforms, in what Brennan Center researchers called the "worst voter suppression we've seen in the modern era." The most egregious example that year took place in Georgia, where Republican secretary of state Brian Kemp ran for governor against Stacey Abrams, the house minority leader for the Georgia General Assembly and the first Black woman ever to run for governor on a major-party ticket. In his capacity as secretary of state, Kemp is alleged to have purged more than 340,000 voters from the rolls. Lawsuits filed against Kemp also accused him of targeting Black, Latino, and Asian communities for disenfranchisement. The election was plagued by massive irregularities, with Kemp ultimately "winning" by 55,000 votes—well within the margin of the votes affected by his reported voter-suppression tactics.

While the Georgia example is particularly striking, it's only the most recent example of openly antidemocratic attacks by conservatives entrenching their own power. In North Carolina in 2016, after Republicans lost the governor's race, the outgoing governor worked with the Republican state legislature to strip the governorship of critical authorities, preemptively weakening the not-yet-inaugurated Democrat. After losing the Wisconsin and Michigan governorships in the 2018 election, the outgoing Republican governors worked with their Republican state legislatures to replicate North Carolina's antidemocratic moves, attempting to preemptively weaken the incoming Democratic governors in their states. When asked why, the Republican Speaker of the Wisconsin State Assembly answered honestly: "We are going to have a very liberal governor who is going to enact policies that are in direct contrast to what many of us believe in." In other words, we lost, so we're changing the rules.

Do a quick survey of America's democratic institutions

today, and you'll see the wreckage this strategy has wrought: gerrymandered U.S. House and state legislative districts; a federal court packed with reactionary conservative judges hostile to progressive policies and democracy itself; labor unions gutted at the state and federal levels through legislative and judicial attacks; and campaign finance and lobbying rules that allow billionaires to buy candidates.[29] The result is a democracy that systematically ignores the will of the people, prioritizing instead the interests of a plutocratic few in the donor class.

The GOP's strategy has worked staggeringly well.

This assault on democracy is a sustained, organized, nationwide campaign pushed by Republican elites and the Koch-funded infrastructure at every level—from the local to the federal; from the legislatures to the courts. In other words, the attacks on democracy aren't just coming from Trump; they're coming from garden-variety Republican electeds and their donors.

And this, in the end, is why Trump isn't the problem. Trump may be louder, crueler, and less competent than most Republicans. But in his contempt for the electorate and democratic norms, in his personification of white rage, in his dedication to advancing the interests of the corporate class, he's not a departure from the modern GOP. He's an avatar of its darkest traits. The Trumpism we see today is just another manifestation of the bigoted, antidemocratic Republican impulses that

---

29. This is of course only a partial list. We dive into the details a bit more in Chapter 6, where we discuss what we need to do to right the ship.

have been festering at the state and federal levels for decades. It is core to the modern conservative theory of change; it's how they ram through their policy agendas and entrench their political power.

And we've let them.

2

The Solution: Constituent Power

If they don't give you a seat at the table, bring a folding chair.
—SHIRLEY CHISHOLM

Everyone in this room has power. The question is,
how do you want to use it? We have an opportunity for
every one of you to be a part of the solution.
—ELLEN STEVENSON, *Social Justice Indivisible (Pennsylvania)*

As the two of us sat down to write the *Indivisible Guide* in November 2016, we didn't know anything about the history of civic engagement in America. Frankly, that would have sounded like a pretty boring topic had you proposed it to us. But we knew something called "constituent power" was real, for a simple and depressing reason: we'd seen it used to destroy the things we cared about most.

We both arrived in Washington in 2008, part of the surge of recent college graduates drawn to D.C. by the promise of the Obama administration. We were idealistic, ready to serve, and looking for cheap rent—which is how we ended up landing together as roommates in a group house in Columbia Heights, a neighborhood a few miles north of Capitol Hill and the White House.[1] By January 2009, we had an incoming president with historic Democratic congressional majorities, committed to moving the most ambitious agenda since Lyndon Johnson's Great Society. It was a heady time to be a young progressive in D.C.

Now forgive us for a couple of pages while we break character. Up to this point in the book, we've been narrating as a pair, but we are in fact two separate people and we had different experiences during this time. So we're going to take a brief interlude and split into first-person narratives to describe our lives as congressional staffers. Bear with us, and take this as a cautionary tale about writing a book with your spouse.

Ezra: *I got a job working for a congressman from Texas, Lloyd Doggett. He was a progressive from Texas, which meant he had a habit of pissing off the Texas Republican Party, and as a result was a regular political target. Lloyd had been elected to Congress in 1994 when I was nine years old, and by the time I went to work for him in D.C., he'd survived primary challenges and redistricting attempts by the uber-conservative Texas*

---

1. Ezra: This place was sort of a flophouse, with six people crammed into a space for four. My room had no windows, so I put a picture of a window up. Leah's room was in the basement and I think was technically a moderate-sized closet. We held a weekly get-together on Wednesdays to meet people in the neighborhood, and during one of the events the power entirely went out, so we drank in the dark and candlelight; on another occasion, a toilet on the second floor started falling through the first-floor ceiling, spurting water down the wall. We loved that house.

legislature. A workaholic populist and brilliant politician, he knew how to keep his district safely behind him.

I started in Lloyd's office in the early days of the Great Recession—actually the same week that the massive invest-ment bank Lehman Brothers failed in September 2008. The country was in turmoil, the economy was crashing, and gov-ernment was relevant and necessary, and Barack Obama won election just a few weeks later.

It was, frankly, an awesome time to be a young staffer on Capitol Hill covering economic and social policy issues. Here I was, a wonky twenty-four-year-old working for a senior mem-ber of Congress at a moment of enormous political opportunity for progressive policy—huge Democratic majorities, moving the most ambitious progressive agenda since the Great Society. For decades, progressive legislation had been stymied, but here we had a rare opportunity to get stuff done. Doggett was also head of the Texas Democratic congressional delegation, which meant wrangling other Texas Democrats as we went toe-to-toe with the Texas Republican governor at the time, Rick Perry. I wholeheartedly threw myself into the fight.

Leah: *I joined the office of Tom Perriello, a young progressive from a red Virginia district who had beaten a wildly xenopho-bic longtime incumbent in a long-shot victory in 2008.*[2] *Having*

---

2. You may remember Virgil Goode as the congressman who caused a national scandal when he infamously objected to the swearing-in of the first Muslim member of Congress, Keith Ellison. Tom had pulled off a long-shot victory in large part by successfully painting Goode as out of touch and more fo-cused on xenophobic crusades than on serving his district.

won by just 727 votes in 2008, we knew we had a tough race ahead in 2010. But, true to his principles, Tom responded not by running to the center but by doubling down on the Obama agenda, voting for key priorities like the Affordable Care Act and the stimulus and then going home to his district to aggressively make the case for Obama's policies.

Virginia's Fifth District was home to at least three very active Tea Party groups, which meant that Perriello's local office was basically constantly under siege. This local insurgency was infuriated by Tom's vote for the Affordable Care Act and dedicated to scrutinizing his (and his staff's) every move. They filled the voice mail in-box with furious calls and the daily news clips with angry letters to the editor. They recorded "gotcha" calls with the staff and put them on YouTube. They protested outside the district offices constantly, eventually causing so much chaos that other tenants in the Charlottesville office park ended up breaking their leases. They attacked Perriello staff with the signs they brought to town halls, and then, when they were banned from bringing signs inside, they protested the fact that their First Amendment rights were being violated.[3] In short, they alternated between being scary and an enormous pain in the ass. It was rough.

On the bright side, somewhere around this time we finally admitted that we were totally in love with each other and

---

3. Leah: The worst violence occurred before I arrived, at the town halls of summer 2009. Members of the Perriello team were kicked, hit, spat on, and had their belongings stolen; the animosity toward Black staff in particular was visceral and frightening. Tom's brother had the gas line to his house cut, in what seemed intended to be an attack on Tom. It was really, really bad.

started dating. We went on our first date the day after the Af-
fordable Care Act passed the House. So that was good. It was
also a huge relief for our housemates, who had gotten very tired
of our awkward flirting.

With that, we return to our shared narrative.

It wasn't just the Fifth District of Virginia experiencing this wave of Tea Party organizing. Across the country, Obama's victory and the Great Recession had sparked a grassroots surge of anger. Tea Partiers organized locally, kept their focus on their elected officials, and never gave an inch. They flooded town halls, wrote letters to the editor, melted the phone lines. They showed up wherever members of Congress went, often wearing Revolutionary War costumes and tricorn hats.[4] They were indefatigable, from Perriello's purplish-red district in Virginia, where they were a constant presence, to Doggett's deep-blue district in Texas, where they showed up to derail his public events with posters of the congressman with devil's horns. They were everywhere. And they were angry. Did we mention that? They were really, really angry.

There were two things that were very apparent to us in our interactions with the Tea Party. First, the popular narrative that the Tea Party movement was just "Astroturf," the product of Koch brother money, simply didn't hold up. They were real people, doing real work. It's true that Tea Party groups were flooded with money and support from Koch-funded entities like Americans for Prosperity, but it was honestly just silly to

---

4. Yes, it was weird.

deny that it was a genuine grassroots movement. Money cannot manufacture that kind of anger.

Second, there was a lot of confusion at the time about why, exactly, the Tea Party was so angry. For those of us on the ground, it was pretty obvious: they were mad that a Black man had been elected president and they were convinced that his legislative agenda was a giveaway to undeserving "others." And, indeed, subsequent academic research has honed in on the strong relationship between racial animus and Tea Party affiliation.

The crazy thing was, what the Tea Party did *worked*. These local bands of angry people with silly hats had a big effect on the national political agenda. Their fury over the nascent health care bill at town halls in 2009 caught members of Congress off guard and deeply rattled the Democratic caucus. Their passionate, intense opposition slowed some pieces of Obama's agenda and halted others. They shaped a political environment in which legislation that did pass was less progressive and more unpopular. This was constituent power—the power of groups of individuals organized geographically by congressional district—focusing on elected officials and changing what was politically possible at the national level. It was awe-inspiring— and incredibly damaging in the moment to the hopes of a couple of young progressive policy nerds.

Their work was not just limited to advocacy, and the Tea Party's most devastating impact on the political system came through actual electoral challenges and victories. Tea Partiers in Massachusetts helped power Scott Brown to victory in the special election for Ted Kennedy's Senate seat, ending the brief window of a filibuster-proof Democratic majority in the Senate and the hope for major legislative change. And they helped deliver a wipeout of epic proportions for the Democrats at every level of government in the 2010 elections. An electorally rebuked Obama called it a "shellacking."

This was a painful period for us. We watched as constant pressure rattled the Democratic caucus, throwing the Obama legislative agenda into chaos. We had fought, unsuccessfully, to keep the Democratic majority in 2010.[5] When that failed, we were forced to recognize that the promise of the Obama administration—or at least the promise of major legislative change—was over.

That was our formative political education, and by 2011 we had had enough. We left Capitol Hill. We went off to graduate school. We got married.[6] We moved back to D.C. And instead of returning to congressional staffer life, we moved on to become anti-poverty and anti–human trafficking policy advocates. For a long time we considered the rise of the Tea Party to be a painful period with no applicable lessons—except perhaps as a cautionary tale for those seeking to make change in Washington.

Then Trump won, and we started going through the stages

---

5. Leah: I lost my job when Tom narrowly lost reelection. True to form, the week after the election, the Jefferson Area Tea Party showed up at the Perriello office to mock me and the other staff for losing our jobs. I thanked them for visiting, told them not to worry, that all the staff would be fine, and offered them tickets to go see the Capitol Gallery. If you're reading this, Jefferson Area Tea Party: Thanks for teaching me the ropes! Hope you're enjoying the Affordable Care Act.

6. Tom Perriello officiated our wedding. Thanks, Tom!

of grief like other progressives. We were facing a future without the White House, Congress, the courts, or most state legislatures. We were facing an administration and Congress that had won on a campaign of anti-immigrant, racist, misogynistic hate. We were facing a president who openly flaunted his belligerence, ignorance, and authoritarian instincts. And he would now control the national levers of power.

The rude awakening many Americans—including both of us—experienced in November 2016 was simple and devastating: we could not count on our existing system to defend us from an unthinkably horrible outcome. The forces powering Trump's rise—a toxic alliance between white supremacy and the corporate class—were strong. Every check we'd imagined would halt Trump's ascension—the parties, the media, the elites, the courts—failed.

There was no cavalry that would be riding to the rescue.

Unless maybe *we* were the cavalry.

In that moment, the lesson of the Tea Party was clear, simple, and urgent: you don't need control of Congress or the levers of power to stop an incoming administration. You need people. Specifically, you need people all over the country, organizing locally and holding their elected officials' feet to the fire.

And one thing was clear in the wake of Trump's election: we had people.

Because something had broken for a lot of people with Trump's election. For many Americans, passively watching was no longer an option. The idea of just signing a petition or donating to a national effort seemed insufficient. The call for the Women's March went viral on Facebook within hours; sister women's marches across the country were rapidly organizing into a nationwide movement. The streets of downtown D.C. were teeming with spontaneous protests.[7] Organizations like Planned Parenthood and the ACLU were being swamped by more volunteers than they could possibly manage. Our previously apolitical friends and family were hounding us for tips on how to effectively lobby Congress. We were getting added to exploding secret Facebook groups with names like "Dumbledore's Army," "The Resistance," and "Our Future." It was clear that people—maybe millions of people—were suddenly becoming civically engaged, many for the first time.

The lightbulb moment came when we were visiting Ezra's family in Austin for Thanksgiving. We were getting drinks with an old friend of Ezra's from college, Sara Clough, who was an administrator of the anti-Trump Facebook group "Dumbledore's Army." We were grilling her on what was going on with this wave of people who seemed to be reacting to Trump by going from zero to sixty, politically speaking. How real was it? What were they doing? Could we help?

Sara told us that the folks in her Facebook group felt like they were hitting a wall. They'd done everything: showed up at protests, written letters to Paul Ryan, called the electors, signed petitions demanding investigations of Trump. But the federal government and Congress were black boxes—tough to

---

7. We were both there in D.C. for the Women's March, along with dozens of Indivisible volunteers. The crowds were overwhelming, and joyfully defiant.

understand, seemingly impossible to influence. They had no idea how to have real impact.

At that moment our thoughts turned back to our firsthand experience with the Tea Party—those local groups of angry people who'd somehow managed to tank the agenda of an *actually* popular president with an *actual* mandate. What we needed was some sort of guide to replicating the Tea Party. Not the violence and racism, obviously, but the smart, effective local advocacy. If people were already organizing all over the country, maybe we could create a playbook that would help.

WHERE DID ALL THESE PEOPLE COME FROM?

When we wrote the *Indivisible Guide*, we intentionally made it as blunt and practical as possible. The strategy was simple: we couldn't do much to pressure Donald Trump, but if we organized locally and effectively, then we—constituents around the country on our home turf—could sure as hell pressure our individual representatives and senators. If we all did it together, we could stiffen Democrats' spines and put the fear of God in Republicans. It wouldn't be enough to stop every terrible Trump effort, but it might be enough to save the Affordable Care Act. It might be enough to make the president back down on his anti-immigrant agenda. It might be enough to turn the tide in 2018 and then some more in 2020.

In short: groups of regular people, organizing locally but all pushing in the same direction, could make Congress listen and reshape the national political environment. It was going to be hard, but it wasn't impossible. The Tea Party had done it, and we already suspected that what was bubbling up around the country in 2016 could match the Tea Party in size and intensity.[8]

We had no idea how right we were.

Indivisible quickly exploded into a burgeoning movement of people building power in their own communities all across the country. In a matter of months, thousands of local groups connected under the banner of Indivisible were organizing locally and coordinating nationally on key policy campaigns. Indivisible groups formed in every single congressional district in the country, from Greene County, Tennessee, to Beaumont, Texas, to Seattle to Brooklyn to Las Cruces, New Mexico.

In living rooms and community centers, churches and synagogues and mosques, coffee shops and libraries, people were pulling together. In the deepest-blue and reddest-red areas of the country, the local "Indivisibles" were reaching out to each other to form communities and to build power. They were mad and scared and ready to organize. Shock and horror were receding. Hope and determination were rising. It would take a little while before the mainstream press and politicians realized what was happening. But from our vantage point, it was clear: a grassroots movement to resist Trump was building.

The first day of the new Congress, January 3, 2017, started off on a bad note. News broke that morning that the chair of the House Judiciary Committee, Congressman Bob Goodlatte of Roanoke, Virginia, was pushing a rule change to gut the Office of Congressional Ethics. The future of the Office of Congressional Ethics is not the sexiest of topics. The fact that there is

---

8. And have fewer silly hats.

an office dedicated to enforcing congressional ethics may come as a surprise to many.[9] But the idea that Republicans would kick things off with a full-frontal attack on the very idea of basic oversight was startling all the same, and it felt like an ominous sign of things to come.

We raised the alarm across our channels, urging our nascent network to call their members of Congress and object. Nationwide outrage was mounting; Republicans were backing away from the plan as their phones rang off the hooks. And then we had a crazy idea: a group in Roanoke had just registered on our map. Maybe they'd be willing to turn up the heat locally on the ringleader, Representative Goodlatte? It seemed worth sending an email to find out.

Ivonne Wallace Fuentes, who had registered the local Indivisible group in Roanoke, responded immediately. Ivonne was a Latin American studies professor writing a book about a Peruvian female politician who'd been brought low by sexism; as she tried to finish her draft in the fall of 2016, she couldn't help noticing the painful parallels with Hillary Clinton. Ivonne had brought a small group together after the election to focus on fighting back against Trump and supporting the immigrant community of Roanoke; she had registered the group on our website the night before, spurred on by anger at Goodlatte. Yes, she could get some people together to take action. Yes, they could go tomorrow.

The next morning, the group that would soon be known as Roanoke Indivisible showed up at Goodlatte's office in down-

---

9. Including, ahem, some former congressional staffers.

town Roanoke. They offered the startled congressional staffer a roll of Saran Wrap ("Be transparent!") and homemade New Year's resolution cards (the inscription: "We hope your New Year's resolution is to be more ethical!"). They brought local media, who were eager to cover this angle now that they had something more interesting to film than the draft of an ethics bill. They recorded their visit and their reactions and emailed the videos to us. We sent it to Rachel Maddow's producers, and that night Rachel Maddow broadcast it to millions.

The effort to gut the Congressional Ethics Office was dead less than twenty-four hours after it became public. Republicans, cowed by the public outcry, dropped the proposal. All it took was a little sunlight and a lot of outrage.

The fact that an under-the-radar attempt to gut an obscure office had triggered a local and national firestorm should have rattled Republicans. The fact that two weeks later Trump's sparse inauguration would immediately be eclipsed by the Women's March—whose attendance nationwide constituted the largest single-day mobilization in U.S. history—should have terrified them.[10] But Trump and his cronies weren't the sort of people who shift course in response to reality. They immediately launched into a series of devastating, vicious, and antidemocratic executive orders designed to put the cruelest parts of Trump's agenda into action.

It was a terrifying moment. It felt like Trump, Steve Bannon, and Stephen Miller were trying to prove that they could break

---

10. We've heard countless stories of Indivisible groups forming on the buses back from the Women's March as women who were inspired by taking their first political action ever sought out their next steps.

the rules, attack our neighbors, and do whatever they wanted. And for a perilous few days, it seemed like nothing would stop them. The thing that sustained us was that we knew—because our in-box was still overflowing—that Trump wouldn't get the last word.

As Trump banned immigration from several majority Muslim countries, nascent Indivisible groups flocked to airports and we hosted a call for more than 35,000 activists, with National Immigration Law Center, Asian Americans Advancing Justice, the ACLU, and the International Refugee Assistance Project—four leading advocates for refugees—on the line to brief Indivisible leaders on the state of play.

As Trump attempted to confirm his horror show of a cabinet, we teamed up with MoveOn, the Working Families Party, and People's Action to call for our very first national day of action—and tens of thousands flooded Senate offices nationwide to put the heat on both Democrats and Republicans. We knew we couldn't win on the confirmations as long as Republicans held together, but we could make each confirmation process as hard and politically damaging as possible. And, perhaps more important, we could draw a line in the sand for Democrats: your constituents expect you to fight, not to rubber-stamp Trump's nominees and agenda.

At the time, this was still far from something we could take for granted. Democratic senators were still talking earnestly about compromise, and many were voting consistently to approve Trump's nominees. The Democratic leadership even announced, during the first week of the Trump administration, a plan to focus on infrastructure—as if that were the most pressing problem at a moment when refugees were literally being barred from our borders. But that all changed quickly. In New York, Indivisible Nation BK showed up with Working Families Party and other protestors at the park outside Chuck Schumer's apartment building to stage a "What the F*ck, Chuck?" rally demanding he take a stronger line against Trump's nominees.[11] When Democrats like Amy Klobuchar, Tim Kaine, and Dianne Feinstein voted to confirm Mike Pompeo, an Islamophobe who had been an apologist for torture, as CIA director, Indivisible groups were outside their local district offices the next day, chanting "Why Pompeo? Why Pompeo?" and demanding answers.

Democrats and their staff were surprised. Some were skeptical of this newfound energy: a senior Dianne Feinstein staffer told the newly formed Indivisible SF, "You'll all have moved on by St. Patrick's Day."[12] But elected officials are pretty good at figuring out where the winds are blowing and adjusting course, and they took notice. By the time a pair of truly egregious nominees—Betsy DeVos for secretary of education and Jeff Sessions for attorney general—came up for votes, the Democratic caucus at least was voting in near lockstep.

Back at Indivisible HQ (also known as our living room), we were still trying to figure out exactly what had hit us. There's no playbook for what to do after you've accidentally launched yourself into the middle of a social movement. We had been in triage mode since the day the *Indivisible Guide* went live. Our

---

11. Just to be clear, we do not endorse either profanity or showing up at elected officials' houses. Well, OK, sometimes we endorse profanity.

12. Protip: One good way to piss off protestors and keep them committed to protesting you is to tell them they'll never be able to keep it up.

every waking hour was dedicated to fighting Trump and urging others to get organized to fight Trump too. We certainly hadn't had time to step back and think about what any of it meant.

We hadn't had a grand vision for a nationwide movement when we wrote the *Indivisible Guide*. Our goals had been pretty simple: we wanted people to show up, use our tactics to scare the crap out of their elected officials, and halt the Trump agenda. We told people to form groups because groups would be better at carrying out the strategy outlined in the guide.

But as we found ourselves in the middle of this growing Indivisible movement, it became clear that the path forward wasn't just about the guide.[13] The path forward lay in the fact that communities had formed in every corner of the country— communities capable of so much more than just showing up at town halls or calling Congress.

And as the Indivisible movement was taking off like a rocket, we learned an important lesson: the basic organizing theory that we believed in wasn't new. It had actually been the norm in American civic and political life for much of the nineteenth and twentieth centuries.

THE SURPRISING HISTORY WE LEARNED
AFTER INDIVISIBLE LAUNCHED

A month or so after we tweeted out the *Indivisible Guide*, we got a call from Marshall Ganz. This in itself was pretty mind-

---

13. Indeed, Indivisible groups were rapidly moving beyond the original guide, innovating on its tactics and taking on new fights well beyond the original focus on Congress.

blowing. Marshall is famous in organizing and political circles as the organizing director for Cesar Chavez's United Farm Workers union and a key architect of the 2008 Obama for America field operation. Somehow he had heard about Indivisible, and he wanted to chat. We were bowled over that this legendary organizing guru was even interested in Indivisible.

We knew that we had not invented organizing and indeed that we were novices in a field with a deep and rich history. We knew there were models, research, theory, practitioners out there. We knew that what was happening with Indivisible— this swell of hyper-local, congressionally focused community engagement—must have had parallels in history, lessons we could draw on. As it turned out, that was what Marshall was thinking too. And he'd literally written some of the history himself, including coauthoring a seminal piece, "A Nation of Organizers: The Institutional Origins of Civic Voluntarism in the United States."

In "A Nation of Organizers," Marshall, Ziad Munson, and Theda Skocpol (the latter would expand the article into a full-length book, *Diminished Democracy: From Membership to Management in American Civil Life*) tell a forgotten history of a core feature of civic life that helped define American democracy throughout the 1800s and into the 1960s. The authors describe how civic-engagement institutions played a pivotal role in mobilizing people to engage with their elected officials. And they raise the alarm about the recent collapse of this foundational feature of American civic life—a collapse that plays into the current threat to our democracy. As for a solution, what they recommend is a renaissance of nationally coordinated local communities. Maybe this isn't sexy, but for us reading this during the rise of the Indivisible movement, it sure as hell was prescient—and that made it riveting.

What "A Nation of Organizers" described isn't the exact same model as Indivisible,[14] but it's the same basic idea of everyday Americans taking it upon themselves to get involved locally and coordinating that combined local power to move the political system nationally. In other words, reading this old academic study, we saw that the basic organizing theory we wrote into the *Indivisible Guide* stretched back nearly two hundred years in American political history.

It turns out that for much of American history, voluntary associations like the Fraternal Order of Eagles, the Independent Order of Odd Fellows, the Benevolent and Protective Order of Elks, and the Loyal Order of Moose were regular major civic-engagement institutions in communities across the country. If you're a millennial like us, their names might sound like they're from Harry Potter, but these were real-life chapter-based organizations that organized millions of local volunteers and wielded power nationally through a federated system, with local, state, and national leadership.[15]

These were not associations of elites but a collection of regular citizens who gathered together locally and often across class

---

14. These old groups often created serious federated structures with fancy titles for their internally elected officials, carried out events with pomp and circumstance, and ran meetings with *Robert's Rules of Order*. Indivisible is somewhat more unceremonious, homegrown, feisty.

15. We're using the past tense, but many of the organizations still exist; they're just shells of their former selves.

lines.[16] Members of a particular Moose "lodge," for instance, identified as "Moose" and shared a sense of personal identity with the Moose in thousands of lodges across the country. This shared identity and national structure allowed the Moose (and others) to work across city and state lines on joint civic and political projects.

Through local chapters spread around the country, these groups became political powerhouses. They provided training, education, and venues for meetings and political debates. Because they were local groups populated by constituents in congressional districts, they were particularly good at influencing legislation. The combination of local leadership and national connectivity was crucial. As Skocpol writes, "The genius of classic American associational life was that joining something small connected members of local chapters to much grander organized endeavors." The Moose got stuff done.

This wasn't just fiddling around the margins: some of their accomplishments were politically enormous. For example, the Fraternal Order of the Eagles orchestrated a national advocacy campaign for state-level pension programs in the 1920s and then played a critical role in setting the stage for the creation of social security. On the enactment of the Social Security Act in 1935, their national leader (the "Eagle Grand Worthy President") received a personal thank-you note from President Franklin Roosevelt along with one of the pens he used to sign the legislation into law. The Eagles also received a pen and thank-you note from President Johnson after the signing

---

16. But notably rarely across racial or gender lines. We'll come back to this.

ceremony for Medicare and Medicaid in 1965.[17] The Eagles got stuff done.

Now, anytime someone tells you a story about a lost golden age of America, they're probably ignoring race, gender, or other lines of difference. And race and gender are a huge part of this story. These civic associations were mostly segregated across lines of difference. There were women's groups and men's groups. There were Black civic associations, many critical to the struggle for racial equality.[18] There were white civic fraternities, including some that made maintaining segregation an active part of their agenda. While race and gender aren't a central part of Skocpol's "diminished democracy," she acknowledges that some of these groups were violent, nativist, and racist.[19]

This segregation had all kinds of implications for the policy these groups lobbied for and the communities they formed. The Fraternal Order of the Eagles, who proudly claim credit for the 1935 Social Security Act, had an all-white membership policy into the 1970s. That the original Social Security Act systematically excluded workers of color from benefits was no accident.

In other words, this is not a story of a harmonious golden

---

17. The president said he was bestowing the pen in recognition of the Eagles' "energetic and dedicated espousal of social justices, and for the generous support you have given to all measures designed to further economic opportunity and the compassionate treatment of the sick and disabled."

18. And, true to form, white legislatures in the South did everything they could to suppress the Black groups.

19. She tells one story of a flourishing all-white, all-Christian group named the Improved Order of Red Men that established "tribes" all over the country.

age free of our greatest historical sins; these civic associations were shaped by and perpetuated the same forces of white supremacy and patriarchy as the world around them. Nonetheless, as with the Tea Party, there are powerful lessons to learn here. For around 150 years of American democracy, these locally led, national associations helped define and shape the contours of democratic politics in America. Through these associations, civic engagement was a normal part of everyday life for millions of Americans.

THE RISE OF TRUMP DURING
AN ERA OF CIVIC DISENGAGEMENT

Think about what this meant: for much of our history, American civic life was dominated by social communities that were also platforms for civic action. In your town—especially if you benefited from racial and gender privilege—there was an opportunity to connect with a social community of like-minded people, one where you could find opportunities to take on leadership and develop your skills and efficacy. This wasn't about one cause or one candidate; it was about participating broadly in civic life and making democracy work. Local, self-governed communities helped to build political power—power that was used to drive local and national change. The meshing of social networks and action made these forms of civic engagement part of the normal pattern of life.

Does this sound like your life right now—or in the fall of 2016? If you're like most adult Americans, the answer is: Probably not. Before 2016, if you were politically engaged, you probably took action through solitary activities: signing a petition, giving your email address to receive a newsletter, or donating money. Socially speaking, you might belong to a church or other religious institution. You might be part of a parents' group or a sports team—or part of a group of parents who go to all your children's sports games. Statistically speaking, you're less likely to know your neighbors, belong to a community group or labor union, or have a social network beyond your family and a small group of friends than at any other point in modern history.

That's because, as of 2016, you were probably part of the multi-decade decline of civic engagement in American life. As faith in government declined in the wake of Vietnam and Watergate, and women entered the workforce in significant numbers, American patterns of communal engagement changed dramatically. Membership and average time devoted to basically all forms of social communities—from PTAs to bowling clubs to churches—dropped dramatically. Over the seventies and eighties, elites left voluntary associations and young people stopped joining.[20] The Moose, the Elks, and other groups largely died out, and a new set of actors started to emerge. At the same time, concerted right-wing attacks on the American labor movement began to take their toll, with union membership falling from over a third of American workers in the post–World War II period to just over 10 percent by the present day.

As broad-based civic groups lost energy, there was a flour-

---

20. This is of course dramatic oversimplification of all the different social trends contributing to this phenomenon, many of which are still being debated.

ishing of more narrowly focused professional advocacy organizations: nonprofits, think tanks, foundations, and political action committees (PACs). An encyclopedia of national associations of this type counted about 5,600 in 1959 and more than 22,000 in 1990. These groups often focused on specific issues, like the environment, civil rights, anti-poverty programs, children's rights, reproductive rights, and more (and there was a flourishing of business associations formed to fight back against all these do-gooders). The rise of advocacy organizations shifted leadership and responsibility from local volunteers to professional wonks, policy advocates, and lobbyists, often based in D.C.[21] Increasingly, policy advocacy became the domain of a small world of professionals, and advocacy became an elite activity, involving policy papers, lobbying, polling, campaign contributions, and media.[22]

This trend was driven, crucially, by a shift in how organizations funded themselves. Historically, national organizations

---

21. To be clear, before Indivisible, this was our world too! We lived and breathed the D.C.-based nonprofit industrial complex. Our pre-Indivisible lives were totally disconnected from any sort of active, engaged network of real people across the country. Frankly, it barely occurred to us that we were missing something—that the gap between having good policy ideas and having people working to push those ideas mattered, that part of the reason we could make only marginal tweaks around the edges to policy was because what we were doing wasn't actually connected to a real base of power. We didn't know any other way.

22. Skocpol has a pretty withering critique of this transformation, noting that all the national organizations fight policy fights among themselves, while "ordinary Americans attend to such debates fitfully, entertained or bemused. Then pollsters call at dinnertime to glean snippets of what everyone makes of it all."

had depended on healthy local chapters both for people power and for their fund-raising needs. By the 1970s, that was changing. With the rise of direct mail, organizations could reach out to individuals regardless of where they lived. You no longer needed a thriving network of local chapters in order to support an organization; you could build a base of financial support from individuals across the country and turn that funding into a professional advocacy operation in D.C. or New York. With the rise of the Internet, digital organizing hubs succeeded in building connections to membership bases of millions—people who could be mobilized both for fund-raising and for everything from signing petitions to taking off-line action.

Each of these shifts helped to create critical pieces of the modern progressive ecosystem. The progressive movement needs policy expertise and advocacy. We need to build individual connections that reach and mobilize people to take action. We need a powerful digital infrastructure.

But at the same time, we've lost something important. The collapse of voluntary associations—coupled with the intentional destruction of the American labor movement—has left gaping holes in the civic ecosystem. Today, fewer and fewer groups in Washington have meaningful connections to large bases of active people outside Washington. And fewer people have a local institution hooking them into civic engagement or encouraging them to take leadership in their community.

While many advocacy organizations maintain a base of supporters who donate and take actions on request, there's no longer any imperative to foster the same level of leadership or cede the same level of control to local volunteers as found in older associations. The broader population of potential activists see their roles as being passive consumers of politics—donors, poll answerers, and media consumers—rather than active participants in the work of making our democracy function.

It's not that Americans aren't organizing and driving change on a national scale; in fact, in the years leading up to the 2016 election, America saw waves of social justice movements. This included the inspired, strategic, and fearless organizing of Dreamers, the Occupy Wall Street movement, the Black Lives Matter movement, and Standing Rock. The Dreamers successfully pressured Democrats to implement protections for young immigrants threatened with deportation. Occupy Wall Street injected discussion of economic inequality and corporate power into the national conversation. The Black Lives Matter movement radically changed Americans' understanding of police violence and the legacy of racial injustice in society. These movements didn't look like the modern national nonprofit space, although they often adopted specific tactics, structures, or partnerships from the nonprofit world in order to maximize their impact. Their success drew on organizing people, not formalizing structures.[23] It's not a coincidence that many of the most impactful, transformative movements have originated largely outside the Washington-oriented nonprofit world.

So in the lead-up to the 2016 election, many progressive Americans assumed the system was going to take care of itself. And why should they have thought anything else? There is a whole

---

23. One very important exception to this rule would be the Fight for $15, a social movement that was also incubated by the Service Employees International Union (SEIU) and the broader labor movement.

professionalized political world that "does politics" every year, spending billions of dollars on political ads, campaign consultants, message testing, polling, marketing materials, and paid canvassers. And in theory the great thing about having professionalized progressive nonprofit structures and national mobilizers in place is that normal Americans need not take time out of their busy schedules to own and lead the work of democracy themselves. Somebody else is taking care of it. Literally, it's somebody else's job—many other people's jobs, in fact. "Political" people.

In 2016, millions of civically minded Americans—including many future Indivisible leaders—understood their role in democracy as voting, keeping up with the news, and maybe giving a bit of money to candidates or signing a petition occasionally. As Sarah Herron, a future leader in Indivisible East Tennessee, told us in an interview, "What was I doing before 2016? I was minding my own damn business." Heather Thornton, who would become a leader of Indivisible Grapevine Area in Texas, told us, "I just let other people handle it; it was in other people's hands that were more knowledgeable than me." Thousands of future activists thought: *It's a good thing we don't have to worry about a horrendous thing like Trump getting elected, because somebody's gonna take care of it, right?*

Oops.

FROM COMMUNITY TO CONSTITUENT POWER

Indivisibles had come together in a moment of shock, fear, and anger after the 2016 election, but what they'd found was something that, for too many, had been missing: community. In interviewing and surveying Indivisible group leaders from across the country for this book, we heard no word more than "community."

Whether in blue, red, or purple states, the local Indivisible groups thrived because they filled this need. Local groups were continuing to grow not just because they were dedicated to taking down Donald Trump; they were growing because in some place, they were patching that missing social fabric back together. As Peter Kollm, a leader with Indivisible Somerville, told us: "I don't know anywhere in my adult life where I've met and gotten to know people from different walks of life before." The most effective groups were driven by friendships and a sense of community as much as they were by political motivation.

This was a throwback to old-fashioned community groups. And it was also critical for the success and growth of the Indivisible movement. Social media had allowed the *Indivisible Guide* to spread and groups to form. And just about all local Indivisible groups have their own email lists, Twitter accounts, Facebook pages, and other online presences and organizing tools. But Indivisible was not and is not an online phenomenon. Indivisibles built up strong personal ties with one another by actually meeting in person—just as Elks, Moose, Eagles, and Odd Fellows in the nineteenth and early twentieth centuries did. Through regular real-life meetings and advocacy events, Indivisible members built strong personal ties with one another that have helped sustain them individually and as a group through the many hard, demoralizing, and depressing moments of the Trump era.[24]

It may seem like a little thing, but these in-person meetings at breweries, community centers, and living rooms are the foundation of Indivisible's uniqueness, strength, and longevity. Indivisible Grapevine Area, for instance, had been holding weekly meetings for more than eighteen months when we talked to them for this book. Heather Thornton, one of the leaders who gives a weekly "sermon" on the week's events, told us that their consistent weekly meeting is key for community outreach: "We're there. We're there if you're scared; if you're angry; if you're hurt; if you just need to be around people."[25] Karen Ziegler, of Tuesdays with Tillis Indivisible in North Carolina, told us of their weekly meetings, "It is a bit like a church on the street: we sing, we socialize, we march around with signs, we chant, and we have speakers." The regular human contact built real community fabric that just didn't exist before Trump.

For Indivisible groups, building local community is about more than emotional support and sustainability. The whole idea of organizing in local communities comes from a basic understanding of how power works in American representative democracy: you have power in the place where you're rooted. Electeds are elected to represent their constituents and not

---

24. And needless to say there were a lot of those moments.

25. Heather also emphasized to us that these meetings "aren't bitch sessions." While they review the most recent Trump administration acts of terror or incompetence, the meetings stay positive and action-oriented. There's no sense in complaining about the world unless you're going to do something to fix it.

anybody else.[26] As a voter, as a constituent, as an organizer, your impact is greatest on your own community and your own elected representatives. Whether they're Democrats or Republicans, and whether you like them or not, they're your voice in the national policy agenda. They're who you need to convince or replace.[27]

This applies to Congress, which was the focus of the original *Indivisible Guide*, but it applies to all other levels of government in our representative democracy. And it turns out that once you get a group of people who are concerned about democracy together in a room, they find that there's a *lot* of work to be done, in every community and at every level of government.

So this isn't just about congressional advocacy, and it certainly isn't just about Trump. The long-term success of the Indivisible effort will depend not on winning a policy fight in Washington or a single election. Our theory is that if self-governing, independent leaders are building community-level progressive infrastructure throughout the country, then from that will flow our advocacy and electoral wins at the local, state, and federal levels. And that's what we're seeing.

It is now possible to consider that America's multi-decade retreat from civic engagement has reached an inflection point. The Odd Fellows aren't coming back,[28] but something new is on the horizon. So what does all this history mean for you?

---

26. There's a fun loophole in American democracy if you're super-famous or rich: then you can have influence over representatives who don't represent you.

27. The second part of this book will dive in detail into how to do that.

28. Sorry, Odd Fellow reader. We're not trying to pick on you here. We just don't think it's in the cards for you, old buddy.

Let's say you're a person who cares about politics and is worried about the direction of the country.[29] You probably get a lot of emails asking you to give money to candidates and political organizations. You probably get a lot of asks to sign petitions. You might be hit up by campaigns to fill volunteer shifts. In essence, you're asked to do things to support the experts, the people who've got this.

Has anyone ever told you that *you've* got this? That you don't need to be an expert to lobby your elected officials to take action? That you don't need to be a professional to bring a group of people together in your community? That your social networks, your professional experiences, your skills— your creativity and passion—are crucial? That the skills you've learned managing your daughter's soccer team, or running a PTA committee, or teaching high school, are some of the skills we need to save democracy? That you're not just a checkbook or a petition signer but a leader in training? That you yourself can run for office?

If not, we're here to tell you now. You have power. We don't mean this in a touchy-feely "Just believe in yourself" sort of way. We mean this in a steely-eyed "This is how power works in American democracy and we desperately need you to understand this; otherwise we're all screwed" kind of way. We're not informing you—we're imploring you. You need to understand this because it's the solution to a buckling and rigged democracy. It is the only way we will be able to build a real democracy in this country.

---

29. And if you don't, why on earth are you reading this book?

We have the chance to put a modern twist on a largely abandoned two-hundred-year-old concept of how American civic life is supposed to work. It's something new, and messy, and exciting—and it won't continue to grow unless we build it together. When Trump is gone and the dust settles, the power we have to demand change will be the power we've built. This will require confronting some very powerful forces lined up against us. These forces are committed to rigging our democracy. They're committed to dividing us and trying to prevent any meaningful reforms. These forces are much larger than any one of us individually, but they can be defeated if we stand together.

We know this works—and not just because we read it in an academic study. We've seen it work with our own eyes. We saw it used against us during the rise of the Tea Party. We saw it work as the *Indivisible Guide* went viral and turned into a movement capable of standing up to Trump and his allies. And we know it's how we will build a truly representative democracy after he's gone. The remainder of this book explains how we can wield this constituent power and what we can build if we do.

How We Win

How to Make Congress Listen

There go the people. I must follow them, for I am their leader.
—ALEXANDRE AUGUSTE LEDRU-ROLLIN, *French politician*

I've run bake sales. This is sort of like a big-ass bake sale.
—BARBARA ANDES, *Roanoke Indivisible*

If you're not in politics, you might not notice that an elected official works very, very hard to craft the right local image so that they can keep getting reelected. The reality is that every elected actually has two jobs: doing their job and *performing* their job. They introduce a bill, then host a press conference so everyone *sees* them introducing the bill. They host a town hall to listen to constituents and invite press so more people *see* them listening. They take calls from constituents, then follow up with responses so that constituents *feel* heard. They maintain entire staffs whose jobs are to deliver services, interact with constituents, get them media coverage, and just generally make them *look good* to the outside world.

What every elected wants—regardless of party—is for his or her constituents to agree with the following narrative:

My elected representative cares about me, shares my values, and is working hard for me.

Your leverage as a constituent comes from your ability to either threaten or reinforce this narrative.

That's the main theme of this chapter and the rest of Section Two. Here we exit the realm of historical political analysis. Now we get to tell some stories about Indivisible. We're not just telling stories for stories' sake. We're doing it to draw out useful lessons about how Indivisibles build and apply constituent power in real life.

But before we get to the stories, let's start with a general primer on advocacy by answering a basic question: What makes electeds tick?

Indivisible Lesson #1: Reelection, Reelection, Reelection
To influence elected officials, you have to understand that they wake up every morning with one thing on their mind: reelection. Your House member runs for office every two years, and your senators every six. Your school board, city council, county board of supervisors, and other local officials (we call them "electeds") face their own lengths of terms too. Functionally speaking, electeds are always either running for office or getting ready for their next election. And that shapes everything they do, from legislation to constituent outreach to media appearances to public events to fund-raising.

You might read this as saying that electeds are cynical and unprincipled. That's not true! Or at least it's often not true. Most electeds believe in their ideals and care deeply about representing their constituents and having a positive impact. But even the best and most dedicated public servants know that if they want to keep doing good things, they need to stay in office. That's why it's all about reelection.

This constant reelection pressure means that electeds are enormously sensitive to their image among constituents. Electeds who have good images as dependable, responsive public servants are likely to get reelected. Electeds with bad images risk a primary challenge, a general election defeat, or a stalled career with no chance for higher office. This is why politicians spend so much time carefully crafting their local images.

And this is what gives constituents power—even outside the voting booth. Constituents are real people living in the communities that electeds represent. They can get local news covering their protest. They can give quotes to reporters criticizing or praising their electeds' actions. They can influence the public image of their electeds by engaging in public actions that are seen by other constituents. It all works because their electeds care about reelection, and that means they have to care about an unruly bunch of constituents who could threaten their local image.

Now, you might have guessed that Congress as an institution has an approval rating on par with toenail fungus.[1] And

---

1. This is from a real poll. In a head-to-head popularity contest, a national poll found that Congress was less popular than toenail fungus, cockroaches, hemorrhoids, and dog poop. The poll was taken in 2013, so presumably the numbers are worse now for anybody paying attention.

that's for a good reason! It's corrupt, self-interested, inefficient, and wasteful. There's broad consensus that the system is rigged and that members of Congress are doing the rigging.

Your member of Congress understands that because they see the same polls as we do. They understand the public mood; that's how they got elected to begin with.[2] They know that their continued employment is literally dependent on convincing voters that they're the exception to the rule—that they're one of the few good people in Congress.[3]

That's where your leverage as a constituent comes in. When it comes to constituent interactions, electeds care about things that make them look good, responsive, and hardworking to the people of their district. They want their constituents to think well of them and they want positive local press. They hate surprises, wasted time, and, most of all, bad press that makes them look weak, unlikable, and vulnerable.

In practice, this means electeds care about some things very much, and other things very little:

ELECTEDS CARE A LOT ABOUT	ELECTEDS DON'T CARE MUCH ABOUT
Constituents from the district/state	People from outside the district/state

---

2. And in some cases a healthy dose of voter suppression and campaign finance creativity.

3. Usually they succeed in the charade. Members of Congress have reelection rates of about 90 percent. Do you think 90 percent of members of Congress deserve reelection? Neither do we.

Advocacy that requires effort (the more effort, the more they care): calls, personal emails, and especially constituents who show up at events in person in the district[4]	Form letters, tweets, Facebook comments (unless they generate widespread attention)
Local and national press, editorials, letters to the editor	Wonky policy analysis
An interest group's endorsement of a bill	Your thoughtful personal analysis of a bill
Groups of constituents, locally famous individuals, or big individual campaign contributors	A single constituent
Their donors and building their donor network	People who don't give them money
A concrete ask that entails a verifiable action: vote for a bill, make a public statement, etc.	Your general ideas about the world
One single ask in your communication (letter, email, phone call, office visit, etc.)	A laundry list of all the issues you're concerned about

---

4. A general rule of thumb for an elected: the amount of effort constituents are willing to expend is a good indication for how much they care. If constituents care enough about an issue only to sign a petition, the elected probably doesn't need to worry. On the other hand, if constituents care enough to show up at their office to talk about the issue, they probably care enough about it to knock on doors for the elected (or their opponent!) in the next election.

One theme you'll notice here is that electeds care first and foremost about their district and about the people in their district. An elected represents a constituency. A senator represents everybody in their state. A House member represents everybody in their district. Their job is literally to represent those people—their constituents—and not other people. Which means they care about their constituents and they don't care about people who aren't their constituents—unless those folks are writing big campaign checks.[5]

If you live in an elected's district, that person represents you, whether you voted for them or not. You're a constituent, and an elected is responsible for representing all their constituents, regardless of whether they can vote, whether they have citizenship, and whether or not they voted *for* that elected. That said, in practice, electeds tend to focus more on constituents who *might* vote for them, or people who can influence other people who *might* vote for them. This is a pretty practical calculation for electeds. Their time is limited, and at the back of their minds they're always thinking about how they can win their next election.

> *Indivisible Lesson #2: Other Electeds Don't Care What You Think, So Focus on Your Own*
> *There's a really important flip side to constituent power: if you don't live in an elected's district, they don't represent you, and they don't care what you think.*

---

5. If you've got deep pockets, electeds will be very interested in your thoughts whether or not you're a constituent. We're not praising this: it's a sort of (usually) legal corruption. Campaign donors get access to talk to electeds, and—lo and behold—the people with access often get their way.

This might seem harsh. We're sorry, but it's literally how electeds operate. If you're from Wyoming and you call the office of a Wyoming senator to give your opinion on a health care bill, the staffer on the other end of the phone is going to ask for your zip code, record your message, tally up the pro-/anti- calls, and tell the senator what his constituents are saying about the bill. If you're from California and you call that same Wyoming office and give your zip code, the staffer is going to thank you nicely for your call, hang up, throw your message in the trash, and go to lunch. The senator from Wyoming cares what people in Wyoming think. That's literally his job. It's just how our representative democracy works.[6]

That means your greatest impact comes from focusing on your own electeds, rather than trying to pressure electeds who represent other parts of the state or country. Trying to directly pressure electeds who don't represent you is quite simply a waste of time.

There is one real, unsavory loophole to this rule: money talks. If you're a major donor, you get special privileges,

---

6. This might seem unfair. Surely elected officials ought to think about the good of the whole, not just their district or state? In principle, representation based on different constituencies is actually quite fair. If our districts weren't rigged and our states were in the same ballpark size-wise, it'd be a very functional way of doing business! The problem is that today's system is wildly unrepresentative and dysfunctional. Gerrymandering has rigged the rules and deprived people of competitive, cohesive districts. And in the Senate about 40 million people in California have the same number of senators as fewer than 600,000 people in Wyoming. That's massively unfair (and Chapter 6 includes some ways to address it). But it's the way the system is set up right now, and harassing the senator from Wyoming isn't going to change that.

because your influence and money will directly help fuel the elected's reelection. So if you're rich enough to give a few thousand dollars to an elected's campaign, congratulations! The elected will care what you think even if you're not a constituent. For everybody else, stick to focusing on your own electeds.

So where do you come in? You, as a constituent, can use what your elected cares about to make sure they pay attention to what *you* care about.

To make this a bit more concrete and show what that looks like, we made a table.[7] Here are examples of actions that electeds might take, what they're hoping to see happen as a result, and what they really don't want to see happen.

ACTION TAKEN	DESIRED OUTCOME	VERY BAD OUTCOME
Congressman sends a letter to constituent about an issue of concern.	Constituent feels satisfied that their concerns were acknowledged and answered.	Constituent posts letter on social media saying it didn't answer their questions, or Congressman Bob didn't answer for weeks/months and is unresponsive and untrustworthy.

---

7. We are after all, in our heart of hearts, policy nerds who love tables.

Congresswoman hosts an in-district event.	Local newspaper reports that Congresswoman Sara appeared at the opening of a new bridge, which she helped secure funding for.	Local newspaper or national media report that protestors barraged Congresswoman Sara with questions about corruption in the infrastructure bill.
Congressman hosts a town hall/listening session.	Local newspaper reports that Congressman Bob hosted a town hall and discussed his work to balance the budget.	Local newspaper or national press report that angry constituents strongly objected to Congressman Bob's support for privatizing Medicare. Video of Congressman Bob stumbling on a question runs on the evening news.
Congresswoman takes a policy position.	Congresswoman Sara votes on a bill and releases a press statement hailing it as a step forward.	Congresswoman Sara's phones are deluged with calls objecting to the bill. Constituents stage an event outside her district office and invite press to hear them talk about how the bill will hurt their families.

You may notice something about this table: these outcomes are not totally within the elected's control. You have the power to make each of the actions result in either a good outcome or a bad outcome for the elected. Some electeds will go to great lengths to avoid bad outcomes—even as far as changing their positions on major policy issues.

You'll notice something else: to have an impact on the outcome, you usually need not just an individual but a group of people. That's important. Electeds and their staff have a limited amount of time and energy and face an overwhelming amount of incoming information from a whole bunch of sources, from constituents to donors to advocacy and interest groups to other electeds. Every day, they have to triage all this and figure out what's most important.

If you're an individual, your preferences do not tend to rank high on the list of what's important.[8] It's not personal; it's just a reality that every elected has a *lot* of constituents, and there's no realistic way to personally engage with all of them. The best an elected can do is try to aggregate individual preferences to get a rough sense of public opinion. That's what's happening when you call in to your elected's office to express your opinion on a bill: someone's taking your opinion down and adding it to their running tally of for/against calls.

A different calculus is at work when someone in power engages with a group—i.e., an organized community of people. They have to take groups more seriously because groups are

8. Again, unless you're a big donor. American democracy in action!

capable of a lot more than a single person, and their influence is broader. They also know groups of constituents can get attention from media, and that media can influence even *more* constituents. In short, electeds pay more attention to groups of constituents because groups are a threat in a way individuals are not.

> ### Indivisible Lesson #3: People Have Opinions, Groups Have Power
>
> *Indivisible's unit of activism isn't the individual—it's the local, volunteer-led group. That's because local groups can build and wield constituent power in ways that individuals can't. In short, local groups of constituents have power because they can either threaten or support electeds' reelection chances. Groups have the numbers, legitimacy, and capacity to do more than individuals—and that means they have power.*
>
> *Part of this is simple math—more people means more voters—but groups are more than the simple sum of their members. The mere fact of having a locally organized, named, permanent group lends legitimacy to the opinions of the individuals who make up that group—and that's power. That legitimacy means they're a source for media and attention in a way that individuals aren't. They have the ability to shape public perception in ways that individuals rarely can. Indivisible Greene County in Tennessee, for instance, can be cited as an entity by the local press and take a position on*

issues in support or in opposition to an elected. That's
important.

   Groups are also more effective at wielding political
power for some very basic practical reasons. They can
develop and execute collective strategies to achieve their
goals, whether that's passing or stopping a piece of legis-
lation, impacting the reputation of an elected official, or
powering a campaign. And because they can build com-
munities of like-minded people, they're sustainable in a
way that one individual's activism might not be.

   In short, if you want change, you can't go it alone. You
need the collective constituent power that comes with
working together toward a shared goal.

That's the theory, but it's not just theory. So let's talk about
how these lessons play out in the real world.

Rewind back to January 2017. Trump has just taken office.
The House and Senate are dominated by conservative majorities. Senate Majority Leader Mitch McConnell and Speaker of
the House Paul Ryan[9] are practically salivating at the chance to
turn their reactionary agenda into the law of the land. They've
spent the past seven years promising that they will repeal the
Affordable Care Act, President Obama's signature domestic
policy achievement, on their first day in office. Now they're
preparing to deliver on their promise.

---

9. Soon after the election, Ryan gushed that Trump will lead a "unified Repub-
    lican government" and that "The opportunity is now here. The opportunity
    is to go big, go bold . . ."

But members of Congress have no idea what's about to hit them.

WOMEN ALL UP IN HIS GRILL

Congressman Dave Brat had a problem.

Back in 2014, Brat, a conservative economics professor, had pulled off a Tea Party–driven insurgent Republican primary challenge to knock out Republican House majority leader Eric Cantor and take a seat the party assumed Cantor would hold into the indefinite future.[10] And for a couple of years, he'd had a very pleasant job: he could rail against immigrants, vote to repeal the Affordable Care Act (also known as Obamacare), and send his constituents long emails complaining about government waste. That was pretty much it. He didn't have to do much constituent outreach and didn't much worry about losing his seat. Virginia's outrageously gerrymandered districts guaranteed him a smooth path to reelection every two years.

But in January 2017 something strange started happening. His suburban Richmond district was in an uproar. He couldn't go anywhere without people—mostly women—demanding to know what he was doing to stop Trump (nothing), whether he'd protect the Affordable Care Act (no), and when he'd host his next town hall (seemingly never, if it was up to him).

---

10. Fun (or rather, awful) fact: Brat's original primary campaign was supported by Steve Bannon, who saw defeating Cantor as a way to kill off the bipartisan immigration reform effort of 2013.

Dave Brat wasn't used to this kind of public scrutiny, and he didn't respond well. He refused to attend or host open public events for constituents, and he did his best to avoid answering constituents' questions. In fact, he appeared to resent the idea that he should have to. "Since Obamacare and these issues have come up, the women are in my grill wherever I go," he groused in a meeting with local conservative activists. "They come up to me and go, 'When's the next town hall?' And believe me, it's not to give positive input."

Now, this is all very human. No one likes negative feedback! But the thing about being in Congress is you don't get to complain about your constituents talking to you. It's literally your job to hear them out. When Brat's kvetching made headlines, the women of Virginia's Seventh District responded in the only appropriate way: by mocking him mercilessly. They leaned into the grilling theme, hosting a "Brat-Worst" event near his office shortly afterward to call attention to his refusal to host public events. They organized town halls and invited him to attend—but made clear they'd go ahead without him if he refused to show up. The local press coverage was devastating. Within weeks, Brat had agreed to host a series of town halls.

Brat was not alone in his confusion, irritation, and alarm. In Colorado, when a crowd of over a hundred constituents showed up to talk to Representative Mike Coffman at a public event in his district, Coffman sneaked out a back door and fled the scene. And who could blame him? After all, the crowd—mostly retirees and women concerned about health care—had broken into a *rousing* rendition of "This Land Is Your Land" while waiting to see him. It was understandably terrifying. Coffman's retreat was caught on film by a constituent; it led the top of the news in his district that night.

In Arkansas, Senator Tom Cotton was surprised to find himself facing a spirited grassroots insurgency demanding answers—in public. Ozark Indivisible had sprung up after the 2016 election, cofounded by twenty-three-year-old Caitlynn Moses, and swiftly surged to a membership of thousands. When its first efforts to lobby Cotton's staff foundered and Cotton abruptly canceled a planned visit, the group decided to show up anyway and brought the local media with them. In a matter of weeks, they had generated enough outrage at Cotton's non-responsiveness to force him back for a town hall.

In deep-red Blount County, Tennessee, Sarah Herron pulled together a community named Indivisible East Tennessee and reached out to meet with their Republican congressman, Jimmy Duncan. Duncan flatly refused their request for a town hall, personally writing a letter in which he described them as "sore losers" and dismissed town halls as "shouting opportunities for extremists, kooks and radicals." This all came as a surprise to his local Indivisible group, a nonpartisan assortment of people concerned about Trump—many of them Republicans or former Republicans. As Sarah told the local newspaper, "When I got my letter from Duncan calling me a kook and a radical, I was heartbroken. I have always voted for Jimmy Duncan, and I felt very dumb that he didn't value me as a constituent." The outraged members of Indivisible East Tennessee promptly staged a well-covered event outside his office, "Kookfest," to highlight the moms, teachers, and business owners of Blount County who just wanted to talk to their elected representative.

Indivisible Lesson #4: Get You Some Earned Media

There's an old joke in politics: "The most dangerous place in Washington is between the congressman and a TV camera." This is a joke for a reason: no politician gets into office if they are not borderline obsessed with their press coverage.

That might sound cynical, but it's really pretty reasonable for electeds. No elected can possibly personally reach all their constituents. The vast majority of the time, they rely on media coverage to shape their image and to get their message out. Elected officials like coverage, especially local coverage, that makes them look like they've got the right values and are connected with constituents in their district. They get very upset about coverage that makes them look weak, out of touch, or just generally bad.

For Indivisibles, getting media coverage is all about building and applying power. It's an effective way to pressure your electeds. You can provide positive reinforcement with media coverage about your electeds standing up to fight for an issue you care about. Or you might get some negative media coverage about your electeds refusing to engage with constituents. Media attention pushes the elected to do what you want—or creates political costs if they don't.

Just as critically, media coverage is a great way to build your own grassroots community's brand and recruit more members. More press means more people know about your Indivisible group, which helps you keep growing your group and building your collective constituent power.

The best way to earn that media coverage is to make journalists' lives easy. Journalists are overworked, underpaid, and always up against a deadline. If you generate timely, useful content for them, more often than not they'll run with it. Reach out to the local TV and newspaper reporters in your community to build relationships. Preadvertise your actions to maximize their ability to cover them. Package what you do in quick, media-friendly bites that allow your overstretched press contacts to quickly add them to the story they're pulling together on a deadline. And then get it all out on Twitter, which is a major source for journalists looking for stories or sources to quote.

In Colorado, Indivisible Front Range Resistance (IFRR) and other Indivisibles held so many protests at Senator Cory Gardner's Denver district office that he up and moved his office location to a harder-to-protest federal building. Katie Farnan, a leader of IFRR, didn't let it slide. She got two local news stations to cover the news that Senator Gardner was trying to hide from his constituents. The local CBS station reported that "Republicans have been dogged by protestors all year, and that has led Senator Cory Gardner to move his Denver field office." Good neighbors that they are, the Indivisibles promptly visited him at his new office to give him an office-warming gift—you know, just to welcome him to the neighborhood and let him know that everyone knew where he'd moved.

Across the country, Republicans and Democrats were facing the same unexpected phenomenon: a wave of constituents demanding their representatives actually represent them. These constituents weren't just asking with polite letters or phone calls—they were showing up in person, making noise, and getting press.

This was unnerving for everyone, but most Democrats adapted faster. Pressure made them change their behavior. Republicans, on the other hand, were stuck between a rock and a hard place. They had no desire to break from the Trump administration, and they weren't prepared to defend themselves from constituents who were upset about their federal policy priorities. They just wanted to go about their business without facing any questions. That's the way their job as members of Congress had always worked before.

The members of Congress didn't realize yet that their jobs had changed.

TOWN HALLS AND SOROS-FUNDED ASTROTURF

In February 2017, Congress went home for what's commonly known as "recess." The word "recess" is actually a bit misleading; it suggests that this period is a break. Recess is not a break. In fact, its actual name is the "District Work Period," when there are no votes or hearings in Washington. This is when members of Congress get free time to meet with their constituents back home.

Recess is also when most members of Congress schedule their listening forums, like town halls, and in February 2017 a lot of Republican members went ahead and put town halls on the books. Under normal circumstances, town halls tend to be sleepy affairs, attended mostly by retirees and other people with flexible schedules and long, confusing lists of grievances.[11] In 2009 the Tea Party had stormed town halls nationwide to great effect, stunning Democratic and Republican representatives alike and dealing a serious blow to the effort to pass health care reform. In 2017, we knew—because our in-box was full of messages from around the country—that Indivisibles were getting ready to turn the tables.

Not a lot of other people knew that yet. The *Indivisible Guide* had received enthusiastic coverage in political media outlets, but the growth of the grassroots movement hadn't yet cracked the mainstream media, so there wasn't a high level of public awareness and understanding of what was brewing nationwide. Back at Indivisible HQ, we'd been doing our best to get Indivisible groups press coverage and to convey to as many people as possible that something very big was happening. It wasn't easy. You try explaining to a political reporter that a massive grassroots resistance movement is taking shape and you know that because there are a zillion new groups called

---

11. Ezra: Seriously, before the Tea Party, town halls and district listening events were pretty darn boring affairs. The highest-risk scenario was that some constituent would come yell at your boss (the member of Congress) about some niche issue. As a staffer, you would get to know the handful of these repeat attendees, and you'd prep the boss ahead of time to try to avoid any sort of uncomfortable interaction. It was pretty low stakes and low drama compared to what would come.

"Indivisible" on Facebook and your in-box is overflowing with random people making plans to pressure their elected officials. Most were skeptical, and reasonably so.

It was early February when we got our first call from CNN. Kyung Lah, a CNN correspondent, was outside a high school in Cottonwood Heights, Utah, where Representative Jason Chaffetz was preparing to face a very large and very frustrated crowd. Indivisible Utah and other grassroots groups had mobilized over a thousand people to pack Chaffetz's town hall. Those who couldn't fit in the auditorium were protesting outside. They'd brought green and red signs so members of the crowd could wave them to signal approval or disapproval as Chaffetz spoke. There was a lot of red that night. In the Q&A session, questioners honed in on Chaffetz's unwillingness as chairman of the House Oversight Committee to investigate any of Trump's rampant ethics issues, a choice that contrasted starkly with the witch hunt he'd waged for years by carrying out transparently partisan investigations of Hillary Clinton's emails. His constituents responded to his weak excuses with chants of "Do your job!"

Their preparation and outrage paid off: the visuals and headlines coming out of the event showed a congressman facing a shocking revolt in his own ruby-red district.

Chaffetz wasn't alone.

Having bowed to constituent pressure to host a town hall, Senator Tom Cotton, over in Arkansas, now looked out over a sea of angry, concerned faces, struggling to find his supporters. The room was overflowing: as Ozark Indivisible's Caitlynn Moses told us, "They'd had to change location twice, and they wouldn't give us a date because they couldn't find a place big enough . . . [T]housands of people came specifically to just yell at Tom Cotton." Questioner after questioner took the mic and demanded to know why he was trying to take away their health care. Kati McFarland, a young woman with a rare genetic disorder, brought the crowd to tears with her story and concluded starkly: "Without the coverage for pre-existing conditions, I will die. That's not hyperbole." In the face of his constituents' emotional, powerful appeals, Cotton seemed unable to cope. The story coming out of the February 2017 congressional recess was one of lives saved by the Affordable Care Act—and put at risk by Trump-supporting senators like Cotton.

> ### Indivisible Lesson #5: Pictures, or It Didn't Happen
> *When you're doing public advocacy, you've got two different audiences: the people who are right there with you in the room and the much wider audience whom you might be able to reach afterward. Getting your story or message out to that larger audience requires making it come alive.*
>
> *This is critically important, because most of the time the visuals of politics are boring: a scripted speech, an interminable committee meeting, an impenetrable hundred-page-long bill. This stuff is important—that impenetrable health care bill might be the difference between someone's life and death—but it's not inherently dramatic. And because boring stuff doesn't get viewers, clicks, or shares, it's less likely to make the news.*
>
> *It's your job to change this dynamic. It's possible that your riveting personal account of confronting your elected*

will catch fire—but it's a lot more likely if you can show, not tell. That's where video and pictures come in. They make the moment come alive for the people who aren't there with you. First, you develop tactics that make politics dramatic—bird-dogging, town hall confrontations, creative events—and then you package that drama so that it can be disseminated widely. If you create delicious content— drama, conflict, visuals, sound bites—then you're doing your local journalist's or TV station's job for them.

In every encounter and every action, you should always be thinking: How will I capture the video or pictures that are most important for my message or my story? And how will I get those things to the people who can spread them: local media, my own network, my social platforms? Storytelling is critical to your advocacy, and these images are critical tools for storytelling.

The fight to save the Affordable Care Act was about more than resisting Trump; it was intensely personal. Trish Florence of Indivisible SATX was fighting for Medicaid for her family. Lisa Dullum with Greater Lafayette Indivisible was a breast cancer survivor and depended on the Affordable Care Act for her own care. Rosemary Dixon with Prescott Indivisible credited the Affordable Care Act for saving her life when she needed a kidney transplant. Kim Benyr of Ozark Indivisible was fighting for the Affordable Care Act while her young daughter, Maddy, was facing terminal cancer. In between events pressuring Tom Cotton, Ozark Indivisible put together a binder full of stories and pictures for their senators and representatives on how the Affordable Care Act had saved their lives and the lives of their children, family, and friends. They delivered the binders in person to bewildered congressional staffers in northwest Arkansas. Across the country, groups like Indivisible Kansas City, Indivisible Lovettsville, and Indivisible Austin compiled stories from people whose lives or financial stability had been saved by the ACA and shared them virtually and in person.

It shouldn't have been a surprise that a bill that would throw millions off their health care was unpopular. But the speed, scope, strategy, and sheer splashiness with which people had organized all over the country was certainly a surprise. These public, visual, media-ready confrontations were suddenly taking place across the country. If you weren't part of the grassroots surge yourself, all this seemed to come out of nowhere.

CNN's Kyung Lah, in Utah, called us to ask the question that was about to be on everyone's lips: Where did all these people *come from*?

We described the *Indivisible Guide*, how it had helped spark grassroots groups nationwide, and that it was these local groups that were doing the work. The town halls that were hitting the national radar now weren't flash protests; they were the product of groups of people who'd started organizing weeks earlier and now had the capacity to turn out constituents in large numbers. We obviously had not personally organized a thousand people to show up at a town hall in Utah. We'd been in touch with the Utah groups—a few weeks earlier they'd reached out for help when police had responded to a routine polite visit to a congressional office by arresting their members—but we'd had only one day's heads-up that the Chaffetz town hall was happening.

Lah explained why she was asking: "Congressman Chaffetz is claiming that this is an Astroturf effort and that many of the protestors are being paid by outside groups."[12]

We had no idea how to respond to this, because it made no sense. We were *paying* people to show up? Like, logistically, how would that even work? But Chaffetz wasn't the only one to fling this bogus accusation at his local grassroots interlocutors. With the Women's March, the airport protests against Trump's Muslim ban, and now the raucous town halls, Republicans nationwide were reeling. Taking their cues straight from the White House, they agreed: the problem wasn't massive popular opposition to their agenda, hypercharged by widespread horror at the election of Donald Trump. That couldn't be it! No, something else was going on.

Dismayed conservatives landed on an explanation: paid protestors, probably funded by liberal philanthropist George Soros, were responsible for this ruckus. Sean Spicer explained to Fox News that what was happening was "a very paid, Astroturf-type movement." Representative Dave Brat urged the press to "Google 'Indivisible' and the Soros-funded movement that is pushing all of this." Right-wingers started hunt-

---

12. "Astroturf" is a term used in politics to describe fake grassroots activism that's paid for by some outside source. For-profit industries often pay for Astroturf when they're trying to pressure electeds or generate public pressure for their goals.

ing for evidence of this shadowy conspiracy.[13] They published exposés "revealing" the secret playbook being used to disrupt town halls (aka the *Indivisible Guide*). A conservative opposition research firm even sent a tracker to follow us at a donor conference and posted creepy, surreptitious video of us on a right-wing news site in a bizarre effort to "prove" that we were Soros funded. (At the time, we weren't.)[14]

These allegations drew on an age-old anti-Semitic smear: that a Jewish banker was pulling strings behind the scenes to create chaos. They were also hilariously false. And while we were nervous about the security implications of becoming right-wing targets, we were mostly struck by the irony of being branded a slick Astroturf operation. As of February 2017, our fledgling organization was the functional equivalent of a bunch of kids in a trench coat pretending to be an adult. We had a website and an email address. We were talking to Indivisible groups, getting press, forming partnerships, sending emails to our growing list, producing policy analysis, and publishing social media updates. From the outside, we were doing a pretty

---

13. Ezra: One of my favorite early articles in this vein came from a hilariously incompetent right-wing news outfit, Daily Signal, that "revealed" that my former employer (an anti-poverty think tank) once had a board member who had once had a fellowship that had been funded by a Soros-backed foundation—therefore proving my deep ties to Soros. Got me!

14. Leah: While we had not actually gotten any funding from Open Society Foundations at this point, the incessant right-wing attacks actually helped bring us together. Later in 2017, when Ezra spoke at a public event, an OSF executive in the crowd came up to him and joked, "Hey, I just wanted to introduce myself, since apparently we're funding everything you're doing." We're now a proud grantee of OSF. Thanks for making that connection possible, right-wing conspiracy theorists!

solid impersonation of an actual nonprofit with staff and a budget. In reality, we were a collective of roughly one hundred frazzled, sleep-deprived volunteers rapidly approaching the end of our collective ropes.[15] Our biggest expenses to date had been T-shirts and pizza for volunteers, which we put on our personal credit card. We'd quit our jobs, but no one had gotten a dime of pay yet.[16] And we sure weren't paying anyone else.

The idea that some deep-pocketed donor was paying for all this was also absurd and darkly hilarious to the Indivisible leaders spending their nights, weekends, and fake sick days building the burgeoning movement nationwide. "Soros-funded Astroturf" became something of an inside joke for the Indivisible movement. Group leaders would show up at mass protests with signs that said "Hey, George, where's my check?" or wearing shirts emblazoned with the moniker "Unpaid Protestor."

At the same time, the right-wing pushback was also taking stranger and scarier forms for groups around the country. In California, Republican representative Dana Rohrabacher's office called the cops on a group of moms from Indivisible OC 48 after a bizarre scuffle in which a Rohrabacher staffer accidentally hit a toddler with a door—the toddler had been delivering

---

15. The combination of these factors produced some very odd moments. We'll never forget the time in March that a staffer at a foundation dressed us down for not being serious because "your environmental policy person hasn't gotten back to me." At the time, our "environmental policy person" was a federal employee who did most of her work on her phone while taking suspiciously long lunch breaks and hiding in the office bathroom.

16. Hence our standard response to all press inquiries about whether we were funded by George Soros: "Not yet, but we'd love to be! Could you connect us?"

Valentine's Day cards—then fell over herself. Rohrabacher followed up by issuing an unhinged press release denouncing the moms as a "mob" of "unruly activists" who were "enemies of American self-government and democracy." Indivisible OC 48's leaders were subjected to vicious online fury and harassment, but Indivisible OC doubled down on its scrutiny of Rohrabacher.

Those organizing in traditionally conservative areas ran into their own problems. Sarah Herron, the leader in Indivisible East Tennessee, noted the fear of social and professional reprisals against those closely affiliated with anti-Trump resistance. One Southern Indivisible organizer who made headlines organizing to pressure her conservative electeds to hold town halls was told by her employer that she'd have to quit Indivisible or quit her job. She handed in her resignation the next day.

But this kind of experience wasn't just confined to red states. New Jersey's NJ 11th for Change was an Indivisible group that had been pushing Republican representative Rodney Frelinghuysen through a well-organized weekly event called "Fridays with Frelinghuysen" (which Frelinghuysen was invited to but never attended). The group was rocked when Frelinghuysen responded to the pressure by reaching out directly to the bank where one group leader, Saily Avelenda, was employed to complain to her bosses. Under pressure from the bank, Avelenda quit her job, then took her story—including the handwritten note Frelinghuysen had sent to a board member of the bank—to the press.

These are just a few of the stories that came back to us. For every one recounted here, there were more stories we heard from grassroots leaders across the country facing threats, ostracism, and even violence in their communities—all for standing up and making their voices heard. But the Indivisible movement kept building. These leaders had gotten involved because the country had fallen into the hands of a vile, dangerous bully. They were not going to put up with harassment in their own communities.

HELP! MY MEMBER OF CONGRESS IS HIDING!

The February 2017 town halls roiled American politics. But after the initial outpouring of public outrage, we started hearing something strange from Indivisible groups: Republican members of Congress were going missing. There was no need to be concerned for their safety—they were still turning up for fund-raisers—but their public schedules were oddly empty. They were avoiding town halls, meeting only in small groups with friendly constituents, and refusing to give out their whereabouts. It was all very mysterious.

Well, actually, it wasn't mysterious at all. We knew exactly what was going on: Republicans were trying to ride out the storm in hiding. They didn't want to field tough questions about supporting Trump, whose popularity was plummeting in their states. They didn't want to accidentally create a viral moment with a constituent desperately begging them to protect their lives by saving the Affordable Care Act. And they *especially* didn't want any negative news coverage.

Remember, no member of Congress wants to look unresponsive, unpopular, or aloof. That's the kind of thing that loses reelections. So it was a rational response: they'd calculated that the risk of hiding from their constituents was lower than the risk of being caught in public. If Indivisibles were going to keep the pressure on, we needed to change that calculus and raise the costs of going into hiding. So our team put our guide hats back on and wrote the *Missing Members of Congress Action Plan*—a new guide for turning up the heat.

The basic idea: members were hiding to avoid negative press, so we needed to make sure that hiding *produced* negative press through creative, attention-getting, funny actions. Across the country, Indivisible groups began orchestrating "empty chair" town halls and other public events. At well-attended town halls in Washington State, Indivisibles used a conspicuously empty chair to play up the absence of their no-show congressman, Dave Reichert.

Indivisible groups in Michigan's Eleventh Congressional District took it a step further at their empty-chair town hall. They brought a live chicken onstage to represent their no-show Republican congressman, Dave Trott. Local news covered the event, noting it was "a not so subtle way of communicating their belief that Trott is being 'chicken' for not being available to speak with his constituents." Subtle or not, it drove the point home about Trott.

In Colorado, Katie Farnan, a leader in Indivisible Front Range Resistance, was fed up with her no-show Republican senator Cory Gardner. In response, she and IFRR worked with ProgressNow Colorado to bring to life "Cardboard Cory," who, unlike his flesh-and-blood counterpart, actually showed up to constituent events all across the state, generating media coverage and making Gardner look ridiculous. They had intentionally created Cardboard Cory to be eye-catching, funny, and eviscerating—and that meant it got attention.[17]

In one particularly memorable incident of local pressure, Representative Darrell Issa, a California Republican who'd traveled to Florida to raise money, found himself under siege by Action Together Suncoast, an Indivisible group in Sarasota. Issa was thousands of miles from home, but the Indivisible groups in his district had alerted their compatriots that Issa was hiding from his constituents and holding a beachfront fundraiser in their hometown. The Sarasota group kayaked out to confront him and demanded that he go home to his constituents to do a town hall. A chastened Issa's spokesperson assured the media covering the event that he planned to hold a town hall.

Live chickens, cardboard cutouts, and kayaktivism are fun and funny—and that's what makes them so politically devastating. People in power can be many things, but they can't afford to be ridiculous. That's why humor, pranks, creative actions, and satire have been so central to nonviolent revolutions worldwide—and why this flavor of pressure tactic is so common within the Indivisible movement.[18]

---

17. In addition to thousands of followers for Cardboard Cory's wickedly sarcastic Twitter account.

18. In Serbia, Srdja Popovic was part of the successful Otpor! movement—a grassroots people power movement to take down the vicious and violent tyrant Slobodan Milošević. Otpor! engaged in tactics designed to force authorities into ridiculous situations. "Laughter was our greatest weapon against the regime," Popovic recalled.

Indivisible Lesson #6: Don't Be Boring

Indivisibles aren't boring. Indivisibles get new recruits and garner a ton of media coverage because we stage visual, interesting actions full of humor, conflict, or poignancy (or all of the above).

But there's a deeper reason why it's important to not be boring. In her book Twitter and Tear Gas: The Power and Fragility of Networked Protest, *sociologist Zeynep Tufekci describes how modern social movements often get stuck in "tactical freeze." They learn to do one thing— a march or type of protest—and they just keep doing that tactic. But if your tactics stay the same, your target will adapt defenses to defang you and learn to work around you. Tactical innovation is necessary to avoid becoming stale and ineffective.*

From the beginning, Indivisibles have been preternaturally successful at getting attention for their advocacy and actions because their advocacy and actions have been unusual and unexpected. The original In-divisible Guide included a handful of tactics—town halls, district office visits, mass call-in campaigns— but this was never meant to be an exhaustive list, and Indivisibles quickly began to innovate their own approaches.

Indivisibles aren't elected officials. We're not part of the political establishment, and we aren't constrained by political debts or professional ties. So we're free to do interesting stuff outside the traditional, staid realm of regular politics. Indivisibles dress like The Handmaid's Tale *characters to protest Republican anti-choicers. They hold die-ins at congressional offices to illustrate the mortal consequences of repeal of the Affordable Care Act. They kayak out to beachfront congressional fund-raisers to demand accountability.*

Innovative tactics catch our advocacy targets off guard. This is also compelling, visually stimulating stuff—the kind of stuff that brings more people into the group and gets media coverage. Being not boring is more fun for everyone involved, and it builds power.

The really funny thing was, the fact that elected officials were going missing was a *good* sign. It meant the strategy of mass, public grassroots resistance was working—or at least, the strategy was working sufficiently well that Republicans had needed to switch course.

TRUMPCARE AND THE NO-SUNLIGHT STRATEGY

In Washington, the pressure was mounting for elected Trump supporters—especially those supporting the president's "Trumpcare" plan to repeal the Affordable Care Act.

We were now months into the Trump administration. Congressional Republicans were well overdue in delivering on their promise to get rid of the Affordable Care Act on the first day of Congress. Republican Speaker of the House Paul Ryan had spent months refereeing a complicated tug-of-war between the ultraconservative House Freedom Caucus members, who

demanded a full repeal of the Affordable Care Act, and traditional Republicans from swing districts, who argued that the
repeal should strip health care from only 20 million Americans
instead of 32 million. (Yes, these were the so-called moderates.)
With every week that passed, there was more press coverage of
the House Trumpcare policy debate: which provisions would
remain, what would be taken away, which constituencies would
be affected. It was all very contentious and ugly and embarrass-
ing for House Republicans—and great for those of us trying to
sink their efforts.

During this months-long process, the House Trumpcare bill
also met with intense public scrutiny and opposition across the
progressive infrastructure, from the national to the hyperlocal
level. Indivisibles teamed up with Planned Parenthood to keep
the heat on congressional district offices. Constituents flooded
congressional phone lines. In red and blue states, person after
person stood up in crowded town halls to say that they would
be dead or bankrupt without the Affordable Care Act. From
California to Arkansas to Florida, they made national news at
these meetings, describing with heartfelt sincerity how they or
their family members would suffer if their representatives were
to support repeal. Face-to-face with cancer survivors, parents
of disabled children, and young people with preexisting conditions, congressional Republicans looked heartless—because
they were acting heartless.

As a result of the media coverage, the public became aware
that Republicans in the House were trying to cut Medicaid and
gut coverage for preexisting conditions. And people around the

country were reasonably frightened and furious. From an advocacy perspective, this was a virtuous cycle: more coverage meant more scared and angry people, which meant more protesting, which meant more coverage. Through it all, Trumpcare's approval ratings kept falling. Even for the most heartless Republicans, this public unpleasantness was creating some real problems.

The public outcry meant that Ryan had to delay the legislative process repeatedly and, in March, admit temporary defeat. On March 24, 2017, the day the House was expected to pass Trumpcare, Ryan was instead forced to pull the bill from the floor when a group of moderate Republicans suddenly ran for the exits. A frustrated Ryan gave a speech declaring that "Obamacare is the law of the land" and would remain so "for the foreseeable future."

For the next two months Ryan kept as quiet as possible while trying to hammer out a compromise that would work for his coalition of extremists and anxious swing seaters. As is typical whenever congressional Republicans negotiate with each other, the bill just got crueler over time. Meanwhile, Republicans' nerves began to recover. By May they were ready to take another shot. As soon as Ryan had the votes for the bill, he moved to put it on the floor. It was understandable that he wanted to act quickly and quietly: at the time, Trumpcare had a staggeringly low 31 percent approval rating. Rushed through without time for most of the Republican caucus to even understand what was in it, the bill passed on May 4 with just two votes to spare. As the vote was taken, Democratic members on the floor chanted, "*Na na na, na na na, hey hey, goodbye!*"—a grim reminder to Republicans of the coming electoral consequences.

The blowback for members in the House who'd voted for the bill was swift and lasting.[19] Indivisible groups were furious, and they let their representatives and the local press know. At Indivisible national, we launched the Payback Project with Women's March, MoveOn, and other allies to amplify efforts to demand accountability for the vote. Stories and pictures poured in from the grassroots across the country. In one particularly evocative and darkly funny demonstration, Indivisible Las Cruces in New Mexico orchestrated "A Wake to Commemorate the Demise of Representative Steven Pearce's Political Career." They staged a reading of the many reasons that Pearce was politically finished and danced around a faux-casket. Similar scenes of constituent fury played out across the country.

But for now the legislative deed was done in the House. Having cleared its first major obstacle, Trumpcare now moved to the Senate, and that meant Republican Senate majority leader Mitch McConnell was up at bat.

McConnell is one of the great villains of our political era, a smart, cynically effective reactionary conservative. And he was ready to do whatever it took to pass this bill. While legislation in the Senate normally requires 60 votes to overcome a filibus-

---

19. Stay tuned for later in the book, when we relish the eventual comeuppance that arrived in November 2018.

ter, McConnell was prepared to circumvent the rule and pass repeal with just a simple majority.[20] With only a slim majority in the Senate, McConnell knew that any public process similar to the House's would further hurt the bill's popularity, which could cost him votes he couldn't afford to lose. So he made a perfectly reasonable and cynical decision: avoid any public debate whatsoever.

To accomplish this, McConnell would employ a strategy defined by secrecy and speed. Instead of holding an open, public discussion of various alternatives to the Senate Trumpcare bill, he would ensure that all negotiations happened behind closed doors. Fewer public discussions would mean less public conflict, which would mean less press coverage, which would mean less public outcry. But secrecy wouldn't work forever; anyone could see that. Bill details would leak. Frustrated negotiating partners would go to the press. Public hearings would unearth damaging details about the bill and the harm it would do. The protest cycle would kick in, just as it had during the multi-month House fight. McConnell couldn't let that happen, and so his strategy was simple: no sunlight, no outrage; no outrage, no problem.

After the House passed Trumpcare, the Senate had thirty-six days in session before the weeklong congressional recess for the Fourth of July holiday. McConnell was desperate not to

---

20. If you want to get wonky and technical about it, McConnell was committing to use something known as "budget reconciliation." It was the same maneuver Senate Republicans used years earlier to pass George W. Bush's giant tax cuts for the rich, and it would be the same maneuver that would be used to pass Trump's tax cuts for the rich as well later in 2017.

allow senators to go home to holiday parades while an unpopular Trumpcare bill was under debate; that would invite unwelcome public pressure. So his strategy was to rework a massive portion of the American economy in thirty-six days behind closed doors, then pass it before anyone could raise the alarm.

At this point McConnell was winning. We had every reason to believe that he would get to 50 votes to pass the repeal.[21] Senators had yet to face public pressure. More independent-minded Republican senators like Lisa Murkowski of Alaska, Jerry Moran of Kansas, and Susan Collins of Maine hadn't seen any real protests at their doorsteps. Protests against what? There was no public Senate bill, nor much media coverage of the hypothetical bill. We weren't totally screwed yet, but things were looking grim.

At Indivisible HQ (now an attic in a coworking space rather than our living room, to the enormous relief of everyone involved),[22] we could see only two ways for the collective progressive movement and the army of Indivisible groups to counter this strategy. First, throw everything we had at raising the temperature in the home states of target senators *right now*. Second, find a way—*any* way—to slow down McConnell.

---

21. Ezra: On June 12, I wrote in my journal, "The fear now is Trumpcare passes the Senate by the end of the month. McConnell has said as much. We need 3 Republicans to defect. It looks tough. Not impossible but tough. If it passes the Senate now, it looks unstoppable after."

22. Leah: The relief was real but also limited. The air-conditioning in that attic kept cutting out. And one of the worst places in the country is an attic in D.C. in the summer without air-conditioning. Summer heat would give way to fall showers, which revealed a pretty healthy number of holes in our roof. This was the command central of the national Soros Astroturf operation.

Our thinking was simple: we needed to grind down progress on the Senate Trumpcare bill so we could make it to the
weeklong July Fourth congressional recess without a vote. If
we could do that, the progressive community could organize in-
state opposition to the bill while senators were home for parades
and other public events. If the bill were to come up for a vote in
June, we were sunk. But if we could push the vote into July, we
might have a shot. It wasn't a sure thing, but a long-shot future
potential win was better than a short-term guaranteed loss.

We could do more to raise the temperature than ever before, for a simple reason: over the past few months we'd started
to build up a real professional national operation. Fueled by
grassroots donations, we'd made our first hires, drawing on
our own pool of volunteers and recruiting campaign staffers
just off the 2016 cycle. By June we had six full-time regional
organizing leads, each covering five to ten states. Since starting, they'd been actively reaching out to groups in their turf to
make contact. With more than five hundred groups each at the
time, this was obviously a work in progress.[23] Now the organizers started raising the alarm bells to the groups they'd touched:
the Senate Trumpcare bill was going to move soon, and it was
going to move fast. We couldn't wait to make a big show of
force when senators were home for recess; we needed to do
whatever we could *right now*.

---

23. In many cases, this was the first person-to-person contact we had with Indivisible groups who'd registered on the site and been putting the guide into
action for months. Organizers had to spend a lot of time convincing group
leaders that they were real, that we were in fact now a proper organization,
and that this was not an elaborate and confusing scam.

We also now had actual policy and communications teams. Angel Padilla, a fellow former congressional staffer and co-author of the *Indivisible Guide*, led the policy team to partner with the leading national health care groups, like Protect Our Care and Planned Parenthood, to coordinate on strategy. For communications, Sarah Dohl, who'd been secretly leading the communications team while moonlighting from her job as VP for a nonpartisan nonprofit, and Emily Phelps, a former Hill press secretary who'd made it her mission to coach and connect fledgling activists to national press, had come on board full-time. Caroline Kavit, who had been volunteering full-time while also working her full-time job at an international human rights nonprofit, joined the staff to lead our design and web work. We were starting to look like a real organization!

Together, the national team launched the "Trumpcare 10" campaign—targeting Republican senators who could potentially be persuaded to vote against repeal. We adjusted our appeals by state to make sure each senator was hearing from their constituents about their own top concern—from Medicaid for Senator Shelley Moore Capito in West Virginia to opioids for Senator Susan Collins in Maine.

Indivisible Lesson #7: Beware of Fairy-Tale Tactics

All too often, we hear the refrain "I just want to do something!" But it's not enough to just "do something." Indivisibles ensure our tactics line up with our goals and your strategy to translate into the change we want to see. There are three common characteristics of good tactics:

1. *Good tactics are strategic. They make good use of your resources and bring you closer to accomplishing your ultimate goals.*

2. *Good tactics are motivational. They're fun and inspiring and show solidarity. Indivisible is a people-powered movement, so people have to want to participate. If you do fun and rewarding things, more people will do them, and that will mean more impact.*

3. *Good tactics build capacity. They improve your fellow Indivisibles' ability to work together and help build and empower new leaders. The best tactics don't just expend group energy—they build up new energy.*

You should always be wary of tactics that don't have these characteristics. We call these latter tactics "fairy-tale tactics": they sound nice, they feel good to do, and they have little to no impact on the real world. Always ask yourself: Are your tactics connected to your strategy? If you can't say how, you might have a fairy-tale tactic on your hands.

There are lots of fairy-tale tactics out there, but one big example is the online petition. With some exceptions, online petitions will have almost no impact on your electeds. Instead, they're usually just used by organizations or political campaigns to harvest your email address and cell phone numbers so you can be targeted for fund-raising later.

> *Indivisibles think hard about their tactics; we think about how they will actually help us achieve our goals. A fairy-tale tactic will at best be a distraction and at worst demotivate your members, who will lose faith that their actions really matter.*

We knew that no online petition drive or Twitter thread was going to change the minds of red state Republican senators. We needed visible displays of people power. We needed senators to understand that this was not politics as usual. Indivisible groups in critical target states like Louisiana, Maine, and West Virginia did precisely that. In Louisiana, Indivisibles showed up at all seven of Senator Bill Cassidy's district offices on the same day, orchestrating "First Do No Harm" rallies from Baton Rouge to Shreveport to Lake Charles and in between. In Maine, Indivisibles led visits and sit-ins at every single one of Senator Collins's offices on the same day. Indivisible Birmingham planned a five-day health care sit-in, "We Dare to Defend Our Rights," at both of their Republican senators' offices. Indivisible Little Rock and Central Arkansas planned a "Vigil to Save the Affordable Care Act" at Senator Tom Cotton's Little Rock office.

While the country's eyes were focused on pivotal swing votes, the nationwide scale of the Trumpcare resistance was critical. A political caucus is like a herd: it's a function of a bunch of people's individual behavior, and they're all looking to one another for cues. So it matters not only how people are going to vote but how enthusiastic those votes might be.

We knew that in any scenario where Trumpcare went down, there'd be a small set of Republicans who took a public stand against it and a larger number of Republicans who'd vote yes if it came to the floor, but who quietly hoped it wouldn't.

Take someone like Republican senator Marco Rubio, for example. Rubio was never on the list of possible flips. He was never going to buck the president publicly, because he's a coward.[24] He was always going to be a public yes vote. But if we generated ferocious opposition in his state, someone like Rubio might quietly start to think his political future would be better served by a scenario in which the bill didn't pass. He might start to mutter to his colleagues about all the anti-Trumpcare pressure he's getting. He might be secretly relieved when a few of his colleagues are blocking the bill. If a lot of those yes votes were thinking like Marco Rubio, the bill would be a lot less likely to pass. There's a big difference between a situation in which forty-seven members of the caucus desperately want to pass a bill and three are holding out, and a situation in which many of those forty-seven have quietly started to lose the will to pass the bill at all. Those nervous yeses make it much safer for a small number of no votes to take a stand.

So at this point we had helped build a nationwide wave of outrage. But it would take more than that to delay the bill into the July Fourth recess. It would take pushing not just our adversaries but our friends.

---

24. Feel free to fact-check this.

THE SCHUMER SHUFFLE

Senate Democrats were in the minority; they didn't have the power to set the agenda. But the Senate Democrats did have the power to delay a vote through a series of procedural maneuvers. What was just absolutely galling to us, though, was that they were not, as of early June, planning to do so. They opposed Trumpcare, of course. They made speeches about it. They declared their unified opposition to it. But they were reluctant to use every procedural tool available to them and force a delay. They were nervous about using maneuvers that might ruffle feathers or make them look like obstructionists.[25] And they had other priorities they wanted to move (and get good press for). In short, they weren't interested in pulling out all the stops to delay business in the Senate.

We knew the Senate Democratic leadership wasn't interested in playing congressional hardball because they were telling us that directly. In the preceding few months, Indivisible had started getting invited to the coordinating tables in Washington where Democratic leadership, progressive movement partners, and advocacy groups strategize, coordinate, and debate. Democrats in Congress weren't sure what was going on with this decentralized "resistance," but they knew we seemed to have ties to people on the ground, and they wanted to be linked up as tightly as possible. Suddenly we had access, but when we disagreed on strategy, as we did now, we still needed

---

25. As you may have noticed, this self-restraint and respect for institutional norms rarely burdens GOP senators or representatives.

to push on our friends. And we worried, because it looked like everything was going according to McConnell's plan.[26]

Things came to a head on Father's Day 2017. We were on the phone with Schumer's staff, asking that he lead Democrats to use the tools at their disposal to block business as usual in the Senate and raise the temperature on Trumpcare—in this case, by using a procedural maneuver called "withholding consent."[27]

Withholding consent? What's that? you might ask. The U.S. Senate operates under rules that give enormous power to the minority—even to one individual senator. To move legislation to a vote quickly, or even to approve the previous day's journal, senators must agree unanimously to move forward. This is "unanimous consent." If any senator raises an objection, the process is delayed. This doesn't kill a proposed legislation, but it slows everything down and consumes the Senate's limited time.

Because this is annoying and time-consuming, the Senate

---

26. Ezra: In a mid-June journal entry titled "Bleh bad," I wrote, "McConnell's strategy is working. He's doing it in secret and there's no public outcry as a result. He is good at what he does. Dems are hoping he fails on his own terms. It's crazy. It won't work. And I just am not feeling good about things." Had I known this would end up in a book someday, I'd probably have chosen a better title.

27. Leah: Ezra and I had just gotten to my parents' house for Father's Day, and Ezra stayed outside for around twenty minutes taking this call with Schumer's staff. He was very sweaty when he came in—which I mostly attributed to the typical June D.C. heat rather than the temperature of the conversation. (Also, Ezra just sweats a lot.)

majority leader and Senate minority leader regularly hammer out unanimous consent agreements to expedite legislative work. A typical unanimous consent agreement looks something like "OK, we'll let you proceed to vote on all this stuff so we can go home early for the July recess to kiss babies and cut ribbons and get ourselves reelected."

But what happens when the Senate minority leader refuses to cut a deal? Well, legislative business slows down. A lot. In this case, it would slow down enough to delay any Trumpcare vote until at least after the July recess. And in the best-case scenario the act of stopping business as usual in protest could help force Trumpcare out of the shadows and back into the news cycle.

The specifics here might sound pretty technical, but we were on solid ground both procedurally and strategically. We were working in partnership with a nationwide grassroots network of people throwing everything they had into stopping this bill. Now we needed Senate Democrats to bring the same urgency to the fight in Washington.[28]

We had gotten on the phone with Schumer's staff because we had a disagreement. We'd put out a call to local Indivisibles instructing them to ask their senators to withhold consent,

---

28. In prep for this moment, Indivisible published an explainer ("I Object!— Withholding Consent and Filibustering"), trained our organizers on the tactic, and held webinars for local Indivisible groups on what exactly "withholding consent" was and why they should be asking their senators to use it. To be effective as a people power movement, Indivisibles have to be able to compete with the two-bit lobbyists who spend all day on Capitol Hill. And those guys (mostly guys) know the rules inside and out.

but Schumer wasn't ready to do that. And his staff presumably wanted to relieve the pressure on their boss and his fellow Democratic senators. On the call, we let them know that while we understood their position, we had big plans for the following week. Local groups throughout the country had been working with our organizers to plan sit-ins at Senate offices—including Democratic offices—demanding that their senators withhold consent. In fact, later that night we'd be getting on a call with Indivisible groups throughout New York State that were planning sit-ins at every single one of Schumer's nine offices, from Syracuse to Albany to New York City, to demand he take this action.

Perhaps more important, Indivisibles and partners in key states where vulnerable Democrats were up for reelection in 2018 were planning their own pressure events. In Charleston, West Virginia, Wood County Indivisible planned a rally at the state capitol. Ohio Indivisible groups in Columbus, Toledo, Cincinnati, and Cleveland planned die-ins. Indivisible in Philadelphia planned a rally outside their senator's office to bring attention to their opposition to Trumpcare. Indivisibles across the country in blue, red, and purple states were joining the national day of action—not just to push Republicans, but to demand that Democrats fight with everything they had.

Now, Senate Minority Leader Chuck Schumer knew—as we all did—that health care was going to be the center of the Democratic message for the next two years. And it was supposed to be a simple message: Democrats are the party of health care and protecting coverage for preexisting conditions; Republicans are the party of taking it all away. At this crucial moment, Senate Democrats didn't want anything complicating that simple, persuasive message. Schumer certainly didn't want protests aimed at him or his caucus suggesting there was more they could do to fight back.

On the phone with Schumer's staff, we assured them there was no reason the upcoming events in New York and around the country needed to complicate that political message. The local groups would be asking their senators, including Schumer, to withhold consent. If they agreed, their constituents would celebrate them enthusiastically. If they refused, well, then things would get complicated. The call ended with no agreement, but everyone knew where Indivisible stood. That night the two of us got on a call with Indivisible group leaders across New York State to go over the plan together.

But then it happened. The next day the news broke: Democrats would in fact be withholding consent to stop McConnell from jamming through the Trumpcare bill. *Politico* reported, "Democrats will start objecting to all unanimous consent requests in the Senate, according to a Democratic aide. They plan to control the floor of the chamber Monday night and try to force the House-passed health care bill to committee in a bid to further delay it." We had won the skirmish.

The Indivisible groups that had planned district office sit-ins for later that week segued seamlessly to a much more positive activity: thanking our friends. Events advertised as sit-ins at Schumer's offices turned into in-person appreciation events. "Keep It Up, Chuck! Thanks for Withholding Consent," read one invitation to a local Indivisible protest turned celebration.

Across the country, Indivisibles who'd been poised to apply pressure now rushed to support their senators who were finally choosing to use their power.

As the Senate Democrats started playing hardball, the broader movement to save the Affordable Care Act amped up its own pressure. By this point a steady drumbeat of opposition was rocking the Hill, from the Little Lobbyists—a group of children with complex medical needs and their parents fighting for the Affordable Care Act—to the near-daily protests that partners such as MoveOn, Planned Parenthood, and Protect Our Care were staging. Days after Democrats announced they were withholding consent, activists from National ADAPT, a disability rights organization, took Washington by surprise. Disability activists stormed Republican offices and hearings, putting their bodies on the line to fight the threat this new bill posed to Medicaid and to their lives. The photos of people in wheelchairs being manhandled and arrested by police shocked the nation and forced the threat of Trumpcare back into the headlines just as the new text of the bill was being released.

The pressure worked: McConnell relented. He didn't have the votes, so he announced the Senate wouldn't consider the Trumpcare bill until after the July Fourth recess. That meant the progressive movement would have at least one more chance to make senators listen to us on their home turf.

Indivisible Lesson #8: Partnerships, Partnerships, Partnerships (Partnerships)

If you're following the Indivisible local group model, you have a powerful engine for change. But you're not going to be doing this alone. In the same way that a group has more power than an individual, coalitions and partners have more power than any single group.

Partnerships are critical to everything you're trying to accomplish. Indivisible is not the entirety of the progressive movement; in fact, we're just one part, and we're pretty new on the scene. Locally or nationally, on basically any issue, advocacy or electoral effort, or campaign, there are other activists and organizations who've been leading the charge. They have strengths you may not, from number-crunching wonks to message-testing guidance to deep expertise, history, and relationships.

That's why it's so important to make sure your strategy is aligned with your partners across the progressive community. The alternative is just inefficient—you'll duplicate efforts—or, worse, it's actively counterproductive to accomplishing your goals. This is true in every case, but it's especially important when you're working to support directly impacted folks. You can't show up on immigrant rights, racial justice, women's rights, LGBTQ rights, or disability rights effectively if you're not taking the lead directly from these communities.

The progressive movement is vast and diverse, and it's impossible for any one organization or any one group to represent the breadth of opinion and the depth of the expertise out there. Partnerships aren't a nice-to-have— they are a must-have. When we win, partnerships are how we do it. When we lose, they are how we continue building toward victory together.

THE ENDGAME TO SAVE THE AFFORDABLE CARE ACT

As the July Fourth recess rolled around, the vast majority of Republican senators were still operating off the "If nobody can find me, nobody can get mad at me" playbook. They shied away from public events. Many refused to announce their public schedules. Some, like Cory Gardner of Colorado, took the unprecedented step of completely skipping out on Fourth of July festivities; others, like Pat Toomey of Pennsylvania, limited all appearances to controlled, friendly audiences. Senator Dean Heller of Nevada made the unusual choice to celebrate the Fourth of July by going to Ely—population slightly more than 4,000—in a remote and conservative small town in his state. The *New York Times* reported that he faced limited opposition, "perhaps in part because, as several people along the parade route said, residents were just surprised to see Mr. Heller there."

But wherever possible, the grassroots found a way to apply pressure. While marching in the Fourth of July parade in the tiny town of Eastport, Maine, Senator Susan Collins was stunned by the constituent outpouring: "Never before, in the fifteen times that I've marched in this parade, have I had people so focused on a single issue." Senator Lisa Murkowski attended a Fourth of July parade in the island town of Wrangell, Alaska, where local news reported that "85 or 90 percent of the people who came up were talking about health care and her being sort of moderate on that issue and potentially not voting for the GOP proposal." In Arizona, Indivisible groups staged protests outside Senators Jeff Flake's and

John McCain's offices, undeterred by the 100-degree heat. And in Kansas, Indivisible KC and Planned Parenthood organized to pack a town hall with Senator Jerry Moran in the tiny town of Palco, population 275. Constituents flooded the venue, demanding their senator oppose the bill. Even Moran's own family pediatrician showed up in support of the Affordable Care Act.

Two weeks of constituent pressure didn't kill the bill immediately, but it certainly set the tone for what came next. The bill McConnell released before recess died soon after senators returned to D.C. Senator Moran, one of the targeted swing votes, joined with a wild card conservative, Mike Lee of Utah, to announce they would both be voting against it. Lisa Murkowski, previously silent, announced her opposition as Indivisibles descended on her office in Anchorage. Indivisibles nationwide staged a wave of demonstrations, with more than 170 events in nearly every state celebrating the collapse of the bill and sending a clear message: the opposition to Trumpcare would not be going away.

But it wasn't over. Within hours McConnell had switched to a new, even more dangerous plan: "skinny repeal." This new bill was underbaked and incomplete. That wasn't a flaw but part of the design: it allowed McConnell to frame it to his caucus as just the first step in a broader Republican effort to address health care. In other words, he was saying: *Sure, we're voting to destroy the Affordable Care Act, but we'll fix everything—in the future!* This was in keeping with the strain of magical thinking that had run through Republican policy on health care for the past decade: there was always some mythical alternate plan on the horizon that would satisfy everyone.

To our alarm, by the end of July this transparently ridiculous justification seemed to be picking up traction with Republican senators. In a bizarre press conference, Senator Lindsey Graham, flanked by fellow Republicans John McCain, Ron Johnson, and Bill Cassidy—four key swing votes—thoroughly trashed the idea of skinny repeal before announcing that he'd vote for it based on private assurances from Paul Ryan that his concerns would be addressed in the future.

Suddenly, skinny repeal was moving fast. With three votes needed to kill it and only Susan Collins and Lisa Murkowski clearly holding out, things looked grim. The only X factor left was McCain, who—his appearance with Graham notwithstanding—was refusing to say how he'd vote. And while McCain talked a lot about standing up to Trump, we'd seen precious little in his voting record to suggest he'd actually do anything about it.

McConnell moved for a vote on skinny repeal late on the night of July 27, 2017. Frankly, we thought there was no way he'd call for a vote unless he knew he had it in the bag. At Indivisible HQ, our team was railing against the bill and driving calls, but we were also preparing for the worst. We drafted a personal note to our sure-to-be-devastated Indivisible group leaders: sorrowful but resolute, trying to highlight what had been saved by stopping the worse, earlier versions of repeal and calling for a pivot to make the GOP pay at the ballot box.

We ordered mediocre Tex-Mex food to the office and waited. And waited some more. The vote was scheduled for midnight. At about 1:00 a.m. we were still at the office with a handful of members of the Indivisible team. The preparations were done, so there was nothing to do but watch the vote in our office, where the air-conditioning had broken down (again).

Then something funny started to happen. Vice President Mike Pence had arrived at the Senate—a clear sign that Mc-Connell expected the bill to pass with 50 votes, requiring the vice president to cast the tiebreaking vote. You don't get the vice president out of bed to cast a vote unless you're pretty sure it's needed—and yet, for some reason, the vote wasn't moving forward. Reporters on Twitter began chattering about the weird body language of Republicans on the Senate floor. They seemed upset. Members of the Republican leadership were trying to corner Susan Collins and Lisa Murkowski, who had announced their intent to vote against the bill. John McCain—who still hadn't declared his intentions—seemed to be excessively happy, and Mitch McConnell looked really mad. Something was up.

Then John McCain walked up to the Senate clerk, stuck his hand out in dramatic fashion, held it for a second or two, and then gave a thumbs-down. Democrats in the chamber audibly gasped. Republicans looked distraught. And Trumpcare was dead.

It wasn't clear precisely what had transpired that night between McConnell and McCain. It's still, honestly, not totally clear.[29] McCain, Collins, and Murkowski held out as a bloc, and—together with the united Democratic caucus—that was enough to kill the bill. Skinny repeal had come within one vote of reshaping the American health care system, robbing millions of people of their health coverage, and throwing countless lives into jeopardy. But it had gone down in defeat.

In Arizona, Alaska, and Maine, there was an outpouring of gratitude for the three Republican senators who'd voted the bill down. Constituents broke into spontaneous applause for Collins at the airport when she arrived in Maine. Thrilled would-be protestors marched to Murkowski's office chanting their gratitude: "Thank you, Lisa!" Well-wishers posted signs thanking McCain along the road leading to his home.[30]

Senators who'd voted for repeal had a rougher August— the month of the longest congressional recess of the year.

---

29. It's worth noting that one of the reasons dramatic reversals don't tend to happen on the Senate floor at 1:30 a.m. is because leadership doesn't schedule votes unless they're pretty sure of the outcome. So the only way something like this happens is if someone switches their vote without telling anyone, which senators don't tend to do because it's not very considerate to make all your colleagues show up for an unnecessary process so that you can heroically cast the deciding vote to kill the bill. All of which is to say that we're very happy John McCain voted against skinny repeal, and it's all very touching, but if he'd just given McConnell a heads-up about his intentions six hours earlier, the vote would have been pulled and everyone could have gotten a good night's sleep.

30. Again, we do not endorse going to politicians' homes—and, honestly, this felt a little creepy to us—but Cindy McCain, John's wife, seemed to appreciate it, so that's nice.

Trumpcare was dead,[31] but it was not forgotten. As senators who had supported Trumpcare went home, intent on turning the page, their constituents let them know they weren't having it. "At Raucous Town Halls, Republicans Have Faced Another Round of Anger over Health Care," a *Washington Post* headline reported on August 11. Senator Cory Gardner, who had supported repeal, chose to hold his first town halls in recent history that month. A headline on the Colorado Public Radio website read, "Rowdy Town Hall Crowds Greet Sen. Gardner. Health Care Vote Leads Concerns." The hundreds of attendees were angry about his vote for Trumpcare and angry he had been hiding from constituents. "The skeptical crowd repeatedly booed him," the public radio station reported. Said one woman concerned with his health care positions, "I voted for Cory and I feel like he's kind of letting us down with some of the promises he made." She echoed a feeling being felt by constituents across the country—awakening to, and disappointed by, the actions and priorities of this Congress and president.

Republicans had not had unified control of the House, the Senate, and the presidency in over a decade. Under President

---

31. Technically, the deadline to pass a Trumpcare bill that year was actually September 30, 2017, so in theory there was still a possibility Trumpcare would make a comeback. Senators Lindsey Graham and Bill Cassidy made a last, halfhearted stab at moving a new bill—Zombie Trumpcare, as we were calling it by that point. It was another scary moment in the fight, but yet again an army of tired but determined activists swung into action. With less than a week to go before the deadline, the zombie bill went down. It did not get back up.

Obama, repeal of the Affordable Care Act had passed dozens of times in the Republican House; a full repeal cleared the House and Senate in 2016, drawing a veto from Obama. Opposition to the Affordable Care Act animated conservative activism and fueled their electoral wins from the moment it passed. Repeal was the central promise, the central organizing principle of the Republican party for almost a decade.

And then they failed.

A few days after the Senate vote, the *Washington Post* ran an op-ed by us and our policy director, Angel Padilla, with the headline "Who Saved Obamacare from the GOP? The American People." In it, we made the point that progressives lacked the Senate, the House, and the presidency. The only power available to us was the power to respond—with our time, our voices, and our physical presence. All we could do was try to make clear what was happening—to shine a light, raise the temperature, and hope the politicians interested in their own political survival would respond.

That's what Indivisibles and countless others did—week in, week out—for most of 2017. Through meetings, die-ins, postcards, op-eds, call-a-thons, district office visits, and creative, heartfelt, hilarious, and emotionally moving tactics laser-focused on their own representatives and senators, that's what Indivisible did.

This deceptively simple, seemingly inconsequential act of coming together in our own communities to demand that our own representatives hear us had an incredible effect. And it worked. Engaged groups of constituents from Palco, Kansas, to Lincoln County, Maine, to Prescott, Arizona—and everywhere in between—changed what was politically possible in Washington, D.C. Together with a powerful coalition of progressive partners, this movement defeated the top legislative priority of the Trump administration and its Republican Congress—and prevented tens of millions of Americans from losing lifesaving health care.

That's the power of organized constituent power. It starts in living rooms and it ends with saving people's lives.

4

How to Build Power Together

We need, in every community, a group of angelic troublemakers.
—BAYARD RUSTIN

We need to be there, but we need to follow the lead of folks
who are more directly impacted by this than we are.
—TRISH FLORENCE, *Indivisible, San Antonio, Texas*

After we finished a draft of what would become the *Indivisible Guide*, we were toying around with titles for the document. The Tea Party, our anti-inspiration, had thrived as a national movement in part because its name had tapped into American history and iconography. It had spoken to their (twisted) values.[1] It had helped knit people together with a common frame of mind.

If we were going to replicate the Tea Party, we needed a frame that people could organize under. We racked our brains

---

1. The original Tea Party was literally a group of white people who dressed up as American Indians to get away with causing mayhem in support of businesses. So actually it was a pretty good fit for an Obama-era white grievance movement!

for historical parallels that spoke to our values—the values
we knew were directly under threat when Trump became
president-elect. But drawing on common reference points in
American history is harder for the left, since, y'know, we understand our country was built on genocide and slavery. There
hasn't ever really been a point where every American is equal
and included, at least not yet.

We brainstormed names.

Leah: *The Great Society?*
Ezra: *No.*
Leah: *The Four Freedoms?*
Ezra: *No.*
Leah: *No Justice, No Bills?*
Ezra: *No, that's weird.*
Leah: *Indivisible?*

We both got chills: this was the perfect name. "Indivisible,
with liberty and justice for all" was more than just a phrase
from the Pledge of Allegiance. "Indivisible" spoke to us. We
were up against an explicitly divide-and-conquer strategy from
Trump. That meant we had to treat an attack on one as an attack on all. If each of us waited our turn for our issue or our
families to be attacked, we would be waiting for our turn to
lose. Our only hope was to stand together—indivisible.

Also, it was a pretty cool word.

The concept of being indivisible was particularly important
for us because we were conscious of the huge amount of privilege we personally had. We were (and are!) a pair of married,

white, graduate school–educated former congressional staffers who now occupied mid-level roles within the progressive elite. We weren't the primary targets of Trump's attacks—but we could stand in solidarity with those who were.

And according to the best research we've got on the post-Trump activism boom, this was pretty common among folks who went from zero to sixty after November 2016. Research on new activists in the Trump era has found that they are disproportionately likely to be women, college- or graduate school–educated, middle- to upper-middle-class, and white.

There are some obvious reasons why women responded to 2016 with righteous outrage: they'd just watched an extraordinarily qualified female presidential candidate lose to an extraordinarily unqualified, hateful charlatan with a self-confessed record of sexual assault. But it wasn't just that. When Indivisible leaders described to us their journey into activism, young mothers came back over and over again to a shared moment: the challenge of explaining to their children how a bully, a man who violated every value they'd tried to instill, had won the presidency. Older women talked about breaking into male-dominated workplaces, about being passed over for promotions and coping with sexual harassment and fighting for their spot at the table and how they'd seen it all reflected in Clinton's loss. And women of every age described a simple, devastating feeling: America was supposed to be a welcoming, caring society. Trump's election shattered any illusion of this.

We've also got a theory about why the average first-time anti-Trump activist is more likely to be white, middle- or upper-class, and college educated. Those of us who radically changed our patterns of political activity after Trump's election did so because something about November 2016 shook the way we understood the world. We'd had some faith that something about the existing system—the parties, the elites, the media, the institutions—would stop this obviously unacceptable, dangerous outcome. We'd believed that open racism and misogyny, a record of serial sexual assault, and sheer malevolent stupidity would be disqualifying for enough voters to keep Trump from the presidency. We'd believed in that illusion of America as a welcoming, caring society.

But the system failed. Americans—specifically white Americans—did not reject Trump, not in the numbers we needed. The bully won.

This kind of faith in the system is more commonly found in people who have benefited from the system—folks with one or another kind of privilege. That means even as we're organizing and taking action, we also have to rethink how we understand the world. We have to think about how it got this bad without us noticing. Because things were not OK before Trump appeared on the scene. And if we don't start from that understanding, we're not going to change it.

If this account of your political awakening hits home but also makes you uncomfortable—if you feel a catch in your throat, a bit of a defensive feeling, a need to explain why you're different—hold on a second. If you were surprised by what Trump's election said about our country, that's because pretty much everything about our society is set up to obscure and justify an unjust status quo. It's the water we swim in and the air we breathe.

And if you weren't politically engaged before 2016, it doesn't make you a bad person. It makes you very normal. The vast majority of Americans were not and are not civically engaged even now, in the Trump era. The scary reality is that, late or not, this massive upsurge in people power over the past few years still constitutes just a small fraction of the American population. To win, we're going to need you *and* everyone you know who's still on the sidelines.

What this does mean for newcomers is you've got responsibility. If you're going to respond effectively to the challenges we face, you need to educate yourself, to learn what's come before, to be conscious of how your identity and privilege informs your activism, and to think about what it means to be part of a multiracial, cross-class, intersectional progressive movement.[2] And then you need to put it into action.

To put it bluntly, it also means you've got an opportunity. If you've got access to societal advantages by virtue of your gender, race, class, or any other identity, you have the chance to use your privilege for good. For too long, we "good progressives" have indulged in a kind of politics that treats the concerns of those with privilege as central and the concerns of the marginalized as, well, marginal. You have the chance to reject that. You have the chance to be part of a different story—a story about the politics of solidarity.

---

2. Intersectionality, a concept developed by Professor Kimberlé Crenshaw, is the recognition that our various identities—race, gender, class, ability, sexual orientation, and more—intersect with each other to shape our experiences with systems of power and oppression.

Indivisible Lesson #9: Don't Get Defensive
About Your Privilege

Trump's victory didn't come out of nowhere. It could only have happened in a society that has consistently devalued the lives and dignity of historically marginalized groups—people of color, including Black and indigenous people, immigrants, queer people, and women. If we're going to defeat Trumpism, we can't just resist Trump; we have to dismantle the structural inequalities that allowed Trump's rise to power.

Many of us within the Indivisible movement have social or economic advantages due to our race, class, gender, ability, sexual orientation, or other factors. Being part of the solution and entering into community with others starts with recognizing that whatever our personal beliefs and convictions, we have benefited from historic systems of oppression. In short, it means recognizing our privilege.

This can be hard: we all want to believe we're not part of the problem. We want to believe we're on the right side of justice. Our lives are complicated and complex. Having privilege because of your race, gender, or sexual orientation doesn't mean things have been easy for you. But it does mean you haven't faced the structural disadvantages that other people have. And it means you need to take that fact into account in how you approach your activism.

Defensiveness and failure to recognize this prevents us from learning, growing, and acting effectively. Honest work to change systems of oppression starts by accepting that we exist within those systems and have to educate

*ourselves on them. And that's why it's crucial to actively
work to examine your own privilege and figure how to be
an effective part of the fight for justice.*

We don't claim to be experts here—which is a little awkward,
because the whole point of this book is that we're supposed to
be experts telling you how to do things. We've messed up and
learned and adapted ourselves; it's all part of the process.[3]

And here's what we've seen: Since Trump's election, Indivisibles have fought for themselves and for their neighbors.
Indivisible Tohono, led by April Ignacio, Gabriella Cazares-
Kelly, and seven other members of the Tohono O'odham
Nation, formed within days of the election in response to the
imminent threat of a border wall on Tohono O'odham lands.
They've pushed their Arizona senators on the border wall, they
held the first candidates' forum ever on Tohono O'odham land,
and April has spearheaded the passage of a bill creating a task
force on missing and murdered indigenous women. As April
says, "We bring our folding chairs with us, and we've let them
all know that we'll no longer be left out of the conversation."[4]

---

3. You'll also notice that we talk about privilege in this chapter in a privileged-
   people-talking-to-other-privileged-people sort of way. That's intentional!
   We're white people who drew on a ton of privilege to build up a new organization in a nonprofit sector that has historically devalued and underfunded the
   leadership of communities of color—a complicated reality that we think about
   every day and that shapes every part of how we show up in the world. We
   generally find that our biggest contribution is talking to people with privilege
   about how we can all do better, so that's where we're going to dig in.

4. This is of course an homage to the great Shirley Chisholm's saying: "If they
   don't give you a seat at the table, bring a folding chair."

Nationwide, Indivisibles have partnered with local immigrant rights organizations and service providers to offer support, from escorting community members to Immigration and Customs Enforcement (ICE) check-ins to showing up for sanctuary city campaigns to raising money for DACA renewal fees. They've joined campaigns for progressive district attorneys, like Larry Krasner in Philadelphia and Wesley Bell in St. Louis, or to remove Confederate monuments in New Orleans and Mississippi. They've showed up nationwide to stand in solidarity after the horrifying events of Charlottesville in August 2017. They've joined national protests to stop the Muslim and refugee ban and to say no to a wall at the border.

This idea of political solidarity is core to Indivisible—it's in our very name. This kind of solidarity is not easy and it's never perfect. We mess up along the way, we make amends, and then we try to do better. But this is how we build power inclusively to win the big fights to come. To illustrate how this can work in real life, in this chapter we tell the story of one of those moments when it was time for Indivisible to show up: the fight to defend immigrant youth under attack by the Trump administration in late 2017.

IMMIGRANT YOUTH ARE HERE TO STAY

It's September 2017, and Donald Trump is the monster who just ended Deferred Action for Childhood Arrivals (DACA). DACA was a sliver of humanity carved into America's barbarous immigration system back in 2012. It allowed youth who came into the United States as infants and children to remain in the country and work legally, serve in the military, and go to college without fear of deportation. While it wasn't a permanent solution, and it was far from complete relief for the millions of undocumented Americans in the country, it was life-changing for hundreds of thousands of young American immigrants.

DACA was an administrative policy; it had been put in place by President Obama, bowing to fierce pressure from young immigrant activists after a bill to provide permanent relief, the Dream Act, failed to clear the filibuster in the Senate.[5] And because it was an administrative policy, it could be unilaterally revoked by the next administration.

Now Trump was axing it. He didn't do the deed himself; he sent his henchman, Attorney General Jefferson Beauregard Sessions III, to announce the heartless act.[6] Sessions seemed barely able to contain his glee during the press conference that would throw the lives of hundreds of thousands of young American immigrants and their families into chaos.

It was a cruel but characteristic demonstration of the xenophobia at the core of Trumpism. Trump launched his presidential campaign with a vicious attack on immigrants as criminals, drug dealers, and rapists. He seized the Republican nomination

---

5. This one is not just on Senate Republicans. The Senate could have successfully passed the bill in 2010 if all the Democrats had held together in support of the Dream Act. They didn't.

6. We can't help but note that his very name is practically a relitigation of the "War of Northern Aggression" (known as the American Civil War outside neo-Confederate enclaves). Jefferson is from Jefferson Davis, president of the Confederacy. Beauregard is from P. G. T. Beauregard, a leading Confederate general who oversaw the first shots of the war at Fort Sumter.

by being more racist, more nativist, and just generally crueler and angrier than the other candidates.

Trump's victory put to rest the fight over immigration that had been raging within the Republican Party for decades. Many Republican electeds had historically taken a less xenophobic approach, either for moral reasons or, more commonly, because their corporate backers benefited from immigration. In both 2006 and 2013, Republican congressional leaders tried to move compromises on immigration, only to see them defeated by factions in their own party.[7] The final blow to the last Republican-backed immigration reform effort came in 2014 when Tea Party candidate Dave Brat[8] successfully primaried Republican House majority leader Eric Cantor by painting him as soft on immigration. This killed all prospects for bipartisan immigration reform for the foreseeable future.

With Trump's victory, the takeover of the Republican Party by its anti-immigrant faction was complete. Republican members of Congress—even those who had long supported immigration reform proposals—fell in line, with few exceptions. The political allure of xenophobia had proved irresistible. Trump's Republican Party was an affirmatively anti-immigrant party.

---

7. The 2013 effort was prompted in part by the wide-scale losses of Republicans in the 2012 elections. The official election autopsy report released by the Republican National Committee blamed its stance on immigration for the loss of Hispanic votes and asserted that "we must embrace and champion comprehensive immigration reform. If we do not, our party's appeal will continue to shrink to its core constituencies only." It turned out to be a pretty good prediction.

8. You may remember Brat from Chapter 3, where he was last seen complaining about all the new lady protestors in his district.

Trump transitioned from anti-immigrant speeches to anti-immigrant policy within days of taking office. One of his first acts was the Muslim ban, limiting travel for people and separating families from certain predominantly Muslim countries. He issued executive orders targeting sanctuary cities and directed ICE agents to pursue any undocumented person in the country, regardless of whether they had a criminal record. Trump began unilaterally revoking immigration protections for hundreds of thousands of people who'd been living in America for years or decades. He drastically slashed the cap on refugee admissions. He proposed a plan to dramatically reduce legal immigration.

The protection for Dreamers provided by DACA was enormously popular: it enjoyed not only a majority of Democratic support, or a majority of Americans' support—it had a majority of *Republican* support. Perhaps as a result, Trump did not move to end it immediately. As of the summer of 2017, DACA was still the law of the land. But, fed up with Trump's inaction, a group of Republican attorneys general threatened a lawsuit against the federal government claiming that DACA was unconstitutional.[9] They wanted Trump to use his power to kill DACA.

The immigrant rights community was prepared for the worst. Over the month of August, chapters of United We Dream, the leading national organization fighting for immigrant youth, organized nationwide demonstrations to pressure Trump not to rescind DACA, with Indivisibles joining and

---

9. This serves as a helpful reminder that Trumpism is not just Trump. Here we have Republican attorneys general from across the country threatening to sue Trump if he didn't move more quickly to end protections for Dreamers.

hosting their own where needed. For instance, Ozark Indivisible in Arkansas and Austin Indivisible in Texas staged protests against their own state attorneys general, urging them to drop out of the anti-DACA lawsuit.

But the xenophobic forces in the White House prevailed. By the time Sessions took to the podium at the Justice Department on September 5, 2017, we all knew what was coming. Within a few hours of Trump's announcement, the National Immigration Law Center sued on behalf of DACA recipients; Executive Director Marielena Hincapié slammed Trump's move as "nothing short of hypocrisy, cruelty and cowardice." Greisa Martínez Rosas of United We Dream, a DACA recipient herself, was defiant: "We will not be thrown back into the shadows."

Trump's decision to rescind DACA was a disaster for hundreds of thousands of DACA recipients. Every recipient had voluntarily given their personal information to the federal government based on assurances from the federal government that the information would not be used against them, which meant that the Trump administration had their home or school address. Would Trump's deportation force come after them? Young people who'd grown up in the United States and built their lives here—who were going to college, supporting their families, serving in the military—were suddenly facing the threat of deportation to countries they might not have seen since they were toddlers.

It's hard to overstate the trauma of this moment. Immigrant youth had put their lives on the line to win DACA. Now they were watching as it was ripped away. One of United We

Dream's first public responses was simple and devastating: they shared to their audience of DACA recipients the phone number for the national suicide prevention hotline.

For the two of us—privileged, white, nonimmigrant folk— it was a moment of shock, rage, helplessness, and guilt.[10] Our partners (and members of our own team whose family and friends were impacted) were managing their own trauma even as they were mounting the next steps in a ferocious battle for their lives and futures. All we could do was try to figure out how to help.

We knew this was an opportunity to use Indivisible's nation- wide constituent power to stand with those under threat—to stand on the principles outlined in the *Indivisible Guide*. Most of us in the Indivisible movement weren't immigrants, but, at our best, we recognized our security and privilege as native-born people and asked a simple question: What can we do?

We were fortunate that we had started with close ties to the partners we'd look to for leadership in this fight. Our *Guide* co- author and now policy director, Angel Padilla, had spent his ca- reer in immigrant rights. And Marielena Hincapié, his former boss at the National Immigration Law Center, had been one of our earliest supporters and advisors in Washington. We'd worked with United We Dream, the National Immigration

---

10. Leah: In a great example of how not to be a good ally, I burst into tears while trying to talk to our team immediately after the press conference. I still regret it: there were members of our team present who were much more di- rectly impacted by Trump's war on immigrants, and I should have been cre- ating space for them, not taking up space with my (not-directly-impacted) feelings.

Law Center, and other immigrant rights organizations to build out our trainings and resources for local Indivisible groups on how to be allies to immigrants. Now we were putting the same principles into action for this fight.

Indivisible Lesson #10: Follow Somebody Else

It's common to hear someone claiming that they're speaking for the voiceless. But in the words of the novelist and activist Arundhati Roy, "There's really no such thing as the 'voiceless.' There are only the deliberately silenced, or the preferably unheard." The job of an ally is not to speak on behalf of a marginalized group; it's to support and fight with them, to ensure that when they're speaking, others are listening.

This is a core Indivisible principle. In campaigns or efforts where we're not directly impacted, we seek out the leadership of communities who are. That means if your Indivisible group is primarily white, or nonimmigrant, or straight, you should look to follow the strategic leadership of organizations serving communities of color, immigrants, and the LGBTQ community. This is for both a moral reason—it's important to center the leadership of the directly impacted—and for really important practical reasons: they've been doing the work, and they have the history, strategy, and analysis that you don't. As April of Indivisible Tohono says: "First and foremost, we need people to understand that if you want to be a good ally, you've got to learn how to listen, and not feel like you're coming in to save us. We're probably smarter than you, because we've had to be. That's been the hardest thing to be in these spaces. It's like we're all on the same team, but you're not listening to what we have to say."

Following isn't just waiting around to be told what to do. It's about proactively building partnerships and trust, learning about the issue, history, and strategy, and thinking about how you can contribute—and then throwing yourself into the fight. This is especially important because community organizations advocating with marginalized communities are often operating on shoestring budgets, with too many needs and too little time. If you want to build a supportive relationship, do your homework in advance and try to identify ways to support what they're doing—monetarily, with volunteers, or with your advocacy capacity—rather than asking them to come to your events or take on your actions.

These kinds of partnerships may not move fast—it takes time and conscious work to build trust. But over time, they can be transformational.

Trump's decision was horrific, but it should have been quickly remedied. Congress could have easily moved to enshrine protections for DACA recipients into law. In a functional system, there would have been an overwhelming bipartisan push to do so immediately.

But we don't have a functional system; we have Congress. And in Congress, the majority party's leadership decides which bills go to the floor for a vote. That meant that the decision to move forward lay with Republican Senate majority leader Mitch McConnell and Republican Speaker of the House Paul Ryan. And both of them were more concerned with satisfying the xenophobes on their right flank than they were with the overwhelming support for DACA from everyone else.

There was a small window of hope: Trump had attacked DACA just days before an upcoming budget deadline. The federal coffers were running dry, and Democratic votes were going to be needed to replenish them. This was Democrats' big chance to demand concessions from Trump. It would be their only chance for months. They could strike now, while the outrage was fresh, and demand protections for Dreamers as part of the deal.

But for that to happen, Democrats would need to prioritize it. Would they press the issue? Were they willing, in this moment, to put their political capital on the line?

It was an open question. Democrats have long had a fraught and tortured history with immigration policy. For decades the consensus had been that Democrats should emphasize security and enforcement to avoid looking "weak" on immigration. If Democrats proved they were tough on border security, the thinking went, that would open up room to negotiate with Republicans on comprehensive immigration reform.

For much of his first term, President Obama followed this line of thought, steadily increasing the overall number of people detained and deported by ICE. He shifted his approach in the latter part of his second term, after it became clear that no amount of appeasement would get Republicans on board for legislative reform.

For immigrant advocates, Democrats were unquestionably the more sympathetic party. But that didn't mean congressional Democratic leadership would be champions without consistent pressure. After all, Obama ultimately created DACA less than five months before his reelection in 2012, but only after Dreamers organized an inside-outside strategy that included protests outside Senate Democratic offices and hunger strikes at Obama reelection campaign offices.

As Trump rose, powered by explicit xenophobia, Democrats often still tried to stick to vague platitudes. They liked immigrants; they said America was a nation of immigrants; they wanted to protect Dreamers. But they still worried about being seen as weak on immigration enforcement and border security.

In the wake of the DACA decision, Democrats were at least *saying* the right things. They were reaching out to Dreamers. They were issuing outraged press releases. House Minority Leader Nancy Pelosi called the decision a "deeply shameful act of political cowardice and a despicable assault on innocent young people in communities across America." Former president Obama described the attack on DACA as "wrong," "self-defeating," and "cruel." Senate Minority Leader Chuck Schumer even changed his official Twitter background page to a stark banner that read, "I stand with DREAMERS."

But it remained to be seen whether the Democratic response to Trump was just words, or a real commitment to action. Public statements were one thing. Putting real political capital on the lines was another. And less than twenty-four hours after Trump rescinded DACA, when the Democratic congressional leadership went to the Oval Office to negotiate a deal on the must-pass funding bill, there was a chance to use that capital. Their votes were needed, so they had leverage—they could insist on a fix for DACA.

No dice. Democrats emerged from the Oval Office with a deal to fund the government for three months. They'd cut out Republican congressional leadership to negotiate directly with Trump—which constituted a major political win in their eyes. They had not asked for or received anything related to DACA in the deal that would now go to Congress for a vote.

Leadership was proud of their dealmaking. They soaked up media praise for their smart negotiating skills. *USA Today* was part of the chorus of national news organizations reporting how handily the Democratic leadership had outmaneuvered Republicans. It described a photo taken during the negotiations that showed Trump smiling and embracing Schumer "after giving Democrats pretty much everything they wanted." But that "everything" did not include protections for Dreamers.

Our partners in the immigrant rights community were horrified. Trump had set off a massive humanitarian crisis and Democrats were treating it like business as usual. Democratic leaders' explanation—that they didn't need to negotiate DACA in this package, that they could move a new Dream Act on its own, and that it would be popular enough that Republicans would have to pass it—belied everything we knew about the Republican Congress. If they actually believed it, they were shockingly naïve.

Indivisible joined with our partners United We Dream and the National Immigration Law Center to publicly oppose the deal. We issued a joint letter criticizing how the proposed deal left out Dreamers: "At a time of great urgency, the message Schumer and Pelosi sent to immigrant youth was, 'wait' . . . Time and time again, Democratic leaders tell immigrants that relief from deportation would come someday down the road—and that someday never comes. We are tired of waiting."

Senate and House Democratic leadership weren't happy. We were stepping on their great news cycle by pointing out that their deal had left Dreamers in the cold. They called an emergency meeting to make the case for their plan—and to convince all of us to stop making such a fuss. In the meeting at the Capitol, House Minority Leader Pelosi and Senate Minority Leader Schumer talked down to the handful of Dreamer advocates in the room—people who themselves risked deportation and whose families were under threat:[11]

> *"You're spreading fear among Dreamers that they're in danger."*
>
> *"You've got to think with your heads, not your hearts."*
>
> *"Trust us. We know what we're doing. We've been doing this a while."*

In the meeting, Greisa Martinez Rosas of United We Dream calmly rejected their rationale and insisted that the congressional leaders explain their plan on how they'd actually win protection for Dreamers like herself. But in response the con-

---

11. Ezra: I took notes during the meeting and wrote them up afterward. These aren't verbatim quotes, but they're close. I was gobsmacked at how these Democratic leaders were speaking to the civil rights leaders in the room.

gressional leadership offered little more than platitudes about how much they cared for Dreamers. We backed Greisa up and told Schumer in front of everybody that he wasn't answering her reasonable concerns or strategic arguments. Schumer was not amused. His office banned Indivisible from future leadership meetings for the next year or so.[12]

Indivisible Lesson #11: Talk Is Cheap, So Ask for More
Electeds and their staffers thrive on strategic ambiguity. They want constituents to feel heard and represented, but they don't want to have to do too much work. This is true even for friendly electeds. They don't want to be tied down; they want to maintain flexibility to act or not act as they see fit.

So that means electeds and their staff love talk. It's simple, it's easy, it signals they're on your side, and it doesn't require any extra work or political capital. They love making symbolic shows of support and opposition. They like to cosponsor bills, sign on to things they know will never pass, and just generally signal that they agree with you. Talk is cheap.

Well, talk isn't good enough for Indivisibles. You want your electeds to use their power to actively fight for you. To

---

12. This would have been a really devastating move to pull on any group whose power comes from inside D.C.: it means you don't have access to insider info on strategy. We were pretty unfazed; we'd made it through our first months without any access, and besides, our other partners just went ahead and looped us in anyway because they wanted to coordinate with us. It's hard to ice out your field for very long.

make sure they listen and follow through, it is extremely important to craft effective "asks" for your electeds.

Good asks for your electeds are specific, strategic, and seeable:

Specific. *Asks are not about philosophizing; they're about prompting specific action. So your ask should be time limited and precise. For instance, "Vote no on x bill" or "Ask x witness about y issue at the hearing on z date."*

Strategic. *The reason you're asking at all is because you want to achieve something. If your elected follows through on your ask, what will be accomplished? For instance, "Cosponsor x bill" builds support for a policy you prefer, while "Make a speech about x issue" might not accomplish anything much at all.*

Seeable.[13] *Look, we'll say it: electeds are really crafty. They're politicians. Trust but always verify. If the action you're asking for cannot be observed and verified, you will not be able to hold your electeds accountable for following through. You can check to see how they voted, you can watch the video of a hearing, you can ask to see the letter they sent.*

Always remember: you've got something you want, so you gotta make the right ask to get it.

Even before that meeting, the die was cast. Once there's bipartisan agreement and congressional leadership has signed on

---

13. You could call this "measurable" or "verifiable," but neither of those words starts with an alliterative *s*, now, do they?

to a deal, it's very hard to stop. Within days the deal passed the House and Senate and went to Trump's desk for his signature. Democratic leadership's only concession to immigrant rights advocates and allies was a promise to use their political capital to pass Dreamer protections ahead of the next funding deadline, three months later.

It was only the first inside-D.C. skirmish in what would become a sustained, grassroots nationwide campaign to enact protections for undocumented youth. Young immigrants and allies flooded the Capitol again and again over the course of fall 2017, taking over the Capitol Rotunda and camping out in Democratic and Republican offices alike. Even business leaders and corporations rallied in favor of DACA. Support was overwhelming across American society.

Leading up to the funding deadline in December, the ask for Democratic leadership was simple: Include a "clean" Dream Act in the budget. The "clean" part was critical. All too often, legislation on immigration involved pitting the rights and safety of one group of immigrants against another. The Trump administration, having destroyed the DACA program, was now demanding additional wins for their nativist agenda in exchange for a legislative fix for DACA: changes to family-based immigration; more money for interior enforcement that would lead to more detentions and deportations; an end to the diversity visa program, which would have a disproportionate impact on immigrants from certain African countries; and funding for Trump's proposed border wall.

Immigrant leaders refused to be used as bargaining chips against their communities. Cristina Jiménez of United We

Dream put it plainly: "My brother has DACA and my parents are undocumented . . . Would you cut a deal which would result in your own mother being chased down and locked into a detention camp to be tormented and abused?"

Indivisibles all over the country joined the fight for a clean Dream Act. In red states and districts, Indivisibles pressured their Republican representatives. Indivisible Midlands of South Carolina hosted a series of in-state actions before heading to D.C. to join United We Dream's protests at the U.S. Capitol, while Indivisible MN03 relentlessly pressured their Republican representative Erik Paulsen to take a stand. In blue states, Indivisibles pushed Democrats to use their political capital. Indivisible Nation BK in Brooklyn partnered with Make the Road New York to support rallies and calls for a Clean Dream—and to turn up the heat on Chuck Schumer. Indivisible SF hosted a rally and lined up 122 pairs of shoes outside Nancy Pelosi's district office in San Francisco—a striking visual representation of the number of DACA recipients who could expect to lose status every day going forward.[14] In Virginia, Roanoke Indivisible staged events where hundreds of handmade butterflies representing the DACA recipients were given to their Democratic senators and to Republican representative Bob Goodlatte.

---

14. Ezra: In the midst of all this grassroots pressure focused on Democrats caving, Representative Joe Crowley reached out to us. Crowley was a Pelosi lieutenant. As the fourth-ranking Democrat in the House, he was widely seen as a likely future Speaker of the House. At a meeting in his office on Capitol Hill, Crowley told us that he thought Pelosi had been smart to cut a deal with Trump in September—and he believed that Democrats could use their leverage in December to protect the Dreamers. A few months later he'd lose his primary to an inspiring young leader named Alexandria Ocasio-Cortez.

At every stage in the process, Indivisible was just a part of a wave led by immigrant activists. Our job was to show that we had their backs—that this was important to everyone, not just those directly impacted. This was about Dreamers, but it was also a fight about who belongs in America. It was critical that nonimmigrant communities show up for that fight. The same impulse that led Indivisibles to storm the airports in response to the Muslim ban drove them to "We Stand with Dreamers" rallies across the country.

All through fall, the pressure built. But we still faced the fundamental problem: getting to a vote on the Dream Act. Every Democrat and the majority of Republicans had agreed to support some form of protection for Dreamers. But there was still no real plan for how to get a vote on the bill without the support of Republican leadership, and they showed no signs of moving.

When they had caved in September, Democratic leadership promised to use their political capital for this fight, and to get it done by December—but they were carefully vague about the actual strategy. We and our partners wanted clarity: Did that mean this would be their top negotiating priority? Did it mean they'd refuse to vote for a budget if necessary? They didn't give clear answers, and they continued to just point the finger at the Republicans.[15]

---

15. This is a pretty common situation when pressuring Democrats. They will argue that congressional Republicans are the real culprits and that all grassroots pressure should focus on them instead. It's an alluring argument, because they're usually right that congressional Republicans are terrible. But the prob-

When December rolled around, Democrats blew through their own self-imposed deadline. They declined to negotiate over the Dream Act as they voted once again to pass a month-long government funding bill. The pain and betrayal of advocates was intense. Democratic congressional leadership had spent the past three months promising that they had a plan—that if advocates trusted them and focused their fire on Republicans, they'd find a way to move the Dream Act by the end of the year. The time for action had come and gone, and Democrats had punted yet again.

The backlash was significant. Immigrant rights groups that had been holding their fire let loose on the failure of Democratic leadership. In New York, Make the Road New York and Indivisible allies from across the city descended once again on Schumer's house in protest. Recriminations began. Representative Steny Hoyer, the second-highest-ranking Democrat in the House after Pelosi, said, "I think we should've frankly been more assertive in September." Yes, that's what the immigrant rights groups and their allies thought too.

Indivisible Lesson #12: Hold Your Friends Accountable
Indivisible is not an arm of the Democratic Party. The willingness to pressure Democrats when necessary hits on a key feature of the Indivisible movement. We're trying to accomplish specific policy goals: stop bad legislation, hold

---

lem is it doesn't matter if Democrats hold the right policy position if they're not willing to fight for it. That's why pressure on Democrats is also critical.

corrupt conservatives accountable, and promote a stark contrast with the antidemocratic policies of the modern Republican Party. We know that as long as we have a two-party system, the way we get there is with a strong, truly progressive Democratic Party. This means that sometimes Indivisibles work with their locally elected Democrats and the party, and sometimes they clash with them—but they always remain independent.

There's a long historical precedent for this relationship between elected Democrats and progressive social movements. An old story from early in Franklin Roosevelt's first presidential term goes like this: A civil rights and labor leader comes into the new president's office with a policy request. Roosevelt responds that he agrees, and he tells the advocate, "Make me do it." We see this dynamic play out repeatedly in political history. Martin Luther King Jr. went to Selma to force Lyndon Johnson's hand on the Voting Rights Act. Dreamer advocates held hunger strikes at Barack Obama's campaign offices to force his hand on protections for Dreamers. Elected Democrats often want to do the right thing, but they need a progressive movement to make them do it.

It's a strategic choice to give tough love. The goal of the Indivisible movement isn't to build a sycophantic personal relationship with those in power. We want a relationship rooted in mutual respect. Our goal is to have elected officials who actually use their power to represent us. That means applying pressure when necessary—pressure that would be difficult to apply if we thought of these electeds as above reproach.

The backlash spooked Democrat congressional leadership.[16] By January, as yet another funding deadline approached, we got word that the Democrats might finally be finding their spines. At the very last minute, Democrats had committed to blocking any budget bill that did not include protections for Dreamers. If that meant the government shut down, then so be it.

It was a huge, historic development: the power of the coalition that had come together to lobby for DACA had changed the political landscape. It had convinced Democrats to fight.

It was a stunning moment. It was also short-lived. The government shut down at midnight on Friday. The next day Trump was up on the airwaves, targeting Democratic senators with a viciously anti-immigrant ad. Even as public opinion polls showed Democrats winning the messaging fight and millions of people, including Indivisibles, flooded the streets of major American cities for the second annual Women's March, the Democratic caucus's will was crumbling. By Monday it was over: Democratic senators were running for the exits. Schumer signed on to a bill reopening the government with the fig leaf of a concession on DACA: a promise to hold an immigration vote in the Republican-controlled Senate. "Big win for Republicans as Democrats cave on Shutdown," tweeted President Trump.

Schumer attempted to frame this as progress, but no one was fooled. Once again, Democrats were trading real leverage now for the hazy promise of future action. And the fact that

---

16. So we heard. As previously mentioned, they weren't really talking to us at this point.

they had collapsed midway through this last gambit meant that Republicans would have no hesitation about calling their bluff in the future. The path forward was bleak.

In the end, there was no final political showdown over DACA. The fight ended with a whimper rather than a bang. In January a federal judge ruled that Trump's administration had possibly violated the law in rescinding DACA, and he paused the rollback until the matter could be more carefully considered. In February the Supreme Court declined Trump's request to expedite the process; it would have to slowly work its way through the courts. As a result, Dreamers were temporarily protected, and, with the pressure off, neither Republicans nor Democrats attempted to address DACA again that year. It was an easy political out for electeds of both parties. No one—neither Democrat nor Republican—had to admit defeat; they could all just throw their hands up and say that it was up to the courts. For now, the legislative fight was over.

WHAT'S CONSTITUENT POWER FOR?

Why tell this story of a fight over congressional strategy that ultimately ended in a stalemate? And why spend so much time focusing on what Democrats should have done differently? After all, Trump and Republicans are the ones who ended DACA and continue to launch assaults on American immigrants. Why not focus on them?

We focus on Democrats not because they're worse than Trump—obviously they aren't—but because the first step in building a political coalition based in solidarity is getting our own progressive house in order. Change doesn't happen if your friends aren't willing to fight for it. And sometimes your friends aren't willing to fight for it unless you push them.

There will always be reasons why it's "strategic" to avoid taking a stand with a marginalized community. There will always be seemingly reasonable people who make the political calculation that we'll be better off if we delay the fight a bit longer. As our partners noted in the letter opposing the funding deal with Trump in September 2017, the message to communities under threat is almost always "Wait."

This is not a new phenomenon. More than five decades ago, Martin Luther King Jr. wrote in his "Letter from a Birmingham Jail":

> *I have almost reached the regrettable conclusion that the Negro's great stumbling block in the stride toward freedom is not the White Citizen's Counciler or the Ku Klux Klanner, but the white moderate who is more devoted to "order" than to justice; who prefers a negative peace which is the absence of tension to a positive peace which is the presence of justice; who constantly says: "I agree with you in the goal you seek, but I can't agree with your methods of direct action"; who paternalistically believes he can set the timetable for another man's freedom; who lives by a mythical concept of time and who constantly advises the Negro to wait for a "more convenient season." Shallow understanding from people of good will is more frustrating than absolute misunderstanding from people of ill will. Lukewarm acceptance is much more bewildering than outright rejection.*

It will never be the right time, unless we—all of us—demand it. Unless we recognize, as Indivisibles did, that whether we're immigrants or not, whether our civil rights are under attack or not, this is our fight too.

In his multivolume biography of Lyndon Johnson, Robert Caro recounts one particularly telling story about how the president thought about political power. Shortly after Johnson became president, there was a heated debate among his political advisors about whether to push for the long-shot civil rights bill. One of the "wise and practical people around the table" argued that "the presidency has only a certain amount of coinage to expend, and you oughtn't to expend it on this." To which Johnson replied, "Well, what the hell's the presidency for?"

Whether it's presidential power or constituent power, if you care about justice, you don't build power to keep it. You build power to spend it. Which is to say, you build power not for power's sake but to make change.

Doing this depends on choosing sides in times of disagreement among friends. When the political outcome is uncertain, we'll often find marginalized groups excluded from the table where some of us are welcomed. Wise and practical people will always advise Indivisibles to hush up and go along. We'll face risks and losses when we push our friends. We'll spark fights within our own network about when and how hard to push. It's precisely in these moments that it matters for folks with privilege to throw in with something more than sympathetic words. Risking our own standing and power does not guarantee victory. Sometimes you lose the fight. But it's possible, in losing, to set the precedent for the next fight. It's possible to keep building toward something better.

Indivisible Lesson #13: Allyship Is a Process, Not an Identity

Each of us enters some situations with some privileges: our gender, our religion, our race, our sexual orientation, our class. You can't choose to not have privilege. But you can choose to use it for good. You can operate as an ally to those directly under threat, the folks who should be leading the fight.

The thing about allyship, though, is that you can't just declare yourself an ally. That's not something you get to decide, in the same way that you don't get to declare yourself "modest" or "a good friend." It's not an identity, a label, or a stamp of approval. It's not enough to share articles on Facebook or wear an "Abolish ICE" T-shirt. It's an ongoing process of reflection, communication, action, and being accountable to others.

Engaging in the politics of solidarity means actually engaging. Your words and feelings are important, but it's how you show up in the world that makes the difference. Alicia Garza, cofounder of Black Lives Matter, argues for a model of "co-conspiracy." As she puts it, co-conspiracy is about "moving through guilt and shame and recognizing that we did not create none of this stuff. And so what we are taking responsibility for is the power that we hold to transform our conditions." Co-conspirators don't make gestures; they make change.

This practice requires that we ask ourselves some questions: How should our analysis shift? How should our strategy adjust? How should we organize in this reality? Who should we be partnering with? Who should we follow? How do we lend to others the power that comes with our privilege? What kind of political capital do we expend, and what status do we risk in service of co-conspiracy? How are we accountable to others?

Indivisibles often operate from positions of privilege and power. When we're at our best, we're not shying away from this reality. Instead, we're embracing what that means and figuring out what it requires of us in the context of widespread injustice.

PRACTICING THE POLITICS OF SOLIDARITY

While Indivisible was not able to help achieve passage of the Dream Act in 2017 or 2018, we established where we'd stand in future fights when immigrant Americans were under attack. And unfortunately there would be no shortage of such attacks.

Trump's administration oversaw the separation of thousands of child refugees from their parents at the U.S.-Mexico border. His border security officers fired tear gas at men, women, and children fleeing violence in Central America. He cheered as the Supreme Court upheld his Muslim travel ban in June 2018. As the midterms neared, with polls looking ominous for Republicans, Trump fabricated a "crisis" at the border, casting a caravan of families and children seeking safety as an "invasion."[17] It was the classic Trump playbook, but when Election Day rolled around, it failed miserably.

A few months into the new Congress, the now Democratic House passed an expansive version of the clean Dream Act for the first time in history, with the strong support of immigrant advocates and allies like Indivisible. This legislation advanced protections not only for Dreamers but also for hundreds of thousands of "temporary protected status" and "deferred enforcement departure" recipients, visa holders from countries that had suffered from war or natural disasters. In appraising the ambition of the House bill, Greisa from United We Dream said, "We showed the country that it is possible to pass legislation that protects people without hurting [others]." The bill passed with the support of every voting Democratic member, as well as a handful of Republicans.

This isn't a story of immigrant advocates achieving any sort of final, complete victory. Nor is the story one of Democrats lining up behind a bold alternative to anti-immigrant Trumpism. As we write this, Dreamers still lack permanent protections: Senate Republicans refuse to even hold a vote on the House-passed Dream Act. Trump still rattles his saber at the southern border. Many Democrats still approach our broken immigration system from a permanent defensive crouch. Over the strong opposition of immigrant rights groups in 2019,

---

17. Trump personally rejected a proposed focus on the economy, and instead his team aired a campaign ad that focused on anti-immigrant fearmongering. The ad was so universally recognized as racist that CNN, NBC, and even the Republican propaganda network Fox News refused to run it.

House Democratic leadership embraced a funding bill giving Trump billions more for his deportation machine. And the idea of compassionate immigration reform—a decades-old goal to fix our cruel and absurdly dysfunctional system—remains a far-off aspiration. We've got more work to do with both our adversaries and our friends.

On a near-daily basis, news breaks of a horrifying violation of immigrant families' rights and dignity by our government. The truth is that over the years we have built—with support from both political parties—an immigration enforcement system so massive, so heartless, and so unaccountable that it's capable of almost anything. Trump didn't create this system, but he removed any checks that might have previously constrained it. Long before Trump became president, U.S. Customs and Border Protection (CBP) and U.S. Immigration and Customs Enforcement (ICE) had been getting away with appalling violations of human rights. They ripped families apart, terrorized immigrant communities, and allowed federal agents to carry out sexual assault and abuse on a wide scale. They faced opposition from immigrant rights advocates—but far too little public outrage or oversight.

We know there's more to come. Trump launched his campaign in 2015 rooted in anti-immigrant hate. He made immigration a focus of the 2016 election. His first acts as president were to attack immigrants. When courts intervened, he found other ways to go on the offense. While many things are uncertain in the Trump era, there's one thing we can be sure about: immigration will be a defining feature of the 2020 presidential contest, because Trump will insist on it. And we know that after he's gone, that virulent strain of xenophobia at the heart of Trumpism will remain.

But we also know that, immigrant or not, undocumented or not, this is our fight too. This is about our democracy. Indivisibles across the country at this very moment are building their power. They're holding their meetings in bars and churches. They're marching to their congressional district offices. They're endorsing candidates and registering voters. And they're following the lead of those directly impacted, standing indivisible against hate, bigotry, and oppression. That's how we build and use power the Indivisible way through the politics of solidarity. That's how we'll build a democracy that represents all our people.

5

How to Make Waves

The women are in my grill no matter where I go.
—*Former representative* DAVE BRAT *(R-VA)*

November is coming.
—*Popular Indivisible refrain directed at electeds year-round*

Remember how we said that the first lesson about elected officials is that they are always running for office? Here's the corollary: elections take place on Election Day. The next election campaign starts the day after that.

This might sound odd. We're conditioned to think of election results as the product of campaigns. When we think about winning, we think about running a great campaign—the TV and radio and digital ads, the polling, the rallies, the speeches. We think about building the kind of turnout operation that gets the right number of people to show up to the polls to win on that one big day.

These things are important. But a lot of the conditions that drive the outcome of an election take hold long before the official campaign gets under way. Elected officials understand this. Sure, their days look different during an election season compared to the legislative season. But it's all part of the same cycle. The reason why your electeds are out kissing babies and riding in parade floats on the Fourth of July in an off year is because they know a lot of those parade-goers are eventually going to be voters.

The same basic idea is relevant for Indivisible as a grassroots activist and community member. Your work might look different based on the season, but it's all part of the continual process of driving change.

> ### Indivisible Lesson #14: The Virtuous Cycle of Advocacy and Elections
>
> *In the political world, it's common to distinguish between two types of work: advocacy and electoral. Advocacy involves activities like building coalitions around a bill or protesting at your member of Congress's office. Electoral work involves activities like endorsing candidates and getting out the vote. These are presented as wholly separate activities, often for wholly different types of people and organizations. Some folks do advocacy, some do electoral.*
>
> *But this isn't how the world actually works. Advocacy and electoral work are part of a continuum. As an activist, if you've got a well-constructed strategy, your advocacy and electoral work reinforce each other to achieve your goals and build power. The advocacy work you do in off years keeps you engaged and builds your strength as you head into the electoral work, which then (ideally) pro-*

duces electeds who are better allies on your future advocacy work. It's a virtuous cycle.

Advocacy produces electoral results. *Advocacy determines the environment in which candidates run for office. The town halls of 2017 were about stopping Trumpcare and the rest of Trump's agenda, but they also provided the content for campaign ads in 2018. Victory in the Trumpcare fight and success in painting the Trump tax cuts as a scam deprived Republicans of any popular accomplishments to run on in 2018. Constituent watchdogs made being a Trump-supporting member of Congress less fun, and that drove a wave of retirements that made it easier for Democrats to take the House in 2018. Determined, sustained advocacy helped cement the public link between Republicans and their most unpopular positions and paint them as unresponsive and out of touch, softening their approval ratings and weakening their reelection chances.*

Electoral power strengthens advocacy efforts. *If you help put someone in office—by endorsing, knocking on doors, getting out the vote—they're going to care about keeping you happy. They're more likely to listen to you when you come calling, because they know they're going to need you in the future. Indivisible groups who went all out to elect candidates in 2018 forged connections to candidates who they'll draw on for their future work in making progressive change.*

There's strong academic research to back up this point. A study found that in areas where there were active Tea Party protests from 2009 to 2010, Republicans were more likely to have electoral victories. Nearly a decade later we're seeing the same phenomenon play out—in our favor. A study of Women's March mobilizations has found that, controlling for all factors, geographies with a bigger showing at their Women's March in 2017 had better Democratic electoral outcomes in 2018. Where grassroots actions flourish in off years, electoral victories follow.

OK, so your advocacy has set the stage for your electoral work. But what does it mean to "do elections"? This is a good question! First, let's talk about the basics.

An electoral campaign is a pop-up operation designed to set up quickly, burn fast, and deliver a win. Campaigns win by getting votes. A campaign starts with a "win number"—the total votes they're going to need—and then builds a strategy to get there. A portion of the electorate will always reliably turn out every election to vote the party line. Campaigns ignore these people: they know these folks are already going to vote for or against them, so they don't waste resources trying to talk to them. Hitting the win number depends on assembling the right combination of three more groups: people who aren't registered to vote yet (electorate expansion); people who *might* agree with you, if you can win them over (persuasion); and people who will probably support you *if* they vote (turnout).

Campaigns get their votes and hit their win number by acquiring and deploying three resources: people, media, and money. People are either staff or volunteers. They run the campaign, knock on doors, make the calls, raise the money, spread word of mouth, and more. Media is, in most races, the way that a campaign reaches the vast majority of voters. Campaigns will mix press coverage (earned media) and ads (paid media) to try to reach as many folks in as effective a way as possible. Money is, well, money. You use it to hire the people and get the media.

The specific combination of these resources is going to vary based on the race, the candidate, the campaign, and other specifics. But at the end of the day, that's what every campaign needs.

Indivisible groups are unique because we are real, locally based, engaged constituents, with networks, resources, and enthusiasm. Why does a candidate speak with a local Indivisible group or seek an endorsement? Because they recognize that it will bring people, media, or money. That's the logic; that's why we matter to them.

If you've built up your Indivisible group, your network, your media profile, and your brand in the community, then campaigns will call you. They'll invite you to events. They'll ask to come speak. They'll ask you to endorse them. They'll ask for your group to help: by knocking on doors, by raising money, sometimes even with basic campaign functions. And if you're considering running for office yourself, your first call will be to the members of your group, because they're going to be your first campaign contributors, your first volunteers, and your pep squad.

It's common to think about elections as your chance to take on the bad guys—to "throw the bums out." And they are! This is important. It's the moment that turns all the work you've done holding your electeds accountable into results. But elections are also your chance to help put the people you actually *want* to represent you in office. It is possible to elect people who aren't just "not bad" but actively good. People who look like our country. People we can believe in. People who won't just hold off the harm but who will fight for the future inclusive democracy we need.

We know this because we've been through some of it already. This chapter tells the story of Indivisibles building the blue wave that came crashing down in communities across the country in November 2018. It was a historic outcome that few people—not even hopeful progressives—dared to predict two years earlier. And it holds some valuable lessons for those interested in building the next blue wave and, you know, saving American democracy afterward.

SURE, THEY MARCHED, BUT WILL THEY VOTE?

In June 2017 the Indivisible national staff was huddled together at Franklin Hall, a Benjamin Franklin– and Franklin Roosevelt–inspired bar near our shared office space in Washington, D.C.[1] We were there, eyes glued to the bar's TV screens, waiting for the returns in the special-election runoff for Georgia's Sixth Congressional District. It was getting late, and we were a bundle of emotions: excited, nervous, and slightly nauseated.

This was the first competitive special election for Congress since Trump had taken office. The seat had been vacated by Tom Price, Trump's incoming secretary of health and human

---

1. Yes, this is a real bar. D.C. is a weird place. (But, to be fair, they've got good nachos.)

services, who'd resigned from Congress to oversee the fight to dismantle the Affordable Care Act. Price's district had long been considered a safe Republican seat; it hadn't gone blue since before the archconservative Newt Gingrich won it in 1978. The Cook Political Report rated the district as leaning Republican by 8 points. To put that in context: to accomplish the herculean task of retaking the House of Representatives in 2018, Democrats would need to take Republican+3 seats. And even Republican+3 districts were seen as a stretch.

But at Indivisible we didn't let any of that bother us. Because, unlike the armchair prognosticators who scoffed at the idea of the Sixth District turning blue, Indivisibles had been out on the ground. We'd seen something they hadn't, something electric: a real wave of resistance energy not only in the Georgia Sixth but in just about every community in the country.

For months this energy had been building and demonstrating its strength nationwide. There had been mass protests at congressional town halls. There had been mass die-ins at congressional district offices. Members of Congress were bombarded from every side by constituents, and that constituent pressure had halted the movement of the Trumpcare bill through the House of Representatives. So we kept telling the people outside the movement: *If you could see the energy we're seeing, you'd understand. We think we can take back the House of Representatives next year. We think it's possible. We really do.*

There was widespread skepticism among the political class. What about gerrymandering? What about voter suppression? What about Donald Trump? Most common was the not-just-a-little-condescending remark, "Sure, it's impressive people are showing up at town halls and marches, but will any of this actually convert into winning elections?"

Now, with this special election in Georgia, we saw a chance to answer that question. Jon Ossoff, the young Democratic candidate, had attracted national attention and raised millions of dollars to make the race competitive. And we knew—because we were talking to the dozen or so Indivisible groups in the district—that he had a grassroots army behind him. Groups like Indivisible Georgia Sixth District and Indivisible North Fulton were mobilizing hundreds of people, many of whom had never volunteered on a campaign before, to blanket the district with canvassers. They had turned Facebook groups for progressive moms into organizing hubs dedicated to action. They were determined to talk to every possible Ossoff voter.

This on-the-ground organizing work was happening everywhere in the country. It wasn't as loud or newsworthy as marches or protests. Local TV stations ate up town hall footage, but they weren't exactly rushing to cover suburban moms or grandmothers who were hosting meetings once a month, who had converted their friends into canvassing squads or taken over their local Democratic parties or run for office themselves.

But, hey, at least it meant they had the advantage of surprise. And we were counting on the first big surprise win in Georgia Sixth.

So that night at the bar we had everything ready to go for our upset victory. We had an op-ed accepted at the *New York Times*, set to publish as soon as Ossoff was declared the victor.

It would go out to millions of readers the next day. In it we described the power of the people united. The resistance was electoralized. The blue wave was coming!

There we waited with bated breath, laptops out, beers in hand. All we needed was for the results to come in, and the next phase of Indivisible could begin.

Then the result came in. Ossoff lost.

Our hearts sank. Sitting at the bar, putting aside our drinks, we scrambled to rewrite our emails and cancel our *New York Times* op-ed. (Well, actually, it was canceled for us.) We knew a lot of people's hearts had been set on this victory, and we were worried for the movement's morale. In our new email to Indivisibles, we sought to console them after this loss—to explain that the fight would continue. It was a safe Republican district. It was never supposed to be in play. The very fact that this had become a competitive race, forcing Republicans to divert time and money to protect a safe seat, was itself a victory.

This was all true, but it didn't feel good. It felt like the story had taken an abrupt wrong turn.

We were especially concerned about the impact of the loss on the Indivisible groups in Georgia's Sixth. They'd worked so incredibly hard for this! It was a tough district, but they'd organized on their home turf and done the work week in and week out. We wanted them to be proud. We didn't want them to think their efforts had been wasted. So we put on a brave face and called to cheer them up. We reached Jessica Zeigler, Amy Nosek, Essence Johnson, and more Georgia Sixth leaders at the

Ossoff "victory" party after the returns had come in. We were ready to thank them for their work and to offer sympathy in the face of a painful loss.

They were *jubilant*.

Passing around the phone, they explained that they hadn't expected Ossoff to win; to be honest, they didn't think he'd run a particularly strong campaign. "*But we're purple now!*" they cheered. They were excited that the election had been so close, that the region and the country now recognized that the Atlanta suburbs weren't a conservative stronghold any longer. They were ready and eager to start holding their new Republican representative, Karen Handel, accountable. They were ready to gear up for the next big fight: a state senate special election. And the 2018 gubernatorial and congressional elections were already on the horizon.

We hung up feeling both elated and a little silly. Here we thought we'd need to console them—and they'd been the ones to cheer us up.

The Indivisibles in Georgia recognized that we don't take back the country by winning one advocacy campaign or one election; we do it by building the kind of local power that can eventually change what's politically possible. They also understood that the 2018 election would not start in 2018, with endorsements or voter registration or get-out-the-vote campaigns. It would start with holding their elected officials accountable from day one. Georgia Sixth Indivisibles might not have won this time, but that was OK: they were playing the long game. And so were Indivisibles across the country.

Indivisible Lesson #15: Mobilizing Versus Organizing

When you think of grassroots power, you might think of masses of people showing up at a protest, chanting, "Show me what democracy looks like!"[2] Or maybe you think of a huge campaign rally or massive Election Day turnout. This is mobilizing: when lots of people take an action of some sort. Mobilizing is spending your power.

Mobilizing is important, but on its own it's not enough for a simple reason: our opponents are entrenched and can outlast one-off mobilizations. What happens after the day of action is over? What happens after the votes are cast? If the answer is Nothing, because people go home, *then the target of our mobilizations will know they can weather the storm.*

Organizing is about building power. It's about building a shared sense of purpose, developing leaders, settling on strategy, creating tactics, and, at the most basic level, just figuring out how to work well with others. If mobilizing is the big demonstration of power, organizing is the part that's quieter but critical for the long haul. Effective groups are always organizing so that they can mobilize at strategically critical moments—for advocacy, for electoral work, for everything in between.

Fundamentally, this depends on developing and sustaining leaders within your group. Effective leaders

---

2. Considered as a title for this book! But we rejected it as too long. Still, one of our favorite chants at rallies.

continually develop volunteers, giving them greater responsibility and leadership roles over time. The best way to do this is the snowflake model, which focuses on building a web of interdependent leaders working to achieve goals together. Each leader functions like an arm on a snowflake, taking responsibility for a task or line of effort that's part of the broader goal. The snowflake model allows groups to tap into the talents of their membership and it ensures the sustainability of the group; as leaders naturally move on, others are continually being groomed to step into their roles.

By continuously developing membership and leadership, Indivisible groups build a muscle they then can flex at key moments over time. The permanence of a local Indivisible group is an essential part of your power. Elected officials and other targets of mobilizations know that they can't just wait it out—because you will still be there long after one particular march or election is over.

"CONGRATULATIONS ON YOUR RETIREMENT"

In April 2017, Indivisible Washington's 8th District, led by founder Chris Petzold, sat down to meet with their Republican representative, Dave Reichert.

This was not Chris's first rodeo. Since before Trump's inauguration, Indivisible Washington's 8th District had been systematically turning up the heat on Reichert. They met with his staff. They held rallies outside his offices. When he refused to host town halls or answer questions from constituents in public, they started systematically showing up to his (rare) public events. They fact-checked him on Twitter and in the media. In short, they were now a constant presence in his life.

Reichert asked Chris a simple question: Why? If their real target was Trump, why were they going after him like this? Chris looked him in the eye as she replied: "We can't stop. We *won't* stop. We're not gonna stop until you quit being a rubber stamp to Trump's agenda."

He had no response. What could he say? He wasn't going to break from Donald Trump—not really; to do so was political suicide. And for Chris and the Indivisible Washington's 8th District team, something had become increasingly clear in those first few months: Trump wasn't the problem—or at least he was only one of the problems. The bigger problem was the people like Reichert who not only weren't checking Trump but were actively advancing his agenda. The ones who pretended to be moderate while handing a blank check to the pro-Trump fanatics. The ones who should have known better.

And that was a problem that Indivisible Washington's 8th District could do something about.

Chris, like many Indivisible leaders, hadn't paid much attention to politics before 2016. She voted, but that was about it. But something snapped for her after the 2016 election; she couldn't sit on the sidelines anymore. In January, she heard about this "Indivisible" guide to advocacy on the radio while driving home from work. Two days later she was leading the newly formed Indivisible Washington's 8th District. She had found a community, and they had found a mission.

If Dave Reichert was annoyed in April, his problems multi-

plied by August. Activists called attention to his unwillingness
to appear in public with a packed and well-covered "Missing
Member" town hall. They placed an empty chair onstage to
stand in for the absent Dave Reichert. A progressive coalition,
including Indivisible Washington's 8th District, drew another
big round of press in July, when progressive champion Pramila Jayapal joined them for an "Adopt a District" town hall,
offering to talk with Dave Reichert's constituents about the
questions that he refused to answer. Indivisible members were
filling local papers with letters to the editor recounting their
unsuccessful attempts to talk with their member of Congress.

Everyone gets a round of bad press occasionally, but this
was doing real damage. A Democratic challenger, pediatrician
Kim Schrier, had started running TV ads about how Dave Reichert was unwilling to listen to his constituents. The star of
the ad? The empty chair from Indivisible's "Missing Member"
town hall. The spot closed with Kim saying that if Reichert
refused to show up, it was time for somebody else to fill his seat.

Reichert was one of many Republicans who'd fully committed to a strategy of hiding from his constituents in the early
months of the Trump administration. And if you're thinking
ahead, it might have occurred to you that while this approach is
pretty effective for avoiding viral YouTube moments, it comes
with one very big drawback. It's possible to hunker down and
hide from your constituents in the first few months of your
term, but it's a lot harder to hide from your constituents when
you also need to ask them for their vote in the upcoming election. And when you do finally appear in public to campaign,
you're going to have company from Indivisible groups. And

they're going to have questions. And your answers will be featured in the local news.

In late August, Indivisible Washington's 8th District got a tip that Reichert would be at a community center health event. This was one of a very small number of public events Reichert still had on his schedule; it had been carefully planned, and he'd expected a friendly audience and a good press clip. Indivisible Washington's 8th District ensured that wouldn't happen. They organized a group of people to meet him outside to protest and a group of people to ask him questions inside to keep him on his toes. Reichert was visibly frustrated as he departed the event, stopping only to tell one of the protestors that their sign was "incorrect."[3]

In early September, Reichert announced his plans to retire.

Reichert was in the middle of his seventh term in office, which by congressional standards meant he was in his prime. He wasn't on anyone's list of likely Republican retirements for the 115th Congress. He also wasn't alone. Republican members felt frustrated, demoralized, and browbeaten. They were facing tough reelections and, honestly, lately they were having a lot less fun. Sarah Herron of Indivisible East Tennessee put it succinctly upon hearing that her own representative, Jimmy Duncan, was retiring on the heels of a wave of bad press: "We definitely changed his job, and then he no longer wanted that job."

Republican Party leaders watched with alarm over the fall

---

3. Her sign said, "You do not have the right to remain silent." So Reichert was technically right, although, practically speaking, it's rarely a good idea for an elected official to remain silent.

as the trickle of retirements turned into a flood. In September, Dave Trott—of the infamous live-chicken town hall—announced it would be his last term. In October, Senator Jeff Flake did the same. In November, Bob Goodlatte—last seen slinking away from his sneaky attempt to gut the Office of Congressional Ethics—announced that he'd be retiring after twenty-six years in office.

In January 2018, Indivisible held a national day of action to congratulate Republicans who'd voted for Trump's tax bill on their forthcoming retirements. Indivisible groups brought cake, balloons, and "Congratulations on your retirement" cards to their Republican members of Congress. The not-so-subtle message was that their tax vote would cost them their next election. It quickly became apparent that some of them had no plans to stick around and try their luck. In the case of Representative Darrell Issa, for example, the day after more than a hundred members of Indivisible San Diego turned up at his office for his nonvoluntary retirement party, he announced his actual plans to retire.

By that point the floodgates were open. Representative Rodney Frelinghuysen, who had never recovered from the revelation that he'd targeted constituent Saily Avelenda of NJ 11th for Change for her political activity, announced his retirement at the end of January. In February, Representative Ryan Costello of Pennsylvania explained the reason behind all the retirements: "I think everybody is aware of what the environment is because they deal with Indivisible people outside their office every week protesting." In March, Costello himself announced his retirement. By April, when Speaker of the House

Paul Ryan shocked the political world with his own retirement, forty-four Republican members of Congress had confirmed they were no longer planning to run for reelection.

It was the inverse of a blue wave—a receding red tide. And it had real implications. Incumbents usually head into an election with significant advantages. They've spent years building up their public images, their ties to the district, and their war chests. Challengers have none of these things. It's one of the reasons why, on average, House incumbents win reelection around 90 percent of the time.

The tide of retirements meant that Republicans were heading into the election season with fewer seasoned incumbents and more open seats to fight for. It was bad for the GOP on the merits, and it also portended an ominous political future for those who remained. If people like Dave Reichert, Rodney Frelinghuysen, and Paul Ryan, who'd spent years climbing the ladder and building their careers in Washington, didn't want to stick around for the 2018 election . . . well, that was a very bad sign for their pro-Trump congressional colleagues.

And there were more bad signs coming.

BILLIONAIRES JUST L♥VE IT

While these retirement announcements were racking up, congressional Republicans were still on a mission. They still had a unified conservative government, and they were going to make use of that power while they had it. The clock was ticking, and they needed a win.

In November 2017, TV cameras and journalists were all

set up outside Senator Cory Gardner's office in Denver. They weren't there for the Republican senator; he wasn't going to show up. (He never did.) The cameras were there for 150 or so other Coloradans who were showing up, organized by Indivisible Denver and Indivisible Front Range Resistance. This was part of Indivisible's nationwide day of action, with similar events happening at other Senate offices of other absent senators all over the country. In Denver that Tuesday, the bundled-up attendees from all walks of life were giving up their lunch breaks to spend a cold afternoon protesting outside for a cause that rarely stirs people's blood: the U.S. tax code.

Having lived through months of photogenic people-powered protests against Trumpcare, the GOP was ready to shift to something boring and popular. The plan was to deliver more than a trillion dollars in tax cuts. The proposal would give the vast majority of the benefits of the tax cut to the rich and corporations, but Trump and his congressional supporters downplayed that part. Their headline was simple: Republicans want to cut your taxes.

At Indivisible, we had two reasons to fight this. First, the Republican plan represented a radical reshaping of our tax code that would further reinforce the power of the corporate class and harm everyone else. This was really bad stuff, and if there was a fraction of a chance we could stop it, we needed to try.

Second, this wasn't just about whether a Trump tax bill passed. It was also about whether the bill was popular and could serve as a feather in Republicans' caps in their reelection campaigns. We weren't sure we could stop this legislative train. But we needed to try, if for no other reason than to ensure

Trump couldn't reap political benefits from the tax cut. Plan A was to kill the bill. Plan B was to make it politically toxic even if it did pass.

Indivisible Lesson #16: Fight to Win, Fight to Delay, Fight to Make It Hurt

Indivisibles pick our battles; we can't fight every fight. But even losing battles can help move progress forward. There are always going to be moments when you know the odds are stacked against you. You might think there's no point in waging a fight you can't win, but winning outright is only one of the reasons to get involved. The fight still might be worth waging if you can delay or score some political points.

When it comes to stopping bad legislation, just delaying can be hugely effective. There are only so many days in a legislative session, and legislative bodies can focus only on a limited number of priorities at a time. When you're in the minority and you fight to prolong a legislative battle—even a losing one—you not only increase the chance for victory; you also limit the possible future damage the majority can do. If your opponents have to spend twice as long on their first priority, their second priority is less likely to move.

Fighting a losing fight can also be worthwhile if you can cause political damage to your opponents. Making the other side fully own their terrible policies can pay off big in the next election and can strengthen your hand headed into the next advocacy fight. When one side is pushing unpopular legislation, a pitched battle—even one they know they can win—is the last thing they want. If you make a big fuss, that brings attention and press— and attention and press assigns responsibility for the policy. If there's no opposition, voters won't know how awful their electeds' policies are and won't know whom to vote against come the next election.

The strategy to win depended on breaking through the eye-glazing discussion of tax rates and brackets to frame the legislation as a corrupt giveaway to the rich—and to do it with humor. At the local level, Indivisibles did this by leaning into theater.

In Denver, outside Senator Gardner's office, the chants, posters, and speeches ranged from nerdy to comedic. One sign featured Rich Uncle Pennybags, the cartoon Monopoly Man. Another read "The Republican Tax Plan: Billionaires Just L♥ve It." Wonkier protestors referenced the nonpartisan Congressional Budget Office, citing the trillions it would add to the deficit. They implored Senator Gardner to listen to them and noted that, one way or another, he'd have to listen in 2020 when he was next up for reelection.

Elsewhere across the country, Indivisible dressed up as billionaires in mock support of the tax bill. They took enormous "Tax March Chickens"—a bizarre thirteen-foot inflatable chicken with Trump-like hair—to public events and protests.[4]

---

4. In a stroke of theatrical brilliance, the Tax March started to help local grassroots groups obtain their own Tax March Chickens after the April march ended. By the fall, these ridiculous chickens were all over the country, generating earned media and attention wherever they went.

Indivisible groups all over the country delivered giant checks to their members of Congress (made out to the elected's donors or simply to "The Top 1 Percent") and demanded to know exactly how much money their representatives would personally receive from the tax cut.

As Republicans moved the bill forward over Thanksgiving weekend in 2017, Indivisibles mounted a national day of action, with around a hundred events in thirty-five states. In Tucson, Indivisible Southern Arizona staged a forty-three-hour vigil outside the offices of Senators Jeff Flake and John McCain. In Maine, a coalition of grassroots groups, including Indivisibles and activists from the Women's March, turned out constituents from all sixteen of Maine's counties to object to the bill. Midcoast Maine Indivisible, Indivisible MDI, Indivisible Sagadahoc, Mainers for Accountable Leadership, and more were driving protests across the state. Susan Collins's offices were full of constituents staging sit-ins and prayer vigils.

Indivisible worked with a constellation of progressive groups to execute a national strategy. Americans for Tax Fairness brought together a table of activists, policy wonks, and others engaged in the fight against Trump's tax bill.[5] The Tax March, an organization that had grown out of the organic marches to demand Trump's tax returns in April 2017, was sup-

---

5. This wasn't just a fight for tax advocates. Women's groups like the National Women's Law Center, Planned Parenthood, and MomsRising joined to make the case for how this bill would hurt women. Environmental groups got involved to fight against the inclusion of drilling in the Arctic National Wildlife Refuge. Health care advocates fought alongside us, recognizing the impact the bill would have on our health care system.

porting local advocacy nationwide. And think tanks like the Institute on Taxation and Economic Policy, the Center on Budget and Policy Priorities, and the Center for American Progress were pumping out daily analyses as the Republican proposal morphed from bad to worse.

Combined, this coordinated effort succeeded in generating national and local attention and media, which was starting to have an effect on the tax bill's popularity. In early October, polling showed that 48 percent of Americans approved of the prospective bill. By mid-December, its popularity was down to 26 percent—a stunning drop for a bill that was ostensibly about giving people more money.

But it wasn't enough to fracture the Republican Senate consensus.

A bit after midnight on December 20, over the din of ferocious protests inside and outside the U.S. Capitol, Republicans passed the Tax Cut and Jobs Act with a 51–48 vote. They'd held their entire Senate caucus together, including the three Republicans who'd broken with them on Trumpcare. A gloating Trump would sign the bill two days later, the only substantial legislative accomplishment of his presidency.

But that's not the end of the story. Yes, Plan A had failed. We had lost the legislative fight. But on the night of the vote, we wrote to Indivisibles on what was to come:

When the Tea Party lost the Affordable Care Act fight in early 2010, they didn't throw in the towel. It was that loss more than anything that fueled their takeover of the rest of the levers of power over the next several years. Today, tomorrow,

*and every day until we have unified progressive control of the
government, no GOP senator should be able to appear in public without answering questions about their support of the tax
scam and their betrayal of their constituents. Some are up for
reelection in 2018. Some are up in 2020. Some are up in 2022.
They will lose and they will be publicly disgraced. We will not
forget. We will not move on. We will take away their majority.
We will hang this around their necks and it will drag them
down.*

Plan B was in motion, and it was going to pay dividends
sooner than we had hoped.

It began in an unlikely spot: a special election for Pennsylvania's Eighteenth Congressional District. Representative
Tim Murphy had resigned in the fall after reports surfaced that
the pro-life Republican had pressured his mistress to have an
abortion.[6] The lines of Pennsylvania's Eighteenth had been
drawn to make it an exceedingly safe Republican seat; Trump
had carried it by nearly 20 points in 2016. It was even redder
than Georgia's Sixth, where our dreams had been dashed a
few months before. But Trump's popularity had continued to
plummet since then. And Conor Lamb, the Democratic candidate, was running an energetic campaign drawing on a wave of
support from groups like Pennsylvania Together, a coalition of
Pennsylvania Indivisibles and other grassroots groups.

National Republicans, alarmed that Lamb was gaining
traction, started pumping money into the race. Their first line

---

6. Reread that sentence. Yes, it's gross and absurd.

of defense? TV ads touting the Trump tax bill. As of the beginning of February, 65 percent of Republican ads for their
candidate, Rick Saccone, featured the tax bill. "Veteran Rick
Saccone supported your tax cut. Now Pennsylvania families
are receiving bonuses and raises. Rick Saccone fights hard for
working families," blared one campaign ad.

Then something strange happened: the tax cut ads vanished
from the airwaves. Saccone stopped talking about the cuts in
his stump speech. By the election in March, not a single Republican TV ad was focusing on the cuts at all. It was like they had
never happened.

The shift in Republican messaging strategy as the election
date neared wasn't an accident. Republican PACs with millions of dollars on the line and an election to win were testing
their messaging. And they'd pulled the tax ads for a reason: the
ads were doing more harm than good. In a safely Republican,
safely Trump-won district, *reminding voters of the Trump tax cut
was hurting the Republican candidate.*

This had never happened before. Tax cuts—even regressive
ones that mainly benefit the rich—are supposed to be popular.
But voters were rejecting the Trump tax bill. By September,
Republican internal strategy memos confirmed what had become obvious: they had lost the messaging war. By a whop-
ping two-to-one ratio, voters agreed that the bill "benefited
large corporations and rich Americans" over "middle-class
families." Republican supporters had promised that Americans
would come to love the tax bill. But that's not what happened,
and polls showed support for Trump's tax bill continuing to fall
over time.

The tax cut couldn't save Saccone. Lamb won. It was the first flipped congressional district of 2018.

The lesson was clear: we might not have been able to stop Trump's tax bill, but we had made it politically toxic and deprived Republicans of a core selling point in advance of the 2018 elections.

Obviously, one basic reason the tax bill was unpopular was that it was terrible policy. The promises that Republicans made—that it would lower most families' tax bills and spur massive growth—never really materialized. But bad, plutocratic bills pass Congress all the time without becoming political liabilities for the party that passed them. Long before the changes to the tax code took effect, Republicans had lost the messaging fight.

This is not a story of triumph by grassroots forces. Republicans won the policy fight. They reshaped the tax code, delivered huge payoffs to their donors, and set us on a course for colossal future budget problems. It would have been better for our country and for all of us had they failed to pass Trump's tax bill. But if we couldn't stop the bill, at least we'd made it hurt. We fought a losing battle, but we set ourselves up to win the war.

And November 2018 was coming.

THE P-WORD

Before November, we had to get through the primaries.

The Democratic primaries of 2018 were distinguished by an unusual feature: they were jam-packed with great candidates.

If you'd ever considered running for office as a Democrat, you knew this was your year. From the most competitive races to the serious long shots, people were rushing to throw their hats in the ring. Which was both great and, for the grassroots, also really stressful.

Indivisibles wanted progressive policies, and they wanted to flip the House. They didn't see much tension between these two goals. When it came to the primaries—or "the P-word," as one of our leaders called them—some decided to stay out. Others got involved, seeing it as an essential moment to choose their future leaders. They looked for the best candidates who could win their districts—which was not always the candidate that the Democratic Party had chosen for them. But everyone was clear on the ultimate goal: a decisive victory in November.

This was Indivisible's first primary season, and we had to build everything from scratch. Indivisible's political director María Urbina and her team worked with an advisory team of Indivisible groups to design a bottom-up, grassroots-driven strategy. The goal was to empower local Indivisible groups with national support as they pivoted from advocacy to elections. Our electoral program, Indivisible435, was dedicated to building local grassroots power everywhere, from the bluest to the reddest district. The name "Indivisible435" was intended to signal our aspiration to support Indivisible group electoral work in all 435 congressional districts. As part of the program, our team published a new guide to navigating primaries and rolled out an endorsement process, allowing local Indivisible groups to nominate candidates who were catching fire at the grassroots level for a national endorsement. A national Indivisible endorsement brought with it additional support and, eventually, funding.

At the national level, we made it clear that primaries were a healthy part of the democratic process. But we also respected that the decision to get involved in a race was up to local Indivisible groups: Indivisible national refused to parachute into districts to pick winners and losers. The local Indivisible leaders were on the ground, they knew their communities, and they knew the candidates best.

Indivisible Lesson #17: Primaries Are Good If We Make Them Good

Primaries have gotten a bad rap as divisive or unnecessary. They're not. They're an important part of how Indivisibles build power and win. Here's why:

Primaries are your chance to shape the direction of a political party. *Given how polarized the parties are, there's little room for real policy debate in a general election. The primary is where you're going to hear candidates share and contrast their ideas—and really talk about who they are—as you observe and decide which policies resonate with you. And this isn't just about an interesting debate of ideas. The positions candidates take while trying to distinguish themselves define their policy agendas if they get elected.*

Primaries build power. *Simply put, electeds care more about people who help them get and stay elected. Early support is simply more valuable than late support. And in cases where your elected isn't listening to you,* *supporting a primary challenger makes clear that there are consequences for ignoring the grassroots.*

Primaries make winning more likely, not less. *Every election cycle, some candidates who look good on paper fall apart. It's a lot better to find that out in the primary than it is in the general election. Competitive primaries work as a stress test, forcing candidates and campaigns to put together a functioning campaign, uncovering anything problematic in a candidate's background, and confirming that a candidate has what it takes. And because a competitive primary forces candidates to start earlier and work harder, the ultimate nominee tends to be stronger by the time they get to the general election. Primaries toughen up candidates to help them win.*

Can primaries be nasty and divisive? Absolutely! But that's why it's important to engage in them from a constructive, healthy place—not a reason to stay out.

This played out in places like Orange County California, where a ton of Democrats were vying to represent a handful of districts. Indivisible OC 48 was on the forefront of this struggle. Formed in the early days of 2017, they had been dedicated to holding their GOP representative Dana Rohrabacher accountable even as he tried to paint them as a violent mob. They continued to publicly press Rohrabacher on health care and on his highly suspect ties to Russia,[7] driving down his approval ratings in a district that had previously been reliably safe for

---

7. Rohrabacher was known in D.C. as "Putin's favorite congressman."

a Republican. Now they were ready to replace the thirty-year incumbent.

The question was: Who were they going to replace him with? There was no shortage of Democrats stepping forward to run. Indivisible OC 48 wanted someone who would beat Rohrabacher, but they also wanted a leader who would actually represent them and their values.

This was a tough question made more urgent by California's highly dysfunctional "jungle primary" system, in which all candidates, regardless of party, compete to be one of the top two vote-getters in order to secure a spot on the ballot in the general election. The jungle primary is practically designed to maximize the odds of weird, unrepresentative outcomes; in this case, there was a real risk that too many Democratic candidates on the ballot in the primary would split the vote, leading to no Democratic candidates on the ballot in the general at all.

The way forward was clear: get the grassroots behind the right candidate and fight like hell to turn them into the top vote-getter. Indivisible OC 48 dove into the task with gusto, hosting a series of candidate policy forums to engage with the candidates in their district, including front-runners Hans Keirstead and Harley Rouda. The Indivisible group even developed its own "Voter Support Score" to systematically gauge grassroots support. The score was based on not just money in the bank but the number of individual donors and amount raised from contributors in the district itself.[8]

---

8. The Democratic National Committee would use a related cutoff for the presidential debates in 2019, welcoming candidates who received at least 65,000 individual donations to the first debate stage.

Keirstead had the endorsement of the California Democratic Party, but Rouda was distinguishing himself for his progressive positions and eagerness to engage with the grassroots. He refused to take corporate PAC money, supported Medicare for All, and worked directly with Aaron McCall of Indivisible OC 48 to build out his positions on ending gun violence and on racial justice.

By the time that Indivisible OC 48 put it to a vote among their members, the choice was clear: Rouda was their candidate. After a supermajority of local Indivisibles voted to endorse him, Indivisible national echoed their support with a national endorsement, doing what we could to boost Rouda as the primary election approached. CNN described Indivisible's support as "a booming bat signal to Democrats" that "confirms the Ohio-born Rouda as the Democratic favorite in the district." Following the Indivisible endorsements, the Democratic Congressional Campaign Committee endorsed Rouda as well, breaking with the California Democratic Party.

As the vote counts rolled in on the night of the primary, the mood for Indivisible OC 48 activists was tense. It seemed quite possible not only that Rouda might lose but that Democrats might be shut out entirely. The election was so close that it took days to ratify the result. In the end, Rouda had beaten Keirstead by 125 votes and became the Democratic nominee to take the fight to Rohrabacher in November. The grassroots won.

And in primaries all over the country, the grassroots were showing up.

In New York City, twenty-year incumbent Joe Crowley was

a moderate congressman with deep ties to the financial industry representing a deep-blue district. A fixture of the Queens
political machine, he was the fourth-highest-ranking Democrat in the House, and the whispers in Washington were that
he was a potential future Speaker. But a twenty-eight-year-old
bartender and activist named Alexandria Ocasio-Cortez was
mounting a spirited challenge, drawing on Justice Democrats,
Democratic Socialists of America, and local Indivisible groups
to help power her grassroots campaign. Her message—people
power, anti–Wall Street, pro-immigrant—resonated with a
broad coalition, allowing her to pull off a stunning primary
upset.

Indivisible Lesson #18: Electability Is a Mirage

*"Electability" is one of the most misguided and pernicious
frames in politics today. It goes something like this: "Of
course I love Senator Smith and her policies, but I just
don't think she can win in the general election." A political hack might give a host of reasons for this assessment:
the candidate's a woman, and there's too much sexism in
America; she's a candidate of color, and there's too much
racism in America; she doesn't have big-money backers,
and there's too much money in politics in America; she's
too left-wing and her policies aren't going to resonate with
voters. The electability concern is rarely a direct attack on
the candidate; it's a "They're just too good for this world!"
argument.*

*These arguments aren't only misguided, they're dan-
gerous. They lead to a suspiciously similar set of can-*

didates every time: candidates who are male, pale, and stale: cookie-cutter politicians who've been in the system for years or independently wealthy guys who can bankroll their campaign out of their own pockets and networks, with policy platforms designed to be as inoffensive as possible. "Safe bets" that look good on paper.

This is how we end up, year after year, with elected officials who are scared to take risks and end up warming seats in Congress. With elected officials who don't represent the diversity and experiences of the people they serve. That's bad for democracy; it undermines the legitimacy and effectiveness of our government when Americans aren't reflected in the people who make decisions for our country. By focusing on a narrow and flawed definition of electability, we lose out on the prospect of real and representative leaders.

It also just doesn't work. Just because a primary candidate has been anointed by the local Democratic Party, is able to self-fund or draw big donors, or is a bland straight white guy with good hair doesn't mean he's a safe bet for the general election. Every year, many of these "safe bet" candidates end up falling apart in the general election. Because ultimately the most important quality of a candidate should be their authenticity and the ability to inspire others—and you.

In Massachusetts, Ayanna Pressley was tired of being told to wait her turn. The first Black woman to serve on the Boston

City Council, Pressley was a leader not because she looked like the traditional white male Massachusetts congressional delegation, but because she didn't. She was an activist and organizer as well as a politician, and her campaign was animated by a fierce sense of outrage with the Trump administration that resonated deeply with the district. Indivisible Somerville endorsed Ayanna Pressley for Congress over incumbent congressman Mike Capuano. Indivisible members had deep respect for Capuano's service as a reliably progressive member of Congress, but Pressley had made the case for a new kind of leadership. Pressley won.

In Florida, Andrew Gillum was an electrifying candidate with a progressive platform. As mayor of Tallahassee, he'd taken on the gun industry and fought against gun violence, from Parkland to Florida's racist Stand Your Ground law. He was the only Black candidate and the only non-millionaire in the Democratic primary, and he'd been largely written off by the political establishment. Indivisible Action Tampa Bay endorsed him, nominated him for a national endorsement, and put their members to work knocking on doors. And Indivisibles statewide, supported by Indivisible organizer Shay De-Golier, joined with a coalition of Black- and brown-led Florida organizations that came together to put him over the finish line for the nomination.

All over the country, candidates at the local, state, and federal level who supposedly had no chance were not just running but winning. Their victories fueled a surging grassroots energy that was transforming the political landscape.

WHOSE HOUSE? OUR HOUSE!

From the very beginning, it was clear that our best—or, rather, our only—chance of checking Donald Trump was to take the House in 2018. Control of the House would prevent dangerous new legislation from moving through a Republican Congress to the president's desk. It would secure the Affordable Care Act from further legislative attacks. It would give Democrats oversight authority and subpoena powers to investigate Trump's crimes and abuses. Control of the House meant that at least one body of our government could restrain Trump. It was a do-or-die moment for American democracy.

Indivisibles didn't need to have this basic political reality explained to them. In every contestable congressional district, they were knocking on doors, making calls, and sending texts to identify voters and get out the vote. The map of districts that were "in play" kept expanding, driven by great candidates, record fund-raising totals, and a grassroots army that was showing up in every corner of the country. Our own Indivisible field program made more than 11 million direct voter contacts in critical races, and we knew that this was just a small fraction of the doors Indivisibles were knocking on directly for campaigns nationwide.

Congressional Republicans were doing their best to charm voters. They were running misleading campaign ads claiming that they were determined to protect preexisting conditions and lower health care costs. Dana Rohrabacher, for instance, was blanketing the airwaves with ads about how his own child had a preexisting condition, so *of course* he was dedicated to protecting others' care. Rohrabacher, like many congressional Republicans pulling similar stunts, had voted to end protection for preexisting conditions months earlier. They knew their policies were unpopular, so they straight-up lied.

But congressional Republicans couldn't erase two years of heartless policy positions, bad press, and disregard for constituents with a last-minute public relations campaign. And Democrats were going on the offensive, building on the ground that two years of determined constituent organizing had laid for them.

In New York's Nineteenth District, where a massive coalition of local Indivisible groups had Representative John Faso in their sights, the Democrats unleashed a devastating ad. It showed video of Republican John Faso outside a 2017 town hall, hugging a woman with a brain tumor and promising to protect her coverage—and then flashing forward to a headline of Faso voting to repeal the Affordable Care Act.[9]

In Minnesota's Third District, Indivisible MN03 spent more than a year hammering the absent Republican Erik Paulsen for his health care vote and demanding a town hall. Now Democrat Dean Phillips was picking up on the theme with an ad featuring an actor dressed as Bigfoot, speaking directly to the camera:

I thought I was good at hiding. Then Erik Paulsen comes along.
I mean, how can you have tens of thousands of people looking

---

9. In a depressingly typical move, the National Republican Congressional Committee countered by running a series of wildly racist ads against the Democratic candidate Antonio Delgado, attacking him for a rap album he'd recorded while in college.

for you all the time and not one of them find you? I started to
wonder—does Erik Paulsen really exist? Where's the proof?
Some blurry photo taken from miles away?

The ad concluded with Bigfoot finding Erik Paulsen at a
pharmaceutical company, apparently taking money in exchange for undermining health care. Democrats were acting
out the script that Indivisibles had written for them over the
past two years.[10] And Republicans were reaping the collective
"reward" of two years of hiding and lying.

As November approached, the final days were a blur for us.
Our national team scattered to work on the ground with Indivisibles in swing states and districts across the country; the two
of us were dispatched to Florida, Texas, Arizona, New York,
and California to rally and canvass with Indivisible groups on
the ground. Everywhere we went, there was a sense of excitement mixed with terror. There was determination. There was
the feeling of being part of something much, much bigger than
ourselves.

In Florida, Indivisibles were knocking on doors for Andrew Gillum, Senator Bill Nelson, and Amendment 4, a
game-changing referendum to re-enfranchise around 1.5 million formerly incarcerated Floridians. In California and New
York, competitive congressional districts like Harley Rouda's
were being flooded with volunteer groups. In Arizona, Indivisibles were fighting to stop a referendum threatening pub-

---

10. It was also a clever homage to fellow Minnesotan Paul Wellstone's iconic
    1990 "Finding Rudy" ad.

lic schools and, with less excitement but an equal amount of commitment, for conservative Democratic Senate candidate Kyrsten Sinema.

Indivisible Lesson #19: Vote Your Heart in the Primary; Vote Your Head in the General Election

Emotions in primaries can run high. People get attached to their candidate, and reasonable folks can disagree. There are real, important differences between different wings of the Democratic Party, and we have to have the space to have those debates. But at the end of the day, we're all here for a reason: we're taking our country back from the antidemocratic forces who are actively rigging the system to work against us. Yes, that means fighting for the best possible outcome in a primary. But it also means winning general elections. That requires supporting the eventual nominee, even if that person isn't our first choice.

This is also just practical. One key way that you make primaries healthy is by committing ahead of time to this basic rule: If everybody agrees that at the end of the day we're rallying around the winner, then that means we can have an honest debate over who we like more in the primary. We can push the candidates, knowing that we're pushing them from our own commitment to shared values and power building.

This electoral strategy is based in both progressivism and political realism. Before Indivisible national issues an endorsement in a primary race, we require that the

> *candidate commit to rallying around whoever wins the primary. If your favorite candidate doesn't win in the primary, it can feel pretty painful. But you cannot take your ball and go home. We know that moral-virtue signaling won't defeat the fascists. We fight like hell in the primary for our ideals. And then we fight like hell to win in the general.*

On November 6 about half our team gathered at Indivisible HQ in Washington, D.C., to wait for the results. The rest were scattered across the country, embedded with Indivisible groups as they finished their final door-knocking shifts.[11] The mood was, frankly, weird. After 2016, no one would trust an election forecast ever again. And this wasn't just another election. This was a pivot point. Either things would start to turn around or they wouldn't. And if they didn't . . . what would we do?

One of the odder things about running a political organization is that you prepare for every election scenario ahead of time. In our case, we had reviewed and cleared the emails we'd send, the talking points for our team, and the press releases in the event of a win, a loss, or total chaos. No one felt ready for the night of the election, but at least technically we were prepared.

Then the results started rolling in—unevenly at first and

---

11. The month before, we had moved into a real office, with air-conditioning, a functioning roof, enough seats for everyone, and no ants. It was a pretty big deal.

then increasingly strongly.[12] House races started getting called. And it became clear: this was, in fact, the historic blue wave that we had dreamed of.

In Arizona, Indivisibles celebrated the defeat of Martha McSally, meaning Jeff Flake—one of the deciding votes for Supreme Court Justice Brett Kavanaugh, Trump's tax bill, and more—would be replaced by Democrat Kyrsten Sinema. In Virginia, the women who'd been up in Dave Brat's grill had finally replaced him with one of their own, Abigail Spanberger. In New Jersey, Tom MacArthur, an author of Trumpcare, went down in defeat to Andy Kim, the founder of an anti-Trump resistance group. In Colorado, Mike Coffman, who'd sneaked away from his constituents to avoid answering questions back in January 2017, was relieved of his duties. Erik Paulsen, of Bigfoot fame, was out of a job. John Faso, who'd resorted to a wildly racist series of attacks on his opponent, Antonio Delgado, lost. In Illinois, registered nurse and health care expert Lauren Underwood defeated Trumpcare supporter Randy Hultgren. Harley Rouda took out Dana Rohrabacher. And across the country, Democrats had claimed the seats of now-retired antagonists like Darrell Issa, Dave Trott, Dave Reichert, and Rodney Frelinghuysen.

There were heartbreaking, infuriating losses. In Georgia and Florida, Stacey Abrams and Andrew Gillum—Black candidates running on inspiring progressive platforms—were

---

12. For a brief gut-wrenching period that night, famed political statistician Nate Silver's FiveThirtyEight website predicted the House would stay in Republican control. While keeping externally calm in front of the Indivisible team, we prepped the "We lost" emails to go out to the movement. Thankfully we never had to send those.

defeated, in no small measure due to voter suppression and restrictive voter laws. In Texas, Beto O'Rourke had made Ted Cruz sweat but came up short in the end. The blue wave wasn't enough everywhere—not in every state or district. The Republican seawalls of gerrymandering and voter suppression had been built up over decades. It would take more than one election to bring them down.

But the blue wave *was* crashing down throughout the country. It was the largest midterm House vote margin for Democrats in American history, and the largest number of flipped Democratic districts since Watergate. Democrats gained forty new House seats, more than three hundred legislative seats, seven governorships, and six new trifecta states where they controlled the governorship and the state legislature. What had seemed politically impossible two years earlier had become political reality.

The incoming House class would have the most women and most people of color ever elected to Congress. It would have the most immigrants elected in modern history. It would have the youngest woman ever elected, the first Native American women ever elected, the first Muslim women ever elected.

It was more than a check on Trump's power. It was a rebuke to his brutal, cynical, culture war politics. It was a reaffirmation of the America we believed in.

IT'S A MARATHON, NOT A SPRINT

It turns out that the blue wave came crashing down even in Georgia's Sixth Congressional District. The women of the district's local Indivisible groups had followed through on their plan after Ossoff's defeat. When Karen Handel, the Republican victor of the special election, took office, the local Indivisible groups were there to hold her accountable every step of the way.

There was a lot to hold her accountable for, because Handel was a very bad member of Congress. She voted for a Trump scam to cut taxes for corporations and millionaires. She voted to deregulate the banks. She voted with Trump fully 98 percent of the time.

At every twist and turn of the legislative calendar, Indivisible groups were there, highlighting how out of step Handel was with the district. They held die-ins to protect health care. They showed up with giant checks addressed to the top 1 percent to protest the Trump tax bill. They made sure to let Handel know, and let the local media know, that Handel was not representing Georgia's Sixth District.

In 2018, Handel faced a very different opponent. Lucy Mc-Bath had become an activist after her seventeen-year-old son, Jordan Davis, was murdered by a white man in an act of racist gun violence. She had fearlessly fought for gun violence prevention in the following years. This year she was taking her fight to Congress. McBath ran a brilliant campaign and, with an unparalleled coalition of grassroots support spanning the district, defeated Karen Handel in November. Newt Gingrich's former congressional district would now be represented by a Black Democratic woman who would fight to end gun violence. Indivisibles had seen the full arc: from hopelessly red to purple to electing a champion.

And that was that, right? No, it wasn't. Because as we mentioned before, the next election campaign begins the day after Election Day. Because there is a virtuous cycle between elections and advocacy. Because elections are important milestones—but they're not the finish line.

Indivisible isn't about winning a game or scoring political points. Indivisible is about building power—not to hold it, but to do good with it. That means we don't pack up and go home after we win or we lose; we keep building and wielding that power. This is how we demand change and build the inclusive democracy we want to see.

So on January 3, 2019, Indivisible held its largest national day of action in our two-year history to that point. More Indivisible groups in more states showed up at more congressional district offices on a single day than ever before. We called these events the "Whose House? Our House!" events. The focus was in support of H.R. 1, the pro-democracy "For the People Act" legislation introduced by House Democrats as their top legislative priority in the 116th Congress. The national day of action was a celebration of the incoming House, but it was also a shot across the bow to all members of Congress. Republican and Democrat alike. It was a simple message: *We're still here, we're not going anywhere, and we expect you to represent us.*

That's the message Indivisibles carry with them in all their organizing and mobilizing. We are active participants in a generational struggle for the soul of American democracy. The forces arrayed against us are powerful, and they've enjoyed a long winning streak. But that streak is coming to an end. We are here, and we demand our representatives represent us. Together, we will replace Trump, defeat Trumpism, and build a truly inclusive democracy in America.

The next chapter describes what that could look like.

A Blueprint for Democracy

6

A Day One Democracy Agenda

Sometimes, the only realists are the dreamers.
—SENATOR PAUL WELLSTONE

I have gone from the fetal position to a determined advocate
for democracy, the rule of law, and the protection of values
and principles upon which this country was founded.
—LAUREN LISI, *Indivisible Fighting 9 (Michigan)*

In 1977, Jimmy Carter entered the White House on the heels of one of the most disastrous periods in American political history. President Richard Nixon had resigned in disgrace after a series of investigations into his abuse of power to undermine his rivals. Vice President Agnew had been forced to resign to avoid federal prison time after evidence surfaced that he had taken bribes and kickbacks while in office. Both men responded to threats by lying, attacking the press, and pursuing a racist political strategy to rally white Americans and conservative Republicans to protect the president. The nation had been rocked by undeniable evidence that the administration had been routinely lying to them. Trust in government was at an all-time low.

The Democratic Party of 1977 had a historic veto-proof majority in the House of Representatives and a big majority in the Senate, too, courtesy of a 1974 blue wave midterm election. The year of Carter's election was the two hundredth anniversary of the Declaration of Independence, and the spirit of reform was in the air. In his inaugural address, the new president acknowledged the challenges facing the bullied, battered, and divided nation, but he did not linger there. Instead he looked optimistically to the future:

> *I believe America can be better. We can be even stronger than before.*
>
> *Let our recent mistakes bring a resurgent commitment to the basic principles of our Nation, for we know that if we despise our own government, we have no future. We recall in special times when we have stood briefly, but magnificently, united. In those times no prize was beyond our grasp.*

A few weeks later, Carter unveiled his plan to reach for a very big prize: a set of bold pro-democracy policies that the *New York Times* called "one of the broadest political reform packages ever submitted by a modern President." The package proposed universal same-day voter registration, public financing of elections, election security provisions, even a constitutional amendment to eliminate the Electoral College. Its aim was simple: to restore the public trust, reform American democracy, and make it more responsive to and reflective of the will of the people.[1]

The Heritage Foundation—a newly formed pro-business, conservative-Christian think tank—went on the attack. The Heritage Foundation declared it a mistake to "take for granted that it is desirable to increase the number of people who vote."[2] In a policy brief released shortly after Carter's announcement, the Heritage Foundation picked apart the democracy proposal piece by piece, vigorously opposing every provision. The chair of the Republican National Committee denounced the package as a Democratic "power grab."

The die was cast. Republican senators rallied against the public-financing portion of the proposal, filibustered it in the Senate, and killed it. None of the other pieces of the democracy reform package got a vote. Democracy reform in the post-Nixon era was dead.

Fast-forward four decades to early 2019. President Trump was embroiled in an investigation into corruption throughout his administration and campaign. He was attacking the press and going on racist tirades, seeking to rally white Americans and conservative Republicans to his defense. His bigotry, corruption, and nonstop aura of chaos had just been repudiated in

---

1. If we were academics, we might say something like *There's actually no such thing as the single, unified "will of the people," because the people are diverse.* But we're not academics, so we're going to stick with "will of the people," knowing full well that the people in a democracy are all special snowflakes.

2. Yes, this is a real quote from the leading Republican think tank. When they tell you who they are, believe them.

a historic blue wave midterm election ushering Democrats into power in the House. A spirit of reform was in the air.

The new Democratic House majority came out swinging with the For the People Act, denoted as "H.R. 1" to signify that it was the first bill of the new Congress and thus their top priority. The package included bold proposals to make American democracy more responsive and reflective of the will of the people: automatic voter registration, public financing of elections, anti-gerrymandering reforms, election security provisions. The media called it "a sweeping anti-corruption proposal," "a broad political overhaul," and "the Biggest Voting-Rights Bill to Appear in Congress Since the Civil Rights Movement."

You can probably guess what happened next. The Heritage Foundation went on the attack with a policy brief arguing that the proposed legislation was "unnecessary, unwise, and unconstitutional," and that maintaining the status quo was the only option "for protecting our liberty and freedom." Mitch McConnell, the Republican Senate majority leader, wrote an op-ed picking apart the proposal piece by piece and promising to oppose the bill at all costs. He labeled it a Democratic "power grab."

The die was cast. The first hearing on the package devolved into a partisan fight, with the *New York Times* describing Republican committee members as "vociferous in their condemnation and occasionally inflammatory in their language." McConnell would block the bill from even getting a vote in the Senate. Democracy reform was dead without Trump ever even touching the bill.

History may not repeat itself, but it often rhymes.

So what can we learn from this? Let's say Indivisibles across the country do everything described in the previous three chapters. Let's imagine Democrats are wildly successful in 2020, winning the House, the Senate, and the presidency. In this best-of-all-worlds scenario, we know what will happen next. On January 3, 2021, the Democratic Speaker of the House will gavel in the 117th Congress. On January 20, the new president will give a soaring inaugural address on the promise of America's future and her plans for reform.

Congressional Democrats will propose something like the For the People Act: pro-democracy reforms to make the government more responsive to the people's will. This legislation will include small-dollar donor matches to balance out big money, and big reforms to tackle voting rights, ethics, and election security. They'll also propose social and economic policies to take on the big issues of the day: the existential threat of climate change; the tragedy of our deficient health care system; the cruelty of our immigration system; the heartlessness of our criminal justice system; the scourge of gun violence; the historical embarrassment of growing inequality and stagnating economic opportunity; the viselike grip of concentrated wealth and political power.

We've got a lot to do.

All of these bills will be introduced with great fanfare and promise. And then Republican politicians and Fox News will kick into gear. They'll brand these policies as a mix of socialism and power grabs. Senate Minority Leader Mitch McConnell—or whichever Koch-funded apparatchik succeeds him—will use the filibuster to kill the democracy agenda in its entirety and to block any other significant progressive change. Democrats will struggle to pass marginal economic policies through the budget process (which is not subject to the filibuster), but any bold reforms will be dead on arrival. A frustrated American public will punish do-nothing Democrats with a rout in the 2022 midterms. The cycle of dysfunction and gridlock will ratchet up another notch, and our democracy will continue its slow collapse.

The backlash to the short and dramatic Trump era may well produce a unified Democratic federal government in 2021. But the national fervor behind this backlash will fade—and the reactionaries aren't going anywhere. Their donors are still their donors. Their base is still their base. The anti-democratic fortress they have built over the past several decades will stand regardless of the outcome of the 2020 elections. The same institutions that sank a post-Nixon pro-democracy platform will sink a post-Trump pro-democracy platform.

The 2020 blue wave will crash on the shores of our jagged and decrepit democratic institutions—a more terrifyingly effective wall than Trump could ever hope to build.

If we fail to reform our system in 2021, we may not have another chance. The demographic bias of the Senate toward conservative and white voters is accelerating. If we fail to change course, the Senate will slip out of our hands for good, permanently frustrating efforts to reform our democratic system or drive progressive change.

At that point, we're looking at a future of either conservative control or divided government. Reactionaries will steadily consolidate their political advantages, using their power to gerrymander districts, further destroy unions, suppress voters, and pack the courts. Our societal problems—climate change, inequality, health care, and more—will get catastrophically worse, while government does nothing.

Does that sound like the future you want? Probably not. So how can we avoid it?

We can't keep playing the same game and expect different results. We have to change the rules to put power in the hands of the people. And we have to do it on day one.

A DAY ONE DEMOCRACY AGENDA

The very legitimacy of our democracy comes from the people, and every piece of the plan in this chapter is designed with that basic political fact in mind. This is a blueprint for democratizing America—for reforming our aging, outmoded institutions so that they actually reflect the will of the people. *All* the people.

Indivisible isn't a think tank, and this isn't a policy white paper. But we do have a clear vision of the reforms needed.[3] We didn't cook up these ideas ourselves. We relied on leading

---

3. Our focus is on federal-level reforms, but versions of many of these policies could be—and in some cases have already been—adopted at the state and local levels. Other policies we miss entirely because of this federal focus. A good example is the elimination of the Electoral College. While that can't be done federally without a constitutional amendment, it can be done through state-level action. This is just one example; many other pro-democracy reforms are achievable at the state and local levels. By all means, get involved in your local Indivisible group to fight for them too.

political scientists, advocates, and experts in American democracy and institutional reform. And we talked to local Indivisible group leaders across the country about the failure of these institutions, and the kinds of change we need.

We asked a simple question: What can we do to change the rules to make democracy more inclusive, representative, and functional?

We've got some ground rules about what's included. First, everything you read below can be enacted *via legislation*. That means Congress could pass every part of it with simple majorities. And the entirety of this blueprint could be on the president's desk on the first day of her administration in 2021.

We've reluctantly (but purposefully) excluded any reform that would require a constitutional amendment. Constitutional amendments have to be approved by three-quarters of state legislatures. To even get an amendment proposed, you need two-thirds of the House and Senate on board.[4] And given the current political climate, we are not remotely close to that being an option.

This is a real constraint. Some of the fundamental flaws of a presidential system with polarized parties that we outlined in Chapter 1 cannot be fixed through mere legislation. We can't institute a parliamentary system. We can't abolish the Senate. We can't reverse the Supreme Court's decisions in *Citizens United v. Federal Election Commission* and *Buckley v. Valeo* to

---

4. You can also propose constitutional amendments if you get two-thirds of states to call for a constitutional convention. That's never been done in the history of the republic. And even if that was done, you'd still need three-quarters of the states to adopt any proposed amendments.

directly force money out of politics. All of these reforms would require constitutional amendments. But our democratic house is on fire *now*. We have to put out the fire, using the tools we've got, before we can talk about major renovations.

With that constraint in mind, we're still going to go big in this blueprint.

Every proposal we cover below is realistic in the sense that it *could* be passed into law in 2021. Not every proposal we cover is realistic in the sense that it's got a lot of political support right this minute. In fact, some of these ideas are barely even on the national political radar. We're offering them up not because we believe that Congress is ready to act on these reforms but because we believe we should be thinking about answers that are actually as big as our problems.

In short, if we have the presidency, the House, and the Senate in 2021, the only thing that stops anything below from becoming law is political will. And that's something we can build. That's why this is a day one democracy agenda.

The policies won't be implemented unless people demand them, so we aim to equip you with what you need to make those demands effectively. For each of the reforms we discuss, we lay out three pieces of information. First, we describe the problem: why an institution is faltering and the impact of that failure on American society. Second, we review the solutions: reforms demonstrated in American history, through existing local and state reforms, or in other industrialized democracies. Third, we discuss what the naysayers say—and why they're wrong.

For those of you in a rush, here's the CliffsNotes version:

1. *Break the gridlock.* The Senate has a procedural loophole—the filibuster—that has morphed into a massive problem for democracy in recent years. Functionally speaking, it gives Senate Republicans veto power over a new president's agenda, even if they've lost the Senate majority. But there's good news: the filibuster is not anywhere in the Constitution, and it can be eliminated with a simple majority vote. Nothing else in this blueprint will become law as long as the filibuster exists, so Senate reformers must act to eliminate it.

2. *Democratize the Senate.* The Senate is an existential threat to progress, and we only have a limited window of opportunity to change it. The Constitution requires that the Senate stay stacked against progress; it's built that way. But nothing prevents Congress from admitting new states to make it more democratic and representative. Congress should admit D.C. as a state and, if their residents so choose, other U.S. territories like Puerto Rico as well. These reforms won't make the Senate fully democratic, but they will provide representation to more people and help undo *some* of the rigging built into the system.

3. *Democratize the House.* Each member of the U.S. House of Representatives represents a district that's vastly larger than the Founders could possibly have imagined. Large House districts mean harder-to-represent constituencies. We should expand the House to make it the "People's

House" again (and make the Electoral College fairer in the process). And at the same time we should take on the broken two-party system by giving people more choices at the voting booth. Proportional representation with ranked-choice voting would give voters those choices and make our politics less dysfunctional.

4. *Democratize the courts.* Reactionaries have succeeded in their multi-decade campaign to block Democratic-appointed judges and pack the Supreme Court with conservative ideologues. This partisan, right-wing court is a threat to twentieth-century social and economic advances and a barrier to twenty-first-century reforms. That's why we have to expand and modernize the Supreme Court and create a less partisan process for selecting and appointing judges.

5. *Democratize voting.* We have to smash voter suppression and dramatically expand access to the vote. More than 20 million American immigrants live, work, and pay taxes in America without representation. Eight million sixteen- and seventeen-year-olds are old enough to get shot at by mass murderers in schools and young enough to die of climate change but not old enough to vote for representatives who can address these issues. Six million Americans with a felony conviction are denied the right to vote. Extending the franchise to these populations at the federal level would be the largest expansion of voting rights in a century.

6. *Democratize the Media.* A healthy democracy requires an informed citizenry, which requires a healthy media. But we're facing a media crisis in this country. The economic model for local journalism has collapsed; independent local news is dying or being gobbled up by conservative ideologues. A propaganda operation in the form of Fox News and Sinclair Broadcast Group poisons the national debate. All the while, Facebook, Google, and other un-regulated social media companies aid in the production and distribution of misinformation. We need to break up media conglomerates and make a historic investment in informing the American people.

While none of these reforms would require more than a simple act of Congress, that doesn't mean they're light lifts. Each requires upending the status quo, and most or all will be opposed by entrenched politicians of both parties. But if we're going to build a truly representative democracy in America, this is how we start.

THE TRICKY PART: DEMOCRATIC WITH A LOWERCASE *D*

Before we get into the specifics of the democracy blueprint, we have to make things a little more complicated. Because if it were as simple as jamming these reforms through in one fell swoop, it'd just be too easy.[5]

---

5. Just kidding! It would still be incredibly hard to build the political will nec-essary to implement this stuff. Sorry. But we still have to try.

The tricky part about the current moment is that we're already in a fairly advanced stage of democratic breakdown. The modern Republican Party has abandoned its commitment to democracy and to democratic norms. And in a two-party system, that makes a democracy reform agenda—which ought to be bipartisan—much, much harder.

In *How Democracies Die*, a pair of Harvard political scientists give a historical, international lesson on how democracies, well, die. Reviewing democratic breakdowns in Latin America and elsewhere, the authors identify pillars of functioning democracies. The one we want to focus on is the idea of "forbearance"—or what non–political scientists might call "restraint."[6] This is the idea that political parties don't run around changing the rules when they get into power. They respect the rule of law and political norms, even when they don't have to.[7] They've got a good reason to do so: one day in the future, they'll be out of power, and they want the other party to do the same. Forbearance is basically the golden rule—do unto others—but for political parties.

It's pretty clear that Republican elites today have abandoned forbearance in favor of court packing, voter suppression, and

---

6. The other one of the two pillars they discuss is "mutual toleration," which basically means that political factions don't treat each other's social, economic, and foreign policy platforms as wholly illegitimate: you can disagree with your opponents without thinking they're out to destroy democracy. We're in a sticky situation with this one, too, because the Koch-controlled Republican Party really is out to subvert democracy.

7. They don't, you know, unilaterally rob a president of a Supreme Court justice appointment (*cough* Gorsuch *cough*).

wanton power grabs.[8] But responding to this is a real challenge for those of us trying to save democracy, because two wrongs don't make a right. Just because the Republicans are blowing up the rules to entrench their own power doesn't mean Democrats can blow up some other rules to entrench their power. If we engage in a tit-for-tat campaign against conservative forces, the cycle of norm breaking will continue to escalate. The forbearance pillar will collapse.

That, political scientists will tell you, is when the whole system breaks down, sending democracy into its death throes.

We face a real conundrum. We desperately need nonpartisan pro-democracy reforms to make our government responsive to the people's will. But when one party has abandoned its commitment to democracy, any reform effort inherently looks partisan.

So how do we advance democratic reforms that *should* be nonpartisan in an era when only one party is into that? It's not enough for us to push through this democracy blueprint. We have to advocate for it carefully and judiciously, in a way that is as nonpartisan and small-*d* democratic as possible.

This is why building independent, progressive political power for this effort is crucial. This can't be about putting power in the hands of Democrats. This has to be about putting power in the hands of the people. Indivisible is not an arm of the Democratic Party, and the reforms we're calling for here would pose threats to both the Democratic and Republican establishment. We aim to democratize, not Democratize.

---

8. See Chapter 1. It's bad and scary.

BREAK THE GRIDLOCK

The Problem

Yes, the word "filibuster" is ridiculous. It's a silly name—and it's also a *very* big problem. In fact, it's not an exaggeration to say that none of the reforms in the rest of this blueprint will be possible if we don't first get rid of the filibuster.

But what is it? The filibuster is a Senate procedural loophole that allows any senator to keep debate open on a bill until the Senate votes to end debate. Under the current rules, ending debate requires 60 votes instead of a simple majority. If you don't have 60 votes, you can't move to voting. That means if your party is in the Senate minority, you don't need 51 votes to vote a bill down; you need just 41 to prevent it from ever getting a vote.

The practical result—in an era when both sides are playing legislative hardball—is that in order to pass just about anything, you need to get 60 votes on your side first.

The filibuster has acquired an odd status as an iconic feature of American democracy. You might remember it fondly from *Mr. Smith Goes to Washington*, a 1930s Jimmy Stewart film that showed a heroic young senator taking a dramatic stand against a corrupt establishment through a marathon speech. It's a nice old movie—and a wildly inaccurate representation of both how the filibuster works in practice and its actual role in American democracy.

In practice, there aren't really "talking filibusters" full of dramatic speeches anymore. In a talking filibuster, someone actually holds the floor and talks while the rest of the Senate waits patiently for them to shut up so that a vote can be taken. The thing is, the Senate is full of old people and they don't like pulling all-nighters, so, in practice, the mere threat of a filibuster is usually enough to kill legislation.

The history of the filibuster is also much murkier than you might imagine. It's often represented as part of the Founders' vision for the Senate's role as a slower and more deliberative body. This is totally ahistorical: the filibuster is actually a fluke. The Senate was originally intended to be a majoritarian institution; a simple majority vote was supposed to allow business to move forward. The filibuster loophole was unintentionally created when Aaron Burr succeeded in eliminating the Senate rule that allowed debate to be cut off with a simple majority vote in the early 1800s.[9] This created an unintended consequence: technically, a senator could now speak indefinitely if he wanted to prevent Senate business from moving forward. But Burr and the other senators had no idea that they had created this loophole, and they would all be long gone before it was ever exploited.

It would be more than thirty years after the filibuster first came into existence that someone actually used the loophole to "filibuster" legislation. Even then, filibusters were rare. Filibuster use didn't really pick up until after the Civil War, when segregationists discovered that they could use it to slam Senate business to a halt whenever anyone tried to move civil rights

---

9. As if you needed more reasons to hate Aaron Burr.

legislation. In 1890, Representative Henry Cabot Lodge proposed a bill to establish federal oversight to protect the voting rights of newly enfranchised Black Americans. It passed the House, but Southern senators filibustered it. And they kept filibustering all types of civil and voting rights bills for decades. That's right, decades. The basic idea behind the 1890 bill—federal protection against anti-Black, antidemocratic Southern voter suppression—wasn't enacted until seventy-five years later, when President Lyndon Johnson signed the Voting Rights Act into law in 1965.

Of course, no one ever made a movie featuring Jimmy Stewart dramatically holding the floor to block anti-lynching legislation. But that would have been a more historically accurate representation of the filibuster.

As the parties became more polarized, the filibuster morphed from a surgical tool to kill civil rights (and some other legislation) to a sledgehammer used to kill everything. The numbers tell the story of how things have changed: during Lyndon Johnson's legislative heyday, from 1965 to 1967, there were seven motions to end a filibuster. During the height of Obama's legislative success, from 2009 to 2011, there were 137.

But there's a big caveat: it's not standard operating procedure for *everything*. The filibuster doesn't apply to giant tax cuts for corporations and rich people; changes to the rules in the 1970s allowed for budgets to move without the filibuster. That's how George W. Bush passed the most regressive and largest tax cuts in history. And that's how Trump did it too. The filibuster also doesn't apply to confirming Supreme Court

justices anymore, either: Senate Majority Leader Mitch Mc-
Connell amended it to give Trump two new justices.

The things the filibuster now blocks are non-budget legislative proposals—i.e., all the democracy reforms discussed
in this chapter, plus the Green New Deal, labor reforms, gun
violence prevention, immigration reform, abortion rights, and
just about any of the big twenty-first-century social and economic policies the rest of the modern industrialized world implemented long ago.

So if you've ever wondered, *Why is super-popular legislation never getting voted on in Congress?*—here's an answer: we
have a Senate in which 11 percent of the country's population, spread across twenty-one disproportionately rural and
conservative states, can prevent a vote from ever taking place.
And not only *can* they—it's become standard operating procedure.

Perhaps you're wondering whether other countries have a
similar legislative brake. We're glad you asked! Through painstaking research, we've compiled an exhaustive list of modern
democracies that give veto power over popular legislation to 11
percent of the population:

- The United States of America
- (End of list)

Of course no other modern democracy allows for such bla-
tant tyranny of the minority. Imagine a system in which ten
friends are deciding where to go to dinner. Nine agree on Olive
Garden, but one says he's not hungry, so the group decides to

starve themselves instead. This is the U.S. Senate in the twenty-first century. Nobody's getting any breadsticks.

The Solution

Reforming the filibuster is one of the least radical positions discussed in this chapter. Don't take it from us; take it from Barack Obama. Reflecting on his own presidency in 2018, Obama said, "Adding the filibuster . . . has made it almost impossible for us to effectively govern at a time when you have at least one party that is not willing to compromise on issues." Obama is far from alone. A host of liberals, centrists, and even one or two conservatives have noted that much of our political dysfunction is fostered by the filibuster.

The good news is that technically speaking, axing the filibuster couldn't be easier. Since the filibuster isn't anywhere in the Constitution, there's nothing to prevent the Senate from going into work tomorrow and killing it with a simple majority vote.

Most likely here's the way this will actually go down: The 2021 version of the For the People Act—or some other package of democracy reforms—will first pass the House. Then that legislation will be sent to the new Democratic Senate. After a round of hearings and amendments, the new Democratic Senate majority leader will call it to be brought to the floor for a vote. Mitch McConnell or his replacement Senate minority leader will then promise to filibuster this "Democratic power grab." At that point the Democratic Senate will face a choice. They can allow McConnell and his allies to kill democracy reform, or they can hold a simple majority vote to eliminate the filibuster and then pass the reforms. This choice should be a no-brainer.

Short of entirely eliminating the filibuster, there are other potential half measures to reform (lowering the filibuster threshold to fifty-five, for instance). But they don't solve the basic problem: the Senate minority, representing a tiny fraction of the U.S. population, is strangling progress. So the real solution to the filibuster is pretty darn straightforward: ax the filibuster, enact your pro-democracy reforms, have a drink, and keep moving.

What the Naysayers Say

There are well-meaning naysayers when it comes to axing the filibuster, and it's worth taking their concerns seriously. Progressive filibuster defenders have a real concern: What happens when the other side gets a Senate majority? If we ax the filibuster in 2021, won't future McConnells use their slim majorities to enact their regressive agenda of tax cuts, Federalist Society judges, gutting abortion rights, and radical cuts to the social safety net?

There are two reasons we don't find this concern persuasive.

First, practically speaking, we've already lost that fight. For the things Senate Republicans care about the most—judges and tax cuts—the filibuster is *already gone*. The current McConnell got rid of the filibuster when it stood between him and a Republican-controlled Supreme Court. We've seen again and again that McConnell and Senate Republicans do not let procedural barriers stop them from achieving their goals. If they need to fully eliminate the filibuster at some point in the future, they'll do it. Nothing about their behavior over the past few years suggests otherwise.[10]

But second, and more important, there's an imbalance here between conservatives and progressives. Gridlock is just better for conservatives. It reinforces their fundamental message that government doesn't work and won't help you. Progressives, on the other hand, are inherently not content with the status quo. We need government to do better, to take on the existential crises we're facing. We win when government delivers real change. That means, over time, the ability to pass major legislation is much more important to us than it is to conservatives.

That doesn't mean we should have just blind faith that everything will work out. To minimize the potential harm a future reactionary government might do, the first legislation in a post-filibuster world ought to be the type of pro-democracy reforms discussed in the rest of this chapter. By making our democracy more representative and functional, we preemptively protect against future reactionary power grabs. The cure for government dysfunction is more democracy, not less.

---

10. Some have argued that the filibuster protected the Affordable Care Act from repeal during the first two years of the Trump presidency. That is flat-out wrong. The reason Republicans never repealed the legislation was not because the filibuster protected it; it was because they couldn't even scrape together 50 votes to do it. The Affordable Care Act's own popularity saved the Affordable Care Act.

DEMOCRATIZE THE SENATE

The Problem

The Senate in its current form is an existential threat to democracy. It's profoundly unrepresentative and dangerously ill-adapted to the current era. It's where progressive policy goes to die.

We know we just went from zero to sixty in one short paragraph, so let's back up a bit. The Senate has two big problems: a math problem and a racism problem.

The first big problem with the Senate comes down to basic math: the two-senators-per-state rule. It may surprise you to hear how controversial this was when the Constitution was written. Many of our leading Founding Fathers hated the idea of an equal number of senators per state. Alexander Hamilton wrote grumpily about Rhode Island's and Delaware's demands for equal representation: "Every idea of proportion and every rule of fair representation conspire to condemn a principle, which gives to Rhode Island an equal weight in the scale of power with Massachusetts, or Connecticut, or New York; and to Delaware an equal voice in the national deliberations with Pennsylvania, or Virginia, or North Carolina."[11] James Madison and George Washington also hated the plan, but they agreed to it because small-population states refused to join the union without it. "They forced themselves to pay what they

---

11. High school history teachers know this grumpy note as The Federalist No. 22.

knew was a corrupt and immoral price in order to get a barely acceptable deal . . . ," Hendrik Hertzberg wrote in the *New Yorker*. But, hey, we got a Constitution out of the deal.

It's hard to believe the Founders would have accepted the same deal today. At the time of Hamilton's frustration, Virginia, the largest state, had a population about twelve times the size of Delaware, the smallest state. Today, California is nearly seventy times the size of Wyoming. *Seventy times*. California's population today is larger than the combined population of the twenty-one smallest states. So Californians get two senators, while the smaller number of residents of those other states get *forty-two* senators.

This baked-in inequality—surprise!—benefits conservatives. Cook Political Report calculates that there are more Republican-leaning states than Democratic-leaning states. Does this mean it's impossible for Democrats to get a majority in the Senate? No. "Democratic" states go for Republican senators and "Republican" states go for Democratic senators all the time. But it does mean the Senate is structurally imbalanced in ways that favor one party over the other.

If you think the Senate is crazily antidemocratic (and anti-Democratic) now, hold on to your hat. Demographically, progressives are increasingly clumping in a smaller number of states. In 2040, half the population will live in just eight states. That means half the population will have sixteen senators, and the other half will have eighty-four senators. As Jamelle Bouie writes in the *New York Times*, "Republicans are on the verge of a durable structural advantage" that will give near-permanent control of the Senate to a Republican coali-

tion of "rural whites, exurban whites and anti-tax suburban-
ites."

The second big problem with the Senate is that even within
this basic framework of being wildly unrepresentative, it's also
extra-racist, because part of the reason that the Senate is so unrepresentative right now is that a lot of Americans, predominantly people of color, don't have any Senate representation
at all.

Washington, D.C., has a population larger than two existing U.S. states, and its residents pay more in federal taxes
than residents in twenty-two other states, but it has no representation in the Senate. Puerto Rico has a larger population
than *twenty-one* states and no representation in the Senate. The
other American territories—American Samoa, Guam, the U.S.
Virgin Islands, the Northern Mariana Islands—have together
a population of over 380,000 people with *no* representation in
the Senate.

It's not a coincidence that all these unrepresented places
are disproportionately populated by people of color. The
history of Washington, D.C., is instructive. In 1867, Black
men in D.C. obtained the right to vote. Just a few years later,
and in large part as a result of backlash among local whites,
the federal government revoked the city's ability to govern
itself and placed it under direct congressional control. This
meant that the increasingly Black city was governed by
the same segregationists who dominated Southern politics.
And it's not just Washington, D.C.: the territories mentioned
above have each been shaped by a legacy of colonization and

imperial devastation that our nation has not even begun to grapple with.[12]

In short, we've got a status quo in the Senate where a lot of near-empty white states are overrepresented and a lot of other Americans—overwhelmingly people of color—are underrepresented. This is bad.

The Solution

Some observers have called for abolishing the Senate,[13] and there's a compelling case for that. But we can't do that without a constitutional amendment, so, for now, we have to keep looking for solutions that can pass. And there's really only one option: admit new states.[14]

If this seems far-fetched, remember that adding new states is how America became the America it is today. It was only sixty years ago that two U.S. territories, Alaska and Hawaii, be-

---

12. We can't possibly do justice to this history here except to note that each of the territories mentioned above has its own complex relationship to the United States and the federal government. Going forward, our interactions with them have to be governed not by what's best for U.S. politics but by what's best for the people of each territory. What we can say on our end is that it is unacceptable to maintain territories without allowing them to be represented in the halls of power.

13. Among those is former representative John Dingell, the longest-serving member of Congress in the history of the republic.

14. Well, this is half-true. One option for admitting new states is to split up existing states. For instance, there have been proposals to split California into two or more states. The decision to create that division would have to come from Californians, but then Congress could admit the new states through a simple majority vote. Frankly, this hasn't gotten a lot of traction yet.

came full-fledged states, adding four new senators to Congress. The battle in Congress to admit these states was contentious, partisan, and—you guessed it—heavily tied up with the fight over maintaining segregationist power in the Senate. But the states were added—and we can add states again.

In 2021, Congress should make D.C. a full-fledged state, giving its more than 630,000 residents representation in Congress. This can be done through a simple maneuver: reduce the "Capitol" to a small, ten-square-mile plot of land covering Congress, the White House, and the National Mall, and make the rest of Washington, D.C., into a new state. The residents of Washington, D.C., have voted in favor of this already. In 2016 a ballot initiative calling for statehood for "New Columbia" passed with an overwhelming 79 percent support. Congress should support the wishes of D.C. residents and admit this new state into the union.

The future for other American territories is more complex, and it depends first and foremost on their own wishes. If any American territory wishes to become a state, it should have that right. Puerto Rico and other U.S. territories should be able to make their own decision on self-determination with the confidence that if they choose statehood, they will be promptly welcomed by the federal government and receive the benefits of representation in Congress.

What the Naysayers Say

Opponents of D.C. statehood make up all sorts of stories. Testifying before a Senate committee in 2014, a representative from the Koch-funded Cato Institute worried that D.C. gaining statehood would mean the federal government wouldn't have unfettered access to snowplows. Yes, snowplows.

In reality, most opponents of D.C. statehood just don't want D.C. to get representation, but they usually try not to say that out loud. Sometimes they let it slip, though. Former Ohio governor John Kasich, a supposed moderate, gave the game away when he explained why he opposes D.C. statehood: "What it really gets down to if you want to be honest is because they know that's just more votes in the Democratic Party." It was the same argument Southern segregationists made against admitting Hawaii in the 1950s: they didn't want any more damn liberals in the Senate.

The most serious objection we'll likely face is the claim that it's unconstitutional to make D.C. a state via simple legislation—that, given its status as the country's capital, D.C. statehood in particular would require a constitutional amendment. But that's why the proposal on the table doesn't call for making all of D.C. a state: it carves out the populated parts of the city to give them representation and leaves the Capitol and White House alone.

Puerto Rican statehood is more complex, given the history of racism and imperialism that has shaped its relationship with the federal government. Progressives have rightfully focused on Puerto Rico's right to self-determination—whether it chooses statehood or independence. However, at a moment when Mitch McConnell is openly describing the idea of D.C. and Puerto Rican statehood as "full-bore socialism," we should be very clear that *if* Puerto Rico were to choose statehood, we would enthusiastically support its recognition and rights as a state.

As for the other potential new states—Guam, American Samoa, the U.S. Virgin Islands, and the Northern Mariana Islands—the most commonly cited opposition to statehood among people who consider it at all is that, well, aren't they really small? And indeed, these territories are smaller than other states. But historically this has never been a permanent barrier to representation when a territory is majority white. Alaska was smaller in population than other states when it joined the Union. In 1860, Nevada had only around 7,000 residents, and even after a silver rush boosted the population, it had fewer than 50,000 residents when it became a state in 1864—fewer than any of the modern-day U.S. territories.[15]

Everyone—especially Black, indigenous, and other people of color who've suffered from our legacy of imperialism, colonialism, and chattel slavery—deserves real political representation. The size of a potential state hasn't stood in the way before, and shouldn't now.

---

15. The story of Nevada statehood is fascinating—and a good example of how admitting new states has always been a political process. In the middle of the Civil War, Union forces wanted another Republican state for the 1864 presidential election and to help pass the Thirteenth Amendment abolishing slavery. Nevada was admitted as a state eight days before the election and voted overwhelmingly for Lincoln and a Republican representative. Lincoln himself didn't have much to worry about: the presidential election was a landslide. But the following year the Thirteenth Amendment would pass the House by just seven votes, with Nevada's newly elected representative providing one of them.

DEMOCRATIZE THE HOUSE

The Problem

The Senate isn't the only problem with Congress. We also have a House of Representatives that isn't representative. There are two big drivers of this problem. First—and this may come as a surprise—the House is too small,[16] and each member's district is too big for them to do an effective job representing all their constituents. And second, our two-party system is just plain broken. It drives zero-sum political battles and deprives voters of real choices. The result is dysfunction, cynicism, and voter apathy.

Let's tackle the size problem first. The House of Representatives was intended to be the "People's House"—more responsive and reflective of the people's will than any other institution in federal government. The typical House member at the founding of the country was often elected by only a few thousand voters.

Take the Pennsylvania House elections of 1794. The Second Congressional District of Pennsylvania saw a hotly contested election between Frederick Muhlenberg, who was then serving as the nation's first speaker of the House, and Samuel Miles, a recent mayor of Philadelphia. Muhlenberg trounced Miles, winning 56 percent of the vote to the mayor's 44 percent. Sounds like an impressive battle of political titans, right? Well,

---

16. We know, we know. Who on earth looks at members of Congress and thinks, *The problem is that there aren't enough of these people?* But bear with us.

it does until you look at the vote count. Speaker of the House Muhlenberg was reelected with 656 votes, defeating Mayor Miles, who drew 510 votes. Your local college student body president probably received more votes.

How things have changed. In 2018, more than 150,000 residents of Pennsylvania's Second Congressional District voted for Democrat Brendan Boyle, a congressman you've probably never heard of.[17] Think about what it means that Boyle received more than 150,000 votes. Forget the House and even Senate elections: no U.S. *president* was elected with more than 150,000 votes until Andrew Jackson in 1828. In short, your personal unknown backbencher congressperson probably received more votes than presidents George Washington, John Adams, James Madison, and Thomas Jefferson, among others. None of the Founders would have dreamed of a constituency so large for a single House member; it would have undermined the whole point of the "People's House."

A lot of the things people hate about Congress are driven by the size of our districts. Big districts mean voters interact less and less directly with their House member. Big districts cost more to campaign in, which gives candidates with deep pockets and big donors the edge over candidates with grassroots support. Big districts make it harder for diverse candidates—i.e., non-white, non-male, non-rich—to get elected. This might seem marginal, but academic research finds that it *matters*: democracies with bigger districts routinely have less trust in government and higher income inequality.

---

17. No offense, Brendan—we're sure you're great.

If that doesn't convince you, we've got one more reason to add House districts: it helps to rebalance the Electoral College. Currently, each state has the same number of electoral votes as it has senators and representatives. If a state is overrepresented in the House and Senate (e.g., Wyoming), it is also overrepresented in the Electoral College. Expanding the House would add more electors, addressing some of the inequities of the Electoral College. This wouldn't totally fix the Electoral College, but it would help bring it closer in line with the popular vote.

Going beyond the size of our districts, we've got another big problem: the two-party system is broken. Yes, the Republican Party has fallen off an ideological cliff. But the Democratic Party isn't winning any popularity contests, either. The truth is that most people don't feel represented by either party. They feel suspicious and jaded and powerless when it comes to choosing their elected officials—and they're right to feel that way. Why shouldn't they? We barely give people a choice.

The vast majority of Americans live in "safe" House districts.[18] Before they go to the polls, they know the Democrat is a shoo-in or the Republican is a shoo-in. In each of the four national elections from 2006 to 2012, more than 90 percent of Americans didn't have a competitive House race. And these elections have gotten less competitive over time. A 2017 analysis found that, since the mid-1990s, the number of competi-

---

18. For the purposes of this, we're defining a competitive election as being decided by less than 5 percent of the vote. In a House election with 200,000 voters, that would mean the race was relatively close: 105,000 votes for one candidate and 95,000 votes for the other, or closer. These are nail-biters in which significant grassroots engagement and turnout could turn the tide.

tive House districts had declined by more than half. There are far fewer competitive House districts now than there were ten years ago, and there were fewer ten years ago than there were fifty years ago.

We hear the shouting already: this is because of that damn partisan gerrymandering! It would be nice if getting rid of gerrymandering would solve the problem, but unfortunately it's not that simple. While gerrymandering is infuriating, it's actually not the main driver of noncompetitive seats in Congress. The reality is that Republicans and Democrats are increasingly sorting themselves into geographically isolated communities, with more and more conservatives living in rural areas and progressives in cities. This demographic trend means, as one analysis summed up, "more and more areas come, in essence, pre-gerrymandered." One political scientist sums it up: "Efforts to substantially change redistricting aren't likely to do much to either mitigate polarization or improve Democrats' electoral fortunes."[19]

This helps to fuel continued polarization, because most members of Congress are more afraid of a primary challenge than they are of a general election challenge. And polarization at the district level drives the polarization at the national level. As we covered in Chapter 1, if there are two polarized parties, each one wins when the other one loses. When you're out of power, your best chance of winning the next election is to play

19. Note that we're talking here specifically about *congressional* gerrymandering. Gerrymandering of state legislature districts can often be even more egregiously partisan.

hardball and block everything. That's how we get continued gridlock, no matter who wins, year after year.

Representative democracy is about the people making choices, but we're increasingly not giving voters much of a choice. As the famed political theorist turned California governor Arnold Schwarzenegger has observed, "There are dictators who win by less" than the typical House member.

But what's a voter to do? Vote for a third party? That's a wasted vote, or worse. Third-party candidates are often spoilers, throwing the election to the candidate who is furthest from your values. When lefties vote for the Green Party, they take down the Democrat; when conservatives vote for the Libertarian, they take down the Republican. Our two-party system just isn't set up for people to vote their conscience in general elections. It's not set up to actually give people choices.

So there we have it. The House is too small. Most districts aren't really competitive. And the result is gridlock, dysfunction, and voter apathy. So what are we going to do about it?

The Solution

We need to build a bigger House with smaller constituencies, and we need a voting system that gives every voter a real say in who represents them.

Expanding the House is the opposite of a radical idea—in fact, it was standard practice for the first 120 years of the republic. From the 1790s to the early 1900s, Congress regularly expanded the House, but House expansions stopped abruptly in the 1920s, when Congress capped the total size at 435. The motivation behind the cap was simple: they were worried about the increase of "foreigners" who were concentrating in cities. The best way to keep these immigrants' political power from increasing was to stop expanding the House.

So there's nothing magic about the 435 number of congressional districts; it was simply the number the House agreed to at the time. While the cap was being debated, one representative said, "There is absolutely no reason, philosophy, or common sense in arbitrarily fixing the membership of the House at 435 or at any other number." The hundred-year-old, unchanging quota is the product of xenophobia and congressional dysfunction, nothing more.

What would the right size of the House be? That's a great question! There are several different options for expansion. If we were to say that every member of Congress's district should be no larger than our smallest-population state (Wyoming), then we'd end up with 545 seats. If we were to expand the House in line with international norms for representative bodies, as a 2018 *New York Times* editorial endorsed, that would give us a House with 593 seats. If we were to expand the House to its 1930 people-per-member levels, we would end up with 1,163 members.

Think 1,163 sounds like a huge House? Had James Madison had his way, the first amendment to the Constitution would have been the Congressional Apportionment Amendment. The amendment dictated that the size of a House constituency would be 30,000, with provisions to allow it, at the extreme end, to ratchet at least as high as 50,000. Had one more state ratified this amendment, we'd have a House of thousands of members today.

So there are a lot of reasonable ways to think about the size the House *should* be—and they all point to a bigger House.

A bigger House would bring representatives closer to their constituents. But it wouldn't change the competitiveness problem, not on its own. If we want *all* Americans to live in a competitive district, we need proportional representation. Let's talk about how this would work.

In our current system, if your party gets 40 percent of the vote in a district, you lose the election and get no congressional representation. In fact, if all your candidate managed was 40 percent, that means your district is so darn lopsided in favor of the other party that the race wasn't competitive at all. You live in a safe district, and your vote effectively doesn't matter. You have that in common with nine out of ten of your fellow Americans.

The basic idea behind proportional representation is that if your party gets, for example, 40 percent of the votes, then your party should get 40 percent of the seats in Congress. That's why it's "proportional" representation. The way you get proportional representation is by changing the rules to elect multiple representatives in each district instead of just one representative per district.

That's not what America has today. Instead, every House district is represented by a single member. If you live in California's Fiftieth District, you have one House member. If you live in Texas's Thirty-Fifth District, same deal. But it doesn't have to be this way; it's not included in our Constitution. In fact, it's a method of electing representatives that is out of step with our own history and international norms.

For the first several decades of America's history, many House members won in races where they were the second or even third or fourth choice of voters in their districts, because districts often elected two or more members. As recently as the mid-twentieth century, states all over the country used multi-member districts or statewide districts to select their House members until Congress mandated single-member districts in 1967. Multimember districts are still used at the state level to fill legislative seats in ten geographically and ideologically diverse states, from Washington to Arizona to West Virginia.

So how would you vote in these multimember congressional districts? The best way is with ranked-choice voting. Under this voting system, you don't just say who your first choice is—you rank your choices. If your first choice doesn't get enough votes to surpass a threshold, your vote for a second choice is counted. You might rank two, three, or more candidates.

To see why ranked-choice voting matters, let's take one particularly painful recent example: the 2016 presidential election. If we'd had ranked-choice voting, Jill Stein voters could have voted for Stein as their first choice and Hillary Clinton as their second. Stein would have been eliminated for failing to amass enough votes, and anyone who chose Clinton as a first or second choice would have gone in Clinton's column. People could have voted their conscience, and Stein wouldn't have been a spoiler candidate. The same logic holds for Libertarians: they could rank a Libertarian candidate first and an establishment Republican second if their heart so desired.

This makes so much sense that a 2018 *New York Times* editorial endorsing ranked-choice voting noted that "nearly everywhere it's in use, voters and candidates say they're happier with it." This includes a growing number of major American cities, such as Minneapolis, Santa Fe, and Oakland, California. Most recently, in 2018, Maine became the first state to use ranked choice to elect its representative to the U.S. House.[20]

How would this combination of reforms play out in the real world? Let's take two examples: Manhattan and Louisiana.

Manhattan has four overwhelmingly Democratic districts where voters regularly elect Democrats by 30 points or more. If you're a Republican running in any of these districts, you're screwed. If you're a voter in Manhattan, you've never voted in a competitive general election. Now imagine a twist: there's one election for all of Manhattan, and the top four vote-getters become members of Congress. Suddenly, to be elected, you need only place fourth, so you need only 20 or 30 percent of the vote. So Manhattan might end up with two Democrats, one Democratic Socialist, and one Republican. And if you're a Manhattan voter, you suddenly have *actual choices* in the general election.

Now let's take Louisiana. Louisiana has a very Republican congressional delegation. Most Louisiana Republicans are afraid of primaries from the right—not general elections. But

---

20. Maine implemented ranked-choice voting after a Trump-like governor won election twice in elections that featured third-party spoiler candidates. The logic was simple: shift to ranked-choice voting to eliminate the negative impact of spoilers going forward. It proved effective in the very next election, when Democratic congressional candidate Jared Golden eked out a victory over an incumbent Republican. Golden didn't get a plurality of first-choice votes, but because of ranked-choice voting, he ended up winning the seat with second-choice votes.

what if they had to run in a general election against not just a Democrat but a Libertarian candidate, or a right-wing populist, or an anti-Trump "moderate"—or all of the above? How might that change their incentives? How might it change the Republican Party?

That's the magic of this reform: it isn't about helping Republicans or Democrats; it's about restructuring the two-party system and ending the era of "safe" districts. Suddenly, Green Party, Libertarian, Democratic Socialist, and other candidates can win in places that used to be considered safe Republican or Democratic seats. Suddenly the Republicans who've been clinging to Trump out of fear of primary challenges have a whole new set of problems. We can't predict everything that would happen with this shift, but what we can say for sure is that if we're going to take on polarization, we have to take on the parties.

In the end, it's a simple proposition: with this reform, nobody lives in a "safe" district anymore. Every constituent has a real shot at electing a representative who actually represents their values. Everybody lives in a competitive district; everybody gets a choice.

This would be a really, really hard reform to pass. But the effects would be dramatic and far-reaching: proportional representation would make elections more competitive, give voters real choices, address hyperpolarization, and improve our political system's responsiveness to the people. That's why political scientists at UCLA and Northwestern conclude in their book on saving democracy that "no other reforms are likely to be effective without it."

What the Naysayers Say

There are three big arguments against expanding the House.

The first is obvious: people hate Congress. Who in their right mind wants more of a bad thing? Opinion polls back up this knee-jerk reaction. Expanding the House isn't a popular idea right now. But polling shows that when you provide additional context about how historically out of whack our current House is, support for expanding the House shoots up. If we believe this is the right policy—and we do—we need to educate the public as to why a larger House would make Congress less terrible.

Second, people worry a big House will be a dysfunctional House—that having more members will limit deliberation, limit the ability to build relationships, and make it difficult to get things done. But the House is totally dysfunctional already! House members skip hearings, play for the cameras, and spend hours every day calling rich people to ask for money. They're not spending their days debating political philosophy and bonding with each other; that's not how it works. As one political scientist studying the House notes, "Whatever idealized deliberation and bonhomie might be lost with a larger House is already long gone, and it isn't coming back." The benefits of a more representative House outweigh the costs here.

Third, expanding the House would mean more districts, and more districts would mean more opportunity for gerrymandering. You literally can't gerrymander states like Delaware and Vermont: they all have just one representative. States with three or four representatives are tough to gerrymander, too: there are only so many ways to carve up those districts. But if you vastly increase the number of districts, you increase the opportunity for gerrymandering. So we get this argument; it's a real threat. And it's why any sort of House expansion should be accompanied by serious anti-gerrymandering reforms to prevent these shenanigans from the outset.

As for proportional representation and ranked-choice voting, there is one very serious concern based in historical experience: How does this impact communities of color? As mentioned above, Congress outlawed multimember districts in 1967. Why then? In the 1960s, Southern states were using multimember districts to water down the votes of Black voters. Combining ranked-choice voting with proportional representation guards against that. FairVote, one of the leading advocacy groups behind improving the fairness of our political institutions, found that combining ranked-choice voting with multimember districts would significantly increase the percentage of racial minorities with the power to elect candidates of their choice. The current system of designating majority-minority districts does indeed help candidates of color in those specific districts, but overall, our system of single-member districts produces a significantly lower proportion of representatives of color. A proportional representation system would help make our elected bodies even more representative.

The other big objection to this idea is that, well, it's just weird. Sure, it sounds nice in theory, but who actually does representation this way? As it turns out, a whole bunch of countries do. A survey of 195 countries found that the *most common* voting system was proportional representation. America's single-member, winner-take-all system is far less common.

This is one of those ideas that might seem out there and wacky but actually has backing across the political spectrum. Supporters of these reforms include the proudly centrist Third Way think tank as well as some of the most progressive members of Congress. Conservative columnist David Brooks has endorsed the reforms in no uncertain terms, arguing that making this shift was the "one reform to save America." The *New York Times* editorial board echoes that sentiment, concluding that implementing these reforms is "the only way a democracy can survive."

Proportional representation and ranked-choice voting are such a challenge to existing power structures that even some of those sympathetic to the reforms are skeptical they can get done, going so far as to label them a "quixotic fantasy." And, indeed, every single member of Congress got elected under the current rules, so why would they want to change them? We understand this—it will be tough. This sort of reform would require overwhelming constituent power demanding change. As a step in that direction, advocates could seek to simply have Congress remove the ban on multimember congressional districts so that proportional representation could be tested by the states. Let the proof be in the pudding—and let that proof fuel wider-scale reform.

DEMOCRATIZE THE COURTS

The Problem

Republicans have appointed fifteen out of the last nineteen Supreme Court justices. This just does not pass the smell test for a legitimate democracy.

Reactionaries have spent decades waging an intensive campaign to pack the federal courts with ideologues—and that campaign has been very, very successful.

Their strategy is simple: when they're in power, they appoint as many judges as they can, as fast as possible. When they're out of power, they block and delay appointments as much as possible.

The gold medal for court packing goes to Senator Mitch McConnell. During Obama's presidency, he used every tool at his disposal to slow and defeat the appointment of federal judges. He waged a low-grade war to delay and reject as many lower court appointments as possible. Most famously, he took the unprecedented step of refusing to even consider President Obama's nomination to fill the Supreme Court seat vacancy created by Justice Antonin Scalia's death.

In the lead-up to the 2016 election, there was every reason to believe Republicans would double down on this strategy. When Hillary Clinton appeared poised for victory, Senate Republicans openly promised to deny her any Supreme Court appointments. NPR reported that Senator Ted Cruz dismissed the idea that the Court needed nine justices to function—the open implication being that Republicans would rather change the size of the Supreme Court than confirm a Democratic president's nominee.[21]

---

21. He wasn't alone. Senator Richard Burr of North Carolina agreed: "I am going to do everything I can do to make sure four years from now, we still got an opening on the Supreme Court." Even Senator John McCain of Arizona, long viewed as a paragon of bipartisan virtue, said, "I promise you that we will be united against any Supreme Court nominee that Hillary Clinton, if she were president, would put up."

Then Trump won, and Republicans made an abrupt U-turn. McConnell and Senate Republicans began expediting federal judicial appointments, packing the courts with reactionary ideologues. They eliminated the filibuster for Supreme Court nominees, allowing Trump to appoint Neil Gorsuch to the seat stolen from Merrick Garland and to confirm Brett Kavanaugh over resounding opposition. In his first two years as president, Trump successfully shifted the ideological makeup of the Supreme Court sharply to the right and confirmed more appeals court judges than Obama and Bill Clinton had appointed in the first two years of their presidencies combined.[22]

The result of this scorched-earth partisan approach to what should be a nonpartisan institution is clear. The Supreme Court now functions as an arm of the Republican Party. Don't believe us? Take it directly from Donald Trump, who in 2018 got into a Twitter fight with Chief Justice John Roberts[23] when Trump asserted that there were "Obama judges" and "Trump judges." Trump was not confused. He understood perfectly well that his job was to complete the transformation of the Court into a partisan institution.

This now Republican institution has played its part well. The Court has attacked organized labor and labor rights, gun violence prevention, and civil liberty protections. It is likely to

---

22. The court reforms we discuss here are all focused on the Supreme Court, but there's nothing stopping a unified progressive Congress from also unpacking the lower courts. Nothing in the Constitution mandates a certain number of circuit court judges: Congress can (as it has in the past) expand and alter the court structure through simple legislation.

23. We can't believe we're writing these words, either.

either repeal or functionally gut the protections of *Roe v. Wade*. The graveyard of progressive policies killed off by Republican justices grows every year.

What's more, the Court has become increasingly antagonistic toward democracy itself. In just the past decade, Court decisions have upheld partisan gerrymandering, gutted the Voting Rights Act, and opened the floodgates to dark money in political campaigns—and this is only a partial list. Ian Millhiser, author of *Injustices: The Supreme Court's History of Comforting the Comfortable and Afflicting the Afflicted*, worries that the conservative Court is so antagonistic toward representative democracy that the U.S. "will, of course, continue to carry out elections, but the results will be preordained."[24]

The biggest long-term victims of this brazenly partisan approach to the courts are the courts themselves.[25] The judiciary doesn't have an army or the power to provide funds to carry out its decisions. The only power it has is the power to persuade Americans and the other branches of government that its rulings are legitimate. The other branches can and have ignored Supreme Court rulings, and there was little recourse left to the courts. Republicans' nakedly partisan approach has endangered the perceived independence of the courts—which is ultimately a threat to the legitimacy of the judicial system and the health of our democracy.

---

24. Of course, this is far from a new phenomenon. No account of the fundamentally partisan nature of the courts is complete without noting that in 2000 five Republican-appointed judges literally stopped a recount in Florida to hand the presidency to the Republican candidate, George W. Bush.

25. Also the American people, America itself, and, you know, the world.

The Solution

We face a conundrum: we absolutely have to address the right-wing imbalance of the current Court right now. But we also have to do it in a way that makes the Court less openly partisan over the longer term. That's a tricky line to walk.

There's no way to rebalance the Court without expanding it. Neil Gorsuch isn't going to politely give his stolen seat back. McConnell isn't going to start seeking broad bipartisan support for justices. It'd be nice if we could hold Brett Kavanaugh and Clarence Thomas accountable for the allegations of sexual misconduct and potential perjury, but removing a Supreme Court justice requires two-thirds of the Senate.

The only solution to unpacking the Supreme Court is to add new justices. The Court's size isn't written into the Constitution. It can change and has been changed throughout American history. A simple act of Congress signed by the president can expand the Court.

But remember, we have two goals: unpack the current Court and depoliticize it for the future. That means we need to think about ways of adding justices that make the Court less political over time.

One proposal on the table is to commit to automatic expansions of the Court going forward. For instance, in 2021, the Congress and the president could pass legislation creating a new rule: every president gets to appoint two additional justices (one every two years). If there's a Democrat, they get to nominate two justices; if there's a Republican, they get to nominate two justices—regardless of vacancies. This would make appointments less random: the path of our society shouldn't rest on the health or illness of a small number of very old people. And it would allow us to both unpack the Court and create a foundation for a more functional, consistent, and less partisan process going forward.

Congress could also impose term limits for Supreme Court justices. In 1919, Congress passed a law allowing federal judges to take "senior status," which allows them to remain official judges but no longer vote or author opinions.[26] This is sort of like auditing a college class: you're still a student, but you don't take the tests or get a grade. That hundred-year-old law creating senior status excluded Supreme Court justices, but it was expanded to the highest court in 1937. A new Congress and president could revise the legislation further, implementing mandatory senior status for Supreme Court justices after an eighteen-year term. The justices could then opt to stay in quasi-retirement or rotate into serving on lower courts.[27]

These options aren't mutually exclusive. Expanding the court, committing to automatic expansion going forward, and instituting term limits is a reasonable combined strategy. Our point here is not to choose the one and only path, but rather to point Indivisibles, national leaders, and other progressive advocates in the right direction. For progressive reforms to sur-

---

26. We were pretty excited to find out about this because initially we had thought term limits would require a constitutional amendment. Brian Fallon, who leads the national court reform organization Demand Justice, gets credit for pointing us in this direction.

27. This isn't some ridiculous hypothetical. Two living former Supreme Court justices, Sandra Day O'Connor and David Souter, have themselves taken senior status and continue to issue opinions in federal appellate courts.

vive, we must unpack the Court. For the Supreme Court to remain legitimate, we must depoliticize it. Any effective reform must tackle both goals.

What the Naysayers Say

One critique of our solution is that it's too cautious. A knee-jerk solution for Democrats in 2021 might be *Let's just add more Supreme Court justices!* This would help address the first part of the Republican court-packing problem. If the incoming Democratic government were to enact a one-off expansion of the Court, they would undo the ideological packing from years of Republican appointments. Such a Supreme Court, full of progressive justices, might reverse bad old decisions like *Citizens United* and uphold new progressive reforms enacted by a unified, post-Trump Democratic government.

But this kind of one-off expansion would exacerbate the second part of the problem. Responding to court packing with additional court packing would further politicize the Court, diminish the Court's power to persuade, and endanger its legitimacy as a core American democratic institution.

Another critique might be that creating automatic Supreme Court appointments won't do anything if the Senate simply refuses to confirm them. We could enter a new stalemate whereby whenever the president and the Senate are of opposite parties, the Senate simply refuses to confirm new justices. Or, as Ian Millhiser cautions, a battle over the judiciary could become "a full-out war. Republicans will retaliate with more court packing if they regain control of the federal government." We know that, given the chance, Republicans will indeed retaliate. They spent years packing the Court without provocation, so imagine what they'll do when provoked.

We agree that these are all frightening prospects. Responding to the history of Republican court packing is a dangerous undertaking, and we shouldn't embark on it lightly. But we also can't accept conservative court packing as the new normal. We can't allow the theft of the Supreme Court to dictate our social and economic policies for a generation. If a Republican-packed Court continues to gut pro-democracy legislation and block world-saving climate reforms and lifesaving health care policies, defenders of democracy will have little other recourse but to demand Court reforms—and that includes expansion.

We can't allow Republican court packing to threaten our other democratic institutions—like free and fair elections, the right to vote, and the right to representation. If we accept this, the game is over. We'll lose by forfeit. And we're not willing to give up like that.

DEMOCRATIZE VOTING

The Problem

In early America, full citizenship was reserved for wealthy white men. That changed slowly over time. In fits and starts, over much of American history, more and more classes of people—poorer whites, naturalized immigrants, Black people and other people of color, women—won the right to vote and participate as full citizens. America has never attained some sort of ideal, permanent, inclusive state of voting rights. The war to stop people from voting is ongoing.

We all know that voter suppression is central to the reactionary strategy. Today that looks like throwing Black people off the voter rolls in Georgia, instituting poll taxes in Florida to block returning citizens from reclaiming their rights, or creating long voting lines by closing polling places in North Carolina.[28] And it shows up in hostility to literally any policy that makes voting easier, more accessible, or even just not an enormous burden for Americans—for instance, early voting, voting by mail, extending voting hours, and automatic voter registration.

Beyond voter suppression, we have to confront the fact that millions of Americans who should have the right to vote are still deprived of that right. The disenfranchisement of millions of Americans distorts and perverts the rest of our representative institutions.

We're going to focus on three broad classes of Americans being systematically deprived of the right to vote: immigrant Americans, younger Americans, and Americans with a felony conviction. Taken together, enfranchising these classes could add more than 30 million people to the voter rolls. To put that in perspective, about 113 million Americans turned out to vote in the historic midterms of 2018. Expanding the electorate to these Americans would make our democracy more representative of *all* our people.

---

28. "Returning citizens" is the preferred term for formerly incarcerated people.

IMMIGRANTS

More than 20 million American immigrants living in this country do not have the right to vote, including both documented and undocumented immigrants. More than 9 million of these people are lawful permanent residents (also known as green card holders) who are eligible to be naturalized and gain full citizenship rights, including the right to vote. The vast majority of the roughly 11 million undocumented Americans have lived here for over a decade. They've worked, gone to school, paid taxes, and contributed to society in every state of the union for years. At least 9 million are of voting age, but they've never been allowed to vote.

These undocumented Americans aren't just treated like second-class citizens; they're treated as if they're invisible. It's an absurd and cruel feature of our immigration laws that this population plays such a critical role in our economy and our national community, yet has no say in our government. Meanwhile, they face an onslaught of racist, degrading treatment from Trump and his allies, and a renewed reign of terror driven by our out-of-control enforcement agencies. These attacks are about making America whiter and keeping the voting population as white as possible.[29]

YOUNGER AMERICANS

We often take for granted that the voting age is eighteen. But it wasn't always so, it isn't the case in a few American cities today, and it's not the case in many other modern democracies.

---

29. In 2018, Trump was caught in the Oval Office saying he wanted fewer immigrants from "shithole countries" and more from mostly white countries ("places like Norway").

Countries like Scotland and Austria have extended voting to sixteen-year-olds. In recent years a few American cities have lowered the voting age to sixteen for local elections, and more than a dozen states allow seventeen-year-olds to vote in primaries. But localities and states can't lower the voting age for federal elections; only Congress can do that.

The last time federal legislation lowered the voting age was 1971. Americans under twenty-one were fighting and dying in Vietnam, and the question was reasonably asked: Why should they be able to die for their country but not vote in their country?

Today's sixteen- and seventeen-year-olds are old enough to be attacked by school shooters and young enough to die from the effects of climate change, but they're excluded from choosing the elected officials who could do something about it. We're requiring our youth to bear the brunt of our public policy failures, but we give them no say in choosing the representatives who create our policies.

AMERICANS WITH A FELONY CONVICTION

About 6 million American citizens are deprived of the right to vote because they've been convicted of a felony. This is far out of step with international norms. In many other democracies, not only can formerly incarcerated citizens with a felony conviction vote, but currently incarcerated citizens can vote as well. The logic is simple: going to prison doesn't erase your humanity or your rights as a citizen.

Voting rights for Americans convicted of felonies vary widely among the states. Maine and Vermont look like many other democracies in the world: they have no disenfranchising restrictions, including for those currently incarcerated. On the other end of the spectrum, twelve states prohibit some or all returning citizens from voting, even after their time is served and they're off parole.

Voter disenfranchisement cannot be understood independent of the legacy of mass incarceration. America has by far the largest incarcerated population in the world. We incarcerate more people than any other country on the planet, including authoritarian countries like China and Russia. This is fundamentally about state-sponsored control and suppression of people of color, and specifically Black people, a legacy that stretches back to the era of slavery. It's not an accident that both incarceration and disenfranchisement rates among Black voters in the former Confederate states are extraordinarily high. But it's also not just the South. Wisconsin, Iowa, Nevada, Wyoming, and Arizona (among others) have extraordinarily high rates of Black voter disenfranchisement. In states with the harshest restrictions, more than 20 percent of all potential Black voters in the country are disenfranchised.[30]

The Solution

Let's start with the obvious. Voting should be a simple, safe, and easy part of everyone's life. There is no reason Americans

---

30. The story gets worse. In the U.S. Census, the federal government counts the nonvoting prison population when apportioning House seats. Lawmakers often strategically take prisons into account as they draw congressional district maps. This practice, called prison gerrymandering, further empowers largely rural, largely white areas. If this feels uncannily like the Three-Fifths Compromise, which gave slave-owning states greater representation, that's because it is.

should not be automatically registered to vote. There is no reason that you should have to miss work to vote. There is no reason that lines at the polls should be hours long. There is no reason that voter suppression should be condoned by the federal government. There is no reason that elections should be vulnerable to foreign threats. It should be easy to vote and hard to steal elections.

The For the People Act includes automatic voter registration, beefs up election security, curbs partisan gerrymandering, expands public financing for elections, protects voting rights, and prohibits voter roll purging. The House has passed this bill already; it should become law in 2021. This is the baseline.

But that's not enough.

America's expansion of the franchise is a rich and storied part of its political history—one of the things we should be most proud of as a country. We should build on this history. The specific reform may vary for each class of currently disenfranchised voter, but don't lose the forest for the trees: more Americans voting is a good thing, and we should encourage this basic level of participation in our democracy. It will make us stronger.

Enfranchising immigrants need not be a partisan issue. Ronald Reagan signed the single largest immigration reform law in American history, providing a path to citizenship and voting rights to nearly 3 million undocumented Americans. Subsequent laws extended a path to citizenship to millions more. So the solution is looking us in the face: we need to provide a path to citizenship for the 11 million undocumented Americans living here, and voting rights guarantees for documented immigrant Americans as well.

This is important first and foremost because immigrants deserve to live in safety and dignity in our country. And a critical part of that is political representation. So, in 2021, a unified progressive government should prioritize a compassionate immigration reform bill that extends citizenship to the millions of undocumented immigrants living in the United States.

For younger Americans, the solution is also pretty clear. Congress can't regulate the minimum voting age for state and local elections, but it can and should pass a law lowering the voting age to sixteen for all federal elections. This would immediately enfranchise about 8 million new voters, and it would open up the opportunity to tie high school civics education to actual practice. This could also have a "trickle-up" effect; research has shown that when younger people in a household gain the right to vote, it encourages more participation among their parents.

At least within progressive circles, this shouldn't be a controversial position. In 2015, Nancy Pelosi, then the House minority leader, publicly embraced lowering the voting age to sixteen or seventeen. In 2019, newly elected Representative Ayanna Pressley introduced legislation to lower the voting age to sixteen, and Speaker Pelosi reiterated her support for the idea.

When it comes to restoring the rights of incarcerated Americans, the simplest voting rights reform—and the one that many criminal justice advocates support—is following Maine's and Vermont's lead. No more restrictions on voting, period. The For the People Act includes a weaker version of this, allowing restrictions for those currently incarcerated. But why go weak? We need to end the epidemic of mass incarceration, and a critical part of that is protecting the right to vote of every person incarcerated or formerly incarcerated by the state.

What the Naysayers Say

We all know what anti-immigrant advocates would say about offering a path to citizenship to the immigrants living in American communities. We aren't interested in arguing with Trump supporters about this. But immigrant rights partners we've talked to have raised a different and important concern.

For years, one of the top goals of the immigrant rights movement has been relief from deportation and a path to citizenship for immigrants. But Congress has been totally incapable of passing any such legislation for decades. As a result of this political reality, many advocates within these communities have turned their focus to securing basic economic opportunity and personal security. In other words, they argue that citizenship shouldn't be a precondition for justice, economic stability, safety, and dignity for immigrant families. They are absolutely right. At a time when immigrant communities are under constant attack by the government, this becomes more important than ever. Citizenship with full voting rights is the ultimate goal, but on the road to that goal we can't abandon protections for non-citizen immigrants. And we shouldn't sacrifice protections for one group of immigrants in exchange for citizenship for another.

As for expanding the franchise to younger voters, the knee-jerk objection to lowering the minimum voting age is that sixteen-year-olds are too young. Opponents say that this population is just not mature enough, or not educated enough about civic life, and won't take the opportunity to vote if it's given to them.

None of these arguments holds up under a basic review of the evidence. As one psychologist in favor of lowering the voting age to sixteen wrote in the *New York Times*, "The skills necessary to make informed decisions are firmly in place by sixteen." And studies show that sixteen-year-olds are just as civically knowledgeable as their slightly older counterparts, or, according to some studies, *more* knowledgeable. Which, when you think about it, makes sense: they're all in school studying American history and government! In fact, cities that have extended voting to sixteen- and seventeen-year-olds have found that their voting rates are far higher than those of the rest of the voting-age population. As with any habit, it helps to start early. In short, if you want more young people to vote, you should make it possible for young people to vote.

When it comes to restoring rights for incarcerated and formerly incarcerated Americans, there's a reason these laws are so prevalent in the states of the former Confederacy: they serve the same purpose that poll taxes and literacy tests once did. And there is still viciously open prejudice against those who've served their time. In 2017, as Florida was considering a historic ballot initiative to restore this population's voting rights, an advocate against the initiative explained his position: "I don't think felons oughta be allowed to vote, the same way I don't think felons ought to be able to own a gun or become lawyers or handle your money or give you investment advice." His argument didn't carry the day. In a statewide election where the Democratic candidates for governor and U.S. senator lost by a slim margin, the rights-restoration initiative received supermajority support from Florida voters.[31]

For those of us who are not formerly incarcerated, young, or immigrants, the question we should be asking ourselves is simple: Do we think more voting is a good thing? Do we believe everyone in our country deserves to have their voices heard? Do we think our society is strengthened by shutting out new voices? For a pro-democracy movement, these aren't complicated questions to answer. If the cure for our democracy is more democracy, one simple way to administer that cure is by opening up the voting booths to more Americans.

DEMOCRATIZE THE MEDIA

The Problem

A healthy democratic republic requires an informed population. Americans need to know what's happening in the world. They need to know what their government and their representatives are or are not doing. The reforms in this chapter aim to make our democracy more responsive to the people. But how informed are the people it's responding to?

The problem we face today is that Americans don't just dis-

---

31. Conservatives took power in Florida in the same election in which voters passed the rights-restoration ballot initiative. In one of their first acts, the Republican state legislature and governor gutted the initiative.

agree about what to do about the social and economic problems facing the country and the world. We disagree about reality itself. This is the direct product of a crisis in American media. It's "a crisis," wrote the authors of "The Death and Life of Great American Newspapers" in the *Nation* more than a decade ago, "that could leave a dramatically diminished version of democracy in its wake." Those words seem prescient now.

Like other crises described in this chapter, America's media crisis has a history that stretches back a few decades. Four decades ago, the vast majority of Americans who got their news at all got it from the three big networks: ABC, CBS, and NBC. Walter Cronkite, one of the few guys[32] whom nearly 30 million people watched every evening, was well-known and well-liked by broad swaths of Americans, in blue, red, and purple states alike. He was the guy who gave them the news—news about the world they could trust to actually reflect reality. But Cronkite got out of the game near the peak of that old world. The rapid expansion of cable news in the 1980s and 1990s, the creation of Fox News in the mid-1990s, and the Internet news explosion in the early 2000s transformed America's media environment. Nobody in American media today—not Rachel Maddow or Anderson Cooper or Sean Hannity—comes close to Cronkite's audience in raw numbers or influence. We live in a different media world today.

At the same time that the national political news environ-

---

32. And it was always white guys. So, just to be clear, we're not saying that this was some perfect era of journalism. As with politics in this era, this level of universality hinged on excluding a lot of people—especially women and people of color—from the conversation entirely.

ment was fracturing, local media was dying. Newspaper circulation has declined literally every year for the past three decades, and the number of journalists, editors, news photographers, and other news staff in our country has dropped precipitously. From 2008 to 2018, nearly 47 percent of newspaper jobs disappeared.

This drastic drop has been driven by simple market dynamics. The economic model for local news has collapsed, especially in the past couple of decades as the Internet gave people alternative options to buy and sell their stuff, and gave ad makers alternative places to place their ads. The decline is so bad that there are now "local news deserts" across the country. Things are grim. Robert W. McChesney, one of the authors of "The Death and Life of Great American Newspapers," told us, "We're just one recession away from the end of traditional journalism altogether."[33] Scary stuff.

It's scary because we can see the results all around us. The journalists who used to cover national politics for local papers don't have jobs anymore. Statehouses and city governments operate with ever less press scrutiny. Today we've got a few surviving national news outlets, we've got cable, and we've got the Internet. The advertising dollars that once paid for your local newspaper have moved over to digital platforms like Facebook and Google, Silicon Valley giants that aren't in the business of news production.

Now, there's nothing inherently wrong with cable or the

---

33. This isn't a U.S.-only phenomenon. Other better-functioning democracies like Canada are also struggling with the demise of local media. The economic model didn't break just here; it broke everywhere there's Internet.

Internet. Cable brought such great things to humanity as seasons 1–6 of *Game of Thrones*. The Internet has brought us many delightful cat videos and memes. And news too! There are now a lot of options for news—news of every size, shape, and flavor. At its best, social media has helped voices long excluded from the mainstream media—people of color, women, LGBTQ persons—make their perspectives heard.

The problem is that some of the options that have flourished in this brave new world are pretty dangerous. And the danger is growing.

If you're reading this, there's a good chance you're a progressive.[34] If so, take a trip to another universe and turn on Fox News, read Breitbart, and visit the Daily Caller. In that conservative world where millions live, Barack Obama is a Muslim socialist, Hillary Clinton is a corrupt traitor, and Donald Trump is a heroic warrior prince. Government is giving away the store to people of color, immigrants are coming to hurt your family, and college kids think you're racist or sexist or homophobic for being "politically incorrect." It's a totally different reality, and it makes compromise, even on the most basic and should-be-bipartisan issues, like voting rights, totally impossible.

To be sure, progressives live in their own media bubbles, too, but it's not really comparable. As with so many of the challenges we face, this problem is not equally felt on both sides of the aisle. It's true that trust in media has declined overall over the past several decades. But this trust has particu-

---

34. If not, good for you for getting outside your comfort zone.

larly dropped among Republicans: today, nearly 80 percent of Democrats trust the media and only about 30 percent of Republicans do. This is a yawning gap, and it plays out constantly in our politics.

A leading force behind this growing distrust is Fox News. Fox shovels a mixture of news and misinformation to the public while actively working to discredit other news sources. Viewers of Fox News tend to be less informed than other consumers of media; in fact, they tend to be less informed than people who don't watch news at all.[35] Under the Trump administration, Fox has become a full-fledged propaganda operation. Trump seems to be in on the scam, regularly calling Fox News competitors "fake news" and the "enemy of the people."

The impact of this propaganda machine on the national political environment is huge. Through this sustained misinformation campaign, Fox News has helped drive the entire American electorate to the right. A 2017 study found that Fox News is responsible for a significant vote swing in Republicans' favor. Without Fox, the popular vote would have gone to John Kerry instead of George W. Bush in 2004, and Obama's 2008 victory would have been an absolute landslide. Of course, Fox was only stronger by the time Trump was running for president in 2016.

The conservative attack on facts and objective journalistic standards isn't limited to national media. In the places where

---

35. In response to a poll by an academic institution that showed non–news watchers were more informed than Fox News watchers, Fox News went on the attack: "We suggest the school invest in improving its weak academic program instead of spending money on frivolous polling."

local news is still available, viewers are increasingly finding conservative coverage. And the source of that conservative local media is often the same: Sinclair Broadcast Group.

Sinclair Broadcast Group isn't as well-known as Fox News, but it has a huge impact on the modern American media environment. Sinclair owns or operates nearly two hundred local television stations that reach about 40 percent of U.S. households. And Sinclair is just as much of a conservative bullhorn as Fox News. Sinclair's chairman believes that "99.9 percent of the media is left of center," and he's used his company's national broadcast footprint to push his conservative agenda. Sinclair mandates that their seemingly objective local news anchors pass down the company line, sometimes verbatim. In one particularly Orwellian example in 2018, dozens of Sinclair anchors across the country were required to read the exact same script about how other sources of media were fake news and a threat to democracy. It was honestly pretty spooky.

Sinclair enjoys just as cozy a relationship with Trump as Fox News does. Jared Kushner, Trump's son-in-law, has admitted that the Trump campaign struck a deal with the media giant to give access to the campaign in exchange for better local media coverage. When the Federal Communications Commission (FCC) slapped down Sinclair's proposed multibillion-dollar acquisition of Tribune Media, Trump himself came to Sinclair's defense. Trump, so often the master of saying the quiet part loud, tweeted, "So sad and unfair that the FCC wouldn't approve the Sinclair Broadcast merger with Tribune. This would have been a great and much needed Conservative voice for and of the People." Trump gets it: in place of thousands of local, independent media sources, we've got a pro-Trump bullhorn pumping propaganda into living rooms nationwide.

But what about that great democratizing force, the Internet? Surely that will save our free and independent media, right? Of course you don't believe that—because you've been living through the meltdown of recent years, just like we have.

First, the Internet itself is under threat. In 2017, Ajit Pai, Trump's political appointee at the FCC, revoked the set of regulations governing "net neutrality"—the requirement that Internet service providers treat all Internet traffic equally. This sounds dry and sort of boring, but it's crucial to information freedom. As one of the holdout FCC commissioners, Mignon Clyburn, says: "Net Neutrality is the First Amendment of the Internet." Without this basic protection, we're at the mercy of big corporations to control the speed with which we access the web—and we're all just waiting to find out what Comcast and Verizon will do with that power. This is a threat to all the independent voices who've used the Internet to connect and to make themselves heard, and especially for communities and activists of color.

Then there are the social media companies themselves— the corporate behemoths that shape the information we see every day. Facebook in particular has transformed the media landscape, driving a series of destructive trends in the media industry and exerting enormous power over the news we consume while taking almost no responsibility for its content or accuracy. In recent years, tweaks to Facebook's News Feed algorithm have driven dramatic surges—or collapses—in entire sectors of the media. It is, functionally, the world's biggest media company, but it's subject to none of the same regulations or expectations.

Free Press, one of the leading American organizations advocating for—wait for it—a free press, notes that rather than spreading joy by connecting billions of people, Facebook has instead divided us into warring camps, helped spread hate, misinformation, propaganda, and has consistently taken advantage of people's personal data, all with "little accountability, transparency or consequence." In 2016, Facebook accepted ads from Putin-linked sources explicitly aimed at dividing Americans and throwing the election to Donald Trump.[36] There's been no real accountability and there's no reason to believe it won't happen again in 2020.

The ad revenue that used to support well-staffed local and national newsrooms is now flooding these online platforms. While Facebook and Google grow, newsrooms shrink, and federal legislators and regulators do little or nothing about it. So, unfortunately, no, the Internet will not save us.

In short, we're facing a set of interlinking problems. The national media environment, which in the mid-twentieth century provided a set of agreed-upon facts to the American electorate, has fractured. The rise of a national conservative propaganda operation has systematically misinformed the public and shifted debate to the right. At the same time, the economic

---

36. It worked! :(

model for independent journalism, especially local journalism, no longer exists. As local news has died off, conservative media conglomerates have absorbed an increasing share of that local coverage. At the same time, the free and open Internet is under attack and massive profit-driven social media platforms hasten the spread of misinformation in relentless competition for the next ad dollar.

Whew! That's a lot of problems. Do you feel a little anxious now? Maybe you need to take a minute. That's fine. Put down the book. Close your eyes for a second. Breathe.

OK, now let's talk about how we're going to fix it.

The Solution

There's no one silver bullet for saving American media. So we're going to offer up two bullets: regulate and break up the conglomerates to unleash more competition, and invest in a new era of independent American media.

Let's start with breaking up the big tech and media conglomerates. The tech giants are too big, and it's a big problem. Today, 70 percent of all web traffic on the Internet flows through Facebook and Google, and that translates into a whole bunch of ad revenue. Facebook had just shy of $56 billion in revenue in 2018, and Google had about $137 billion. If Google were a state, that revenue would make it the second largest— just behind California in terms of revenue. Sinclair Broadcast Group for its part is one of the largest broadcasting companies in the country, and it has plans to expand even further. They're huge, and they use their power to extract wealth from us and, purposefully or not, undermine our democracy.

We need to break up the megacorporations and enact regulations to protect the American public from their excesses. A hundred years ago, Republican president Teddy Roosevelt trumpeted the importance of breaking up and regulating big corporations to protect the public interest. In his day he was going after the oil, beef-packing, and other industries, but the logic behind breaking up the conglomerates ("bad trusts") was all the same.[37] When corporations get big—we mean really big—they can use their bigness to squash competitors, prey on consumers, and avoid accountability. Roosevelt took this to heart and went toe-to-toe with corporate giants like Standard Oil that were exploiting their monopoly power precisely this way.

The dangers of megacorporations are as real today with big media and tech conglomerates like Sinclair Broadcast Group, Facebook, and Google.[38] As media and tech companies get bigger and bigger, profits soar, and we all lose. These are the Standard Oil of our day, and the harm they do to consumers, society, and democracy is just as real. The solution now is the solution a hundred years ago: break up these massive corporations to loosen their stranglehold on the American public. In their place we'll get more competition and more options for

---

37. Fun historical fact: Roosevelt's successor, William Howard Taft, was actually a much more zealous anti-monopolist, but he's mainly remembered for an apocryphal story about getting stuck in a bathtub.

38. This very book is being published by an imprint of Simon & Schuster, which is both one of the largest publishers in the world and is also owned by one of those giant media conglomerates, CBS Corporation. We'll see if this footnote survives editing!

all of us, and we'll reduce the power that any single massive private corporation has over American society.

To promote free and open competition, breaking up these bad trusts needs to go hand in hand with a plan to promote a media system that gives more people a voice in our democracy. That starts with reinstating net neutrality. It's a basic step to protect freedom of the Internet, and it should be enshrined into law so that no future Republican administration can use the FCC to revoke it again.[39]

Proponents of breaking up Facebook include an early Facebook investor and mentor to founder Mark Zuckerberg, who wrote that the platform and its peers like Google harm "public health, democracy, privacy and competition." One of Facebook's original cofounders (and a former roommate of Zuckerberg's) also supports breaking up the tech giant, writing in 2019 that "we are a nation with a tradition of reining in monopolies, no matter how well intentioned the leaders of these companies may be. Mark's power is unprecedented and un-American."

So we've taken on the harm done by the tech and media giants, but how do we support real, crucial journalism? We start by acknowledging that independent local and national journalism is a societal good. We need it for our democracy to function. And, unfortunately, private markets aren't producing enough of it. The twentieth-century economic model for quality journalism—especially quality local journalism—is not

---

39. After taking the House in 2018, the Democrats passed a bill to do precisely this.

coming back. If the market isn't going to supply this societal good on its own, that means we need public investment.

There hasn't been a major new investment in public media since the Public Broadcasting Act of 1967. That legislation created stuff you might just take for granted now—the Corporation for Public Broadcasting, the Public Broadcasting Service (PBS), and National Public Radio (NPR). Is the media environment the same as it was half a century ago? Of course not. It's been completely transformed in all the ways we described above. So why haven't we reimagined how to support new public services in this new media environment?

It may sound crazy, but why not try revitalizing journalism in America by *investing* in journalism in America? Compared to our peer democracies, the United States drastically under-invests in media. Every year America spends about $3 per person in public funds for public broadcasting—around the cost of a venti regular coffee at Starbucks once a year.[40] By comparison, Germany invests more than $140 per person per year. That's a lot of coffee.

A big reason America has such a crumbling media infrastructure is because we don't pay for it. Imagine an alternative: a real commitment to actually creating a healthy media environment that produces an informed electorate. McChesney supports the creation of a new universal media voucher that could be used at any nonprofit media source. All Americans would get an annual $200 voucher that they could donate to

---

40. Perhaps unsurprisingly, Trump has repeatedly proposed eliminating even this meager funding.

the nonprofit media source of their choice—almost literally democratizing the media by allowing people to vote with their vouchers for the media they want to see. Free Press proposes a big new "Public Interest Media Endowment" that would support local journalism, investigative reporting, media literacy, noncommercial social networks, civic-technology projects, and news and information for underserved communities. This seems worth the cost of a few more cups of coffee to us.

How could we fund this new investment in independent American media? Providing a $200 voucher to every adult American to invest in nonprofit media would cost around $40 billion per year. To add on top of that, a Public Interest Media Endowment would cost just a couple of billion more. We could pay for it like the modern GOP pays for just about everything it wants, from military increases to corporate welfare: by simply racking up more debt. Or you could reverse some small portion of the Trump tax cuts for the rich, which cost about $230 billion per year. Or if you don't like that, Free Press recommends adding a small tax on the hundreds of billions that companies like Facebook and Google collect in ad revenue.

Regardless of how we pay for it, if we want a vibrant democratic society, we need an independent and flourishing media environment. The free market isn't going to produce that for us, so public investment has to do it.

What the Naysayers Say

Supporters of big tech and media say that government shouldn't be picking winners and losers in the market, and that the companies themselves can self-regulate their behavior. Others who are more amenable to oversight still argue that breaking up companies is too extreme a move, or that the real problems will remain even if the companies are broken up into small pieces.

There will always be arguments against breaking up a monopoly. Reasonable people can disagree on where to set the threshold of "too big." But at this point, pretty much no one is prepared to argue that Facebook is having a positive effect on our media environment, or that it's successfully regulated itself. Facebook now occupies such a pivotal role in our world that slight tweaks to its algorithm can spell doom for the rest of the media ecosystem. That's just too big. And no one would argue that one company, Sinclair Broadcast Group, having functional control over so many local media markets is good for democracy. That's just too big.

The most common line of argument against public investment in reviving American media is that media should not be publicly funded. Of course some of this comes from reactionary conservative types who don't want government to spend money on anything beyond corporate subsidies and military boondoggles. The same Heritage Foundation, which helped kill Carter's democracy reform package in the 1970s and opposed the For the People Act in 2019, has come out swinging against public funding for media. They call the fifty-year-old practice of taxing Americans to fund public media "sinful and tyrannical."

But it's not just right-wing reactionaries who have concerns about publicly funded media. Authoritarianism, politicization, and bureaucratization are all risks with a publicly funded program. If government controls the media, and government is controlled by politics, won't politics infect our press? If government picks winners and losers in the media, how can it be truly free and independent? These are all valid questions.

These concerns are not new. In the 1960s, as a unified Democratic federal government was considering the Public Broadcasting Act, lawmakers worried about public funding interfering with editorial independence. In laying out the program, President Lyndon Johnson declared that the system "will be carefully guarded from government or from party control. It will be free, and it will be independent, and it will belong to all our people." Imagine if fears about independence had prevented us from creating NPR. The concerns were valid then and they're valid now—but they were also solvable then and are solvable now.

There will always be conservative hacks who bray about left-wing media bias in NPR and PBS; there's no getting around that. But fifty years later NPR is still here; PBS is still here; the Corporation for Public Broadcasting is still here. And the popularity of these institutions remains quite high. A 2018 poll found that Americans trusted PBS and NPR news more than any other news source, including networks like CBS and ABC, cable news like Fox and MSNBC, and national papers like the *New York Times* and the *Wall Street Journal*. Even GOP voters oppose cutting funding for public media by a nearly two-to-one margin. So, yes, it is indeed possible to craft a public investment for media that doesn't lose public confidence. We've done it.

Critics of voucher proposals raise a related concern: Won't right-wingers give their vouchers to right-wing hack media companies? Yes, yes, they will! By limiting eligible recipients to not-for-profit media organizations, a media voucher program could cut down on the influence of the most egregious profit-stealing fake news sites. But part of accepting that we live in a democracy is accepting that people are going to do dumb stuff, and we've got to let them. As wacky as it sounds, that's the whole theory of democracy—so why not apply it to our media too?

CONCLUSION

We're not starry-eyed idealists. What drives us now is necessity. American democracy is crumbling while the existential threats to our country and the earth mount. We have a choice between waging a long-shot fight for a real American democracy that can solve these problems or giving up. We choose to fight.

We don't have time to wait. The country faces permanent conservative control of the Senate—and, by extension, the courts—if we fail to act soon. The planet faces calamitous consequences if America fails to overcome its dysfunction and tackle climate change fast. If we fail to retake power in 2020 and build an inclusive democracy in 2021, we may not have another shot. The stakes for the country and the planet are high.

The reforms presented in this chapter are democratizing reforms: they would make our federal system of government more responsive to and representative of the people. Combined, these reforms can stave off minority, oligarchic rule in America, and each reform would reinforce the others to create an increasingly inclusive and representative democracy after Trump.

That "after Trump" part is key. President Trump will not sign any part of this blueprint into law. Nor will Senate Majority Leader Mitch McConnell allow any of the reforms in this chapter to come to a vote. The only pathway to bringing this vision off the page, through Congress, and onto the president's desk is to wrest control of our government from the reactionaries who currently control it.

We know that the post-Trump era will not come on its own. That era is within our grasp, but it will take all our combined power to successfully reach for it. The Indivisible lessons described in Section 2 are intended to guide that effort. We believe that the grassroots energy that surged after Trump's election can translate into power. Then, and only then, will we have our chance at building the democracy described in this chapter.

Even then, we know full well that the reforms laid out here will not be easy to achieve; real change never is. We know this vision for American democracy will be attacked from all sides. McConnell and establishment elected Republicans will smear it as a radical "power grab" made by political rabble-rousers. Establishment Democrats will call it unrealistic or impossible. Politicians of all stripes who have acquired power through existing structures will laugh at us, and fight to kill the reforms or blunt their impact.

But this inclusive American democracy is achievable if we demand it.

In this book, we've given you a lot of theory. We've talked about the political philosophy and strategies behind the forces undermining our republic. We've explored the history of American civic engagement. And we've laid out a blueprint of reforms that will ensure that our democratic system better represents all of us. This is complex, sometimes abstract stuff.[41]

But Indivisible is not a thought experiment. The thousands of Indivisible groups organizing themselves around the country right now are defined by action—by their energetic involvement in our democracy. Because we all know that power concedes nothing without a demand. We know that electeds can't resist the demands of their electorate indefinitely. They may try to ignore it. They may try to delay. They may try to fight back. But ultimately electeds must give in to what the people want—if the people consistently and forcefully insist on it.

This is the challenge for all of us fighting for an inclusive democracy in America. We will not save democracy by defeating Trump. We will not save democracy by winning any individual election. We will not save democracy by defeating one bad bill or by implementing one good reform.

We will save democracy by standing together in communities across the country and demanding that the system bend to the will of the people—*all* the people. We'll do this by working across lines of difference. We'll do this by organizing ourselves and partnering with others. We'll do this by leading and by following.

---

41. Sorry, we're both policy nerds at heart.

This is how we defeated the attack on the Affordable Care Act in 2017. This is how we built the blue wave in 2018. This is how we'll wage the coming battle to defeat Trump and his lackeys. And this is how we'll build a real democracy once they're gone. This is how we win.

ACKNOWLEDGMENTS

It turns out that writing a book isn't easy, and it's not a solo activity (or even a duet, in our case). Our two names are on the book spine, but every part of this book is the result of many people's time, care, attention, and generous contributions. So let's talk about who made this book possible.

The Indivisible groups. First and foremost, this book would not have happened without Indivisible group leaders around the country. Not only have they built this movement, but they also provided us with literally hundreds of stories for this book. Particular thanks to the leaders who took time for deep-dive interviews with one or both us: Indivisible East Tennessee, Indivisible Grapevine Area (Texas), Ozark Indivisible (Arkansas), Indivisible NY 27th, Prescott Indivisible (Arizona), Greater Lafayette Indivisible (Indiana), SATX Indivisible (Texas), Indivisible Action Tampa Bay (Florida), Indivisible New Orleans (Louisiana), Indivisible Lincoln County (Maine), Indivisible Las Cruces (New Mexico), Roanoke Indivisible (Virginia), Indivisible Front Range Resistance (Colorado), Indivisible Tohono (Arizona), Indivisible Nation BK (New York), Indivisible OC 48 (California), and Indivisible Greene County (Tennessee). And to the hundreds of other

Indivisibles who sent in their stories from across the country. There are just too many stories to tell from this movement, but know that, whether named or not, we're so proud to be in this movement with you.

The Indivisible national volunteers and staff. Indivisible the organization started as a collective of over one hundred volunteers: friends, colleagues, anyone who was willing to drop everything in their lives and spend the first six months of 2017 on our Slack channel. For our first few months, Indivisible was powered by the late nights and fake sick days of these dedicated volunteers, brought together by some combination of hope, fear, and a desperate need to do whatever we could. Our organization exists today because of this team. There are too many folks to name individually, but we want to specifically remember Julia Fox, who led Indivisible's early organizing efforts and who passed away tragically in 2018. Thank you, Julia.

Today, Indivisible is a national organization dedicated to supporting this decentralized Indivisible movement. When we talk about how we flexed our movement muscle to kill Trumpcare, how we turned the tax scam into a political liability, or how we helped build a historic blue wave, that "we" isn't Leah and Ezra; it's us and the dozens of members of our staff who are in this fight together with us. We can't possibly recognize the specific and amazing individual contributions of every team member, but we can thank them for building this movement and bearing with us as we attempted to simultaneously run the organization and write a book.

The brain trust. Think tankers, political scientists, policy experts, advocates, academics, and other smart and attractive people helped us in conceiving of and crafting the diagnosis and reforms presented in this book. We particularly want to thank (in alphabetical order!) Lee Drutman, Judy Estrin, Brian Fallon, Marshall Ganz, Christie George, Martin Gilen, Jeremy Haile, Hahrie Han, Charlotte Hill, Marielena Hincapié, Tim Karr, Nancy MacLean, Bob McChesney, Sean McElwee, Heather McGhee, Ian Millhiser, Rick Perlstein, Tom Perriello, Sabeel Rahman, Jack Santucci, Daniel Schlozman, Waleed Shahid, Theda Skocpol, and Todd Tucker, and of course our national policy director, Angel Padilla; our national political director, María Urbina; our chief communications officer, Sarah Dohl; and our chief operating officer, Matt Traldi, for their guidance and in some cases careful review of early versions of our drafts.

The book team. Our editors, Jen McDonald, Yochi Dreazen, and Bob Bland, were extraordinarily helpful throughout the drafting process, from initial outlining to final product, as was our publisher, Julia Cheiffetz. Our agent, Gary Morris, helped demystify the publishing world and shepherded us through the whole process. Our fact-checker, Alexis Sottile, ran a fine-tooth comb through the manuscript, catching everything from wrong dates to misremembered events. Abby Porter arranged, recorded, and transcribed all the Indivisible group leader interviews and helped out on countless tasks along the way to ensure that this book could actually become a real book. Emily Reyes led the painstaking process of converting all our citations into usable endnotes. Our family members were a core part of the book team, too, reviewing drafts and debating various titles and cover designs along the way (and also helping us make it through the past three years alive and well). That includes Sara Anderson, Shayna Brown, Megan Conley, Mark Greenberg, Rosa Greenberg, Danny Levin, Ronda Levin, and Gabby McEntee.

We have certainly failed to include everyone who helped make this book a reality. That's on us, as are any and all errors that remain in the final text. In the grand tradition of Indivisible, we hope you'll helpfully point out the errors so we can fix them in the next edition. As always, we're building this all together.

NOTES

INTRODUCTION

2 **when he attacked immigrants as rapists and drug-carrying criminals:** "Here's Donald Trump's Presidential Announcement Speech." *Time*. June 16, 2015. https://time.com/3923128/donald-trump-announcement-speech/.

6 **Trump lackey cited America's Japanese internment camps:** Bromwich, Jonah Engel. "Trump Camp's Talk of Registry and Japanese Internment Raises Muslims' Fears." *New York Times*. November 17, 2016, sec. U.S. https://www.nytimes.com/2016/11/18/us/politics/japanese-internment-muslim-registry.html.

6 **his plan was to find common ground with Trump on infrastructure:** Steinhauer, Jennifer. "Senate Democrats' Surprising Strategy: Trying to Align with Trump." *New York Times*. November 16, 2016, sec. U.S. https://www.nytimes.com/2016/11/17/us/politics/democrats-house-senate.html.

7 **The Tea Party was super-racist and sometimes violent:** Miller, Carlin. "Tea Party Getting Violent? 10 House Dems Report Threats, Vandalism." CBS News. March 26, 2010. https://www.cbsnews.com/news/tea-party-getting-violent-10-house-dems-report-threats-vandalism/.

10 **Robert Reich posted it to his Facebook page:** Reich, Robert. "Indivisible Town Hall Tip: How to Respond to Evasive Members of Congress." Facebook. July 3, 2017. https://www.facebook.com/RBReich/videos /1621262431219680/?__xts__[0]=68.ARDO6-Zmfz2Ak3aXUaVsTlU _byG8g2-VixDGhlEn_NXyIG-mVrJeA-VUeiawbRlHcCWAbyQohBte C2SKvwhbgHKktewfKWbbhFulmAjMF3_UodgnDJBEYO_MErqXR -_mALO4H8jt5dA1UJJx6hkwn95aSIszOxFYlSNbfmuSEbyK-2PoYBkjo Los5BdHw5tLcrkikVmqU5IuF4oBSxt22wtOS9NbMvW43Dq_4YIWqEX CTrtcp7Wpbq9WNCjmxai-NL9DzKw2UR24KiGx5kLcHke0CEM6bQ3w 6Y8TrUswQYpnc_pyw0xCGi9ZVzaaYDMEczlHglVAeuOELmurTjR5aw SHsdw_rxQlfFJnyw&__tn__=H-R.

CHAPTER 1: THE PROBLEM:
A BUCKLING AND RIGGED DEMOCRACY

30 **wrote an essay called "The Perils of Presidentialism.":** Linz, Juan J. 1990. "The Perils of Presidentialism." *Journal of Democracy* (Johns Hopkins University Press) 1 (1): 51–69. https://doi.org/10.1353/jod.1990.0011.

32 **"segregation is not humiliating":** Matthews, Dylan. "Woodrow Wilson Was Extremely Racist—Even by the Standards of His Time." Vox. November 20, 2015. https://www.vox.com/policy-and-politics/2015/11/20/9766896/woodrow-wilson-racist.

32 **a concession to segregationist Southern Democrats:** Kaiser, Robert G. " 'Fear Itself: The New Deal and the Origins of Our Time' by Ira Katznelson." *Washington Post.* March 1, 2013, sec. Opinions. https://www.washingtonpost.com/opinions/fear-itself-the-new-deal-and-the-origins-of-our-time-by-ira-katznelson/2013/03/01/a4030f2c-7b72-11e2-a044-676856536b40_story.html.

33 **"walk forthrightly into the bright sunshine of human rights":** Traub, James. "The Party of Hubert Humphrey." *Atlantic.* April 7, 2018. https://www.theatlantic.com/politics/archive/2018/04/did-hubert-humphrey-doom-the-democratic-party/557282/.

34 **"we just delivered the South to the Republican Party":** Oreskes, Michael. "Civil Rights Act Leaves Deep Mark on the American Political Landscape." *New York Times.* July 2, 1989, sec. U.S. https://www.nytimes.com/1989/07/02/us/civil-rights-act-leaves-deep-mark-on-the-american-political-landscape.html.

34 **a backlash among white evangelicals:** Balmer, Randall. "The Real Origins of the Religious Right." Politico. May 27, 2014. https://politi.co/2QalpUg.

35 **liberal Republicans and conservative Democrats retired:** Parker, Clifton B. "Politicians More Polarized Than Voters, Stanford Political Scientist Finds." Stanford News. December 20, 2017. https://news.stanford.edu/2017/12/20/political-parties-polarized-voters/.

42 **Republicans have *vaulted* to the right:** "The Polarization of the Congressional Parties." Voteview.com. March 21, 2015. https://legacy.voteview.com/political_polarization_2014.htm.

42 **"the core of the problem lies with the Republican Party":** Mann, Thomas E., and Norman J. Ornstein. "Let's Just Say It: The Republicans Are the Problem." *Washington Post.* April 27, 2012, sec. Opinions. https://www.washingtonpost.com/opinions/lets-just-say-it-the-republicans-are-the-problem/2012/04/27/gIQAxCVUlT_story.html.

42 **Republican Party is the "root cause":** Mann, Thomas E., and Norman J.

Ornstein. "How the Republicans Broke Congress." *New York Times*. December 2, 2017, sec. Opinion. https://www.nytimes.com/2017/12/02/opinion/sunday/republicans-broke-congress-politics.html.

42 **brothers spent years in "bare-knuckle legal brawls":** Schulman, Daniel. "The 'Other' Koch Brother." *Vanity Fair*. May 19, 2014. https://www.vanityfair.com/style/society/2014/05/frederick-koch-brothers.

43 **reshape America in line with their radical reactionary agenda:** If you want to go deeper on this, check out Jane Mayer's *New Yorker* article "Covert Operations" and her book *Dark Money*; Nancy MacLean's book *Democracy in Chains*; and Theda Skocpol and Alexander Hertel-Fernandez's research on the Koch funding network, "The Koch Network and Republican Party Extremism." In short, it's scary, well-documented stuff.

43 **Stalin's Russia and Germany during the rise of the Third Reich:** Confessore, Nicholas. "Father of Koch Brothers Helped Build Nazi Oil Refinery, Book Says." *New York Times*. January 11, 2016, sec. U.S. https://www.nytimes.com/2016/01/12/us/politics/father-of-koch-brothers-helped-build-nazi-oil-refinery-book-says.html.

43 **platform he ran on included, among other initiatives:** "Astounding: David Koch's 1980 VP Run: Kill Medicare, Social Security, Minimum Wage, Public Schools." Daily Kos. April 10, 2014. https://www.dailykos.com/story/2014/4/10/1291095/-Astounding-Charles-Koch-s-1980-VP-Run-Kill-Medicare-Soc-Sec-Min-Wage-Public-Ed.

44 **Biff was based on Donald Trump:** Stuart, Tessa. "'Back to the Future' Writer: Biff Is Donald Trump." *Rolling Stone* (blog). October 21, 2015. https://www.rollingstone.com/politics/politics-news/back-to-the-future-writer-biff-is-donald-trump-190408/.

45 **funded conservative academic institutions and think tanks:** "Lawmaking Under the Influence of Very Special Interests." Progress Florida, n.d. Accessed July 30, 2019. https://www.progressflorida.org/sites/all/files/thinktankreport/spn-report.pdf.

45 **A real argument made in a real book:** Lott, John R., Jr. 2000. *More Guns, Less Crime: Understanding Crime and Gun Control Laws*. University of Chicago Press.

46 **Carter governed as a conservative Democrat:** Khan, Jibran. "Jimmy Carter's Conservatism That History Forgets." *National Review*. May 10, 2018. https://www.nationalreview.com/2018/05/jimmy-carter-more-conservative-administration-than-history-remembers/.

46 **trumpeting fiscal conservatism and deregulation:** Leonard, Andrew. "No, Jimmy Carter Did It." Salon. June 4, 2009. https://www.salon.com/2009/06/04/jimmy_carter_did_it/.

46 **the "era of big government is over":** Mitchell, Alison. "State of the Union: The Overview; Clinton Offers Challenge to Nation, Declaring, 'Era of Big Government Is Over.'" *New York Times*. January 24, 1996, sec. U.S. https://www.nytimes.com/1996/01/24/us/state-union-overview-clinton-offers-challenge-nation-declaring-era-big.html.

46 **health care proposals of the conservative Heritage Foundation:** Krugman, Paul. "Heritage on Health, 1989." *New York Times*. The Conscience of a Liberal (blog). July 30, 2017. https://krugman.blogs.nytimes.com/2017/07/30/heritage-on-health-1989/.

48 **Lee Atwater explained the strategy:** Rosenthal, Andrew. "Lee Atwater's 'Southern Strategy' Interview." *New York Times*. Taking Note (blog). November 14, 2012. https://takingnote.blogs.nytimes.com/2012/11/14/lee-atwaters-southern-strategy-interview/.

48 **Willie Horton:** Withers, Rachel. "George H. W. Bush's 'Willie Horton' Ad Will Always Be the Reference Point for Dog-Whistle Racism." Vox. December 1, 2018. https://www.vox.com/2018/12/1/18121221/george-hw-bush-willie-horton-dog-whistle-politics.

50 **one *New York Times* article on Trump's closing argument:** Shear, Michael D., and Julie Hirschfeld Davis. "As Midterm Vote Nears, Trump Reprises a Favorite Message: Fear Immigrants." *New York Times*. November 1, 2018, sec. U.S. https://www.nytimes.com/2018/11/01/us/politics/trump-immigration.html.

50 **thirty were men, and all thirty-one were white:** Segers, Grace. "Democrats Have More Diverse Slate of New House Members Than Republicans." CBS News. November 14, 2018. https://www.cbsnews.com/news/democrats-have-a-more-diverse-slate-of-new-house-members-than-republicans/.

50 **precisely one Black Republican was elected:** Will Hurd, a representative from Texas, won election in 2018. The only other Black Republican serving in Congress is South Carolina senator Tim Scott.

51 **Today, whites make up about 60 percent of the population:** Poston, Dudley, and Rogelio Sáenz. "The US White Majority Will Soon Disappear Forever." Chicago Reporter. May 16, 2019. https://www.chicagoreporter.com/the-us-white-majority-will-soon-disappear-forever/.

51 **In 1960, there were fewer than 10 million immigrants:** Radford, Jynnah, and Luis Noe-Bustamante. "Immigrants in America: Trend Data and Demographics, 1960–2017 | Pew Research Center." Pew Research Center (blog). June 3, 2019. https://www.pewhispanic.org/2019/06/03/facts-on-u-s-immigrants-trend-data/.

51 **And this proportion is growing:** "The Foreign-Born Population in the

United States." 2011. Census.gov. CSPAN Presentation. https://www.census
.gov/newsroom/pdf/cspan_fb_slides.pdf.

51 **America's richest 1 percent took home about 10 percent:** Stone, Chad,
Danilo Trisi, Arloc Sherman, and Roderick Taylor. "A Guide to Statistics on
Historical Trends in Income Inequality." Center on Budget and Policy Priorities. Policy Futures. Updated December 11, 2018, 23. https://www.cbpp
.org/sites/default/files/atoms/files/11-28-11pov_0.pdf.

51 **Today, the top 1 percent take home more than 20 percent:** "Income Inequality." Inequality.org, n.d. Accessed July 16, 2019. https://inequality
.org/facts/income-inequality/.

51 **the total number of white people:** Sáenz, Rogelio, and Kenneth M. Johnson.
"White Deaths Exceed Births in a Majority of U.S. States." Applied Population
Lab. June 18, 2018. https://apl.wisc.edu/data-briefs/natural-decrease-18.

51 **racial wealth gap is huge and growing:** Collins, Chuck, Dedrick
Asante-Muhammed, Josh Hoxie, and Sabrina Terry. "Report: Dreams Deferred." Institute for Policy Studies. January 13, 2019. https://ips-dc.org
/racial-wealth-divide-2019/.

53 **broader Southern strategy shift in the 1970s:** Frances Fox Piven and Richard A. Cloward provide an overview of this transition in their book *Why
Americans Still Don't Vote*, which focuses on the fight to expand voting rights,
leading ultimately to the 1993 Motor Voter Act.

53 **the "Lenin of social conservatism":** Lapham, Lewis H. September 2004.
"Tentacles of Rage: The Republican Propaganda Mill, a Brief History." *Harp-
er's* 309 (1852): 16. https://msuweb.montclair.edu/~furrg/gned/lapham
tentacles04.pdf.

54 **lock people—especially Black and brown voters—out of the system:** If
you're interested in a history of GOP attacks on voting rights in the past several decades, check out Ari Berman's *Give Us the Ballot: The Modern Struggle
for Voting Rights in America*. In it he tracks the GOP's multi-decade legal assault to undermine the Voting Rights Act. A central antagonist in Berman's
history is John Roberts, a twenty-six-year-old Reagan administration staffer
who helped wage a campaign inside the Justice Department to weaken the
Voting Rights Act—and who would go on, as chief justice of the Supreme
Court, to write the majority opinion gutting the Voting Rights Act in 2013.

54 **calling voter suppression to dampen progressive turnout "a great idea":**
Brice-Saddler, Michael. "GOP Senator: It's a 'Great Idea' to Make It Harder
for 'Liberal Folks' to Vote." *Washington Post.* November 16, 2018, sec. Politics. https://www.washingtonpost.com/politics/2018/11/16/cindy-hyde
-smith-its-great-idea-make-it-harder-liberal-folks-vote/.

54 *twenty-five states* **enacted reforms making it harder to vote:** "New Voting
    Restrictions in America." Brennan Center for Justice. Updated January 7, 2019.
    https://www.brennancenter.org/sites/default/files/legislation/New%
    20Voting%20Restrictions.pdf.

54 **"worst voter suppression we've seen in the modern era.":** Roth, Zachary,
    and Wendy R. Weiser. "This Is the Worst Voter Suppression We've Seen in
    the Modern Era." Brennan Center for Justice. November 2, 2018. https://
    www.brennancenter.org/blog/worst-voter-suppression-weve-seen-modern
    -era?utm_source=facebook&utm_medium=socialmedia.

55 **alleged to have purged more than 340,000 voters from the rolls:** Durkin,
    Erin. "GOP Candidate Improperly Purged 340,000 from Georgia Voter Rolls,
    Investigation Claims." *Guardian.* October 19, 2018, sec. U.S. News. https://
    www.theguardian.com/us-news/2018/oct/19/georgia-governor-race-voter
    -suppression-brian-kemp.

55 **preemptively weakening the not-yet-inaugurated Democrat:** Hersher,
    Rebecca. "North Carolina Governor Signs Law Limiting Power of His
    Successor." NPR. December 16, 2016. https://www.npr.org/sections/the
    two-way/2016/12/16/505872501/north-carolina-governor-signs-law-limiting
    -power-of-his-successor.

55 **Republican Speaker of the Wisconsin State Assembly answered honestly:**
    Beauchamp, Zack. "The Wisconsin Power Grab Is Part of a Bigger Republi-
    can Attack on Democracy." Vox. December 6, 2018. https://www.vox.com
    /policy-and-politics/2018/12/6/18127332/wisconsin-state-republican-power
    -grab-democracy.

56 **prioritizing instead the interests of a plutocratic few in the donor class:**
    This is outside the scope of what we want to cover here, but there are two
    excellent books on just how unrepresentative and unresponsive American
    government is to the public will: *Democracy in America?* by the political sci-
    entists Benjamin Page and Martin Gilens; and *Winner-Take-All Politics* by the
    political scientists Jacob Hacker and Paul Pierson. Both books are rigorous
    works by well-known academics with fancy credentials, and both focus on
    how the political system in modern America systematically reflects the inter-
    ests of elites rather than middle- or lower-class Americans. Basically, if you
    have a gut feeling that American democracy is rigged in favor of the rich and
    corporations, these books provide academic research to back up that feeling.

CHAPTER 2: THE SOLUTION: CONSTITUENT POWER

63 **with posters of the congressman with devil's horns:** King, Michael.
    "Health-Care Hysteria Dogs Doggett." *Austin Chronicle.* August 7, 2009.
    https://www.austinchronicle.com/news/2009-08-07/819416/.

64 **relationship between racial animus and Tea Party affiliation:** Xavier, Jonathan. "How Racial Threat Has Galvanized the Tea Party." Stanford Graduate School of Business. July 15, 2016. https://www.gsb.stanford.edu /insights/how-racial-threat-has-galvanized-tea-party.

66 **we had people:** For a very readable blow-by-blow of the rise of grassroots energy, take a look at Ryan Grim's book *We've Got People*.

69 **gut the Office of Congressional Ethics:** Lipton, Eric. "With No Warning, House Republicans Vote to Gut Independent Ethics Office." *New York Times*. January 2, 2017, sec. U.S. https://www.nytimes.com/2017/01/02/us /politics/with-no-warning-house-republicans-vote-to-hobble-independent -ethics-office.html.

72 **many were voting consistently to approve Trump's nominees:** Andrews, Wilson. "How Each Senator Voted on Trump's Cabinet and Administration Nominees." *New York Times*. January 31, 2017, sec. U.S. https://www.ny times.com/interactive/2017/01/31/us/politics/trump-cabinet-confirmation -votes.html.

72 **a plan to focus on infrastructure:** Short, Aaron. "Chuck Schumer Under Fire from Left-Wing Activists." *New York Post*. January 28, 2017. https://ny post.com/2017/01/28/chuck-schumer-under-fire-from-left-wing-activists/.

73 **But that all changed quickly:** Caldwell, Leigh Ann. "Democrats Sour on Trump Infrastructure Proposals." NBC News. June 5, 2017. https://www .nbcnews.com/politics/congress/democrats-sour-trump-infrastructure -proposals-n768446.

73 **an Islamophobe who had been an apologist for torture:** Wise, Lindsay. "New CIA Director Mike Pompeo on Torture, Muslims, Terror, Iran, NSA Spying." McClatchy DC Bureau. November 18, 2016. https://www.mcclatchydc .com/news/politics-government/election/article115635853.html.

75 **he'd literally written some of the history himself:** Skocpol, Theda, Marshall Ganz, and Ziad Munson. 2000. "A Nation of Organizers: The Institutional Origins of Civic Voluntarism in the United States." *American Political Science Review* 94 (3): 527–46. https://doi.org/10.2307/2585829.

76 **Maybe this isn't sexy:** Robert Putnam, a political scientist at Harvard, actually did write a sexy analysis of American civic engagement: *Bowling Alone*. Well, "sexiness" is in the eye of the beholder, but the book was hugely popular and launched a thousand think pieces on the decline of American society. But whereas Putnam focused on the decline of basic social ties (e.g., bowling leagues), the analysis in "A Nation of Organizers" focuses on the bygone era of nationally coordinated, locally led civic associations with direct ties to democratic participation. This analysis, while far less known outside the halls of academia, is far more relevant to the current predicament facing our democ-

racy. Don't get us wrong: it's all well and good to have a bowling league. But bowling leagues themselves don't defeat fascism or concentrated corporate power.

76 **gathered together locally and often across class lines:** Skocpol, Theda. 2003. *Diminished Democracy: From Membership to Management in American Civic Life*. SOE Curriculum Lab. University of Oklahoma Press.

77 **"much grander organized endeavors":** Ibid.

78 **some of these groups were violent, nativist, and racist.:** Ibid.

78 **all-white membership policy into the 1970s:** Graham, Fred P. "Fraternal Clubs That Bar Negroes Are Held Taxable." *New York Times*. January 12, 1972, sec. Archives. https://www.nytimes.com/1972/01/12/archives/fraternal -clubs-that-bar-negroes-are-held-taxable-court-forbids.html.

78 **Social Security Act systematically excluded workers of color:** Katznelson, Ira. 2013. *Fear Itself: The New Deal and the Origins of Our Time*. First Edition. Liveright Publishing Corporation.

78 **bestowing the pen in recognition of the Eagles':** "Remarks by Hon. Jim McDermott 'Commending the Fraternal Order of Eagles on Its 110th Anniversary.'" *Congressional Record*. September 23, 2008. https://www.congress .gov/crec/2008/09/24/modified/CREC-2008-09-24-pt1-PgE1869-4.htm.

81 **5,600 in 1959 and more than 22,000 in 1990:** Skocpol, Theda. 2003. *Diminished Democracy: From Membership to Management in American Civic Life*. SOE Curriculum Lab. University of Oklahoma Press.

82 **With the rise of direct mail:** Karpf, David. 2012. *The MoveOn Effect: The Unexpected Transformation of American Political Advocacy*. Oxford Studies in Digital Politics. Oxford University Press. https://books.google.ca /books?id=xlifgdlbCIkC.

82 **building connections to membership bases of millions:** The evolution of digital organizations is charted with great insight by Dave Karpf in *The MoveOn Effect*. Karpf describes the rise of digital organizing hubs whose work and fund-raising depend on their lists of members, millions of people connected to a central national organization through emails, cell phone numbers, and social media followers. These national organizations use their lists to mobilize their membership to make donations, sign petitions, or take other off-line action.

CHAPTER 3: HOW TO MAKE CONGRESS LISTEN

95 **Congress was less popular than toenail fungus:** Jensen, Tom. "Americans Like Witches, the IRS, and Even Hemorrhoids Better than Congress." Public Policy Polling. October 8, 2013, 42. https://www.publicpolicypolling.com

/polls/americans-like-witches-the-irs-and-even-hemorrhoids-better-than
-congress/.

96 **Members of Congress have reelection rates of about 90 percent:** "Reelection Rates Over the Years." OpenSecrets.org. Center for Responsive Politics. 2018. https://www.opensecrets.org/overview/reelect.php.

104 **Ryan gushed that Trump will lead a "unified Republican government":** LoBianco, Tom. "Ryan: Trump to Lead 'Unified Republican Government.'" CNN. November 9, 2016. https://www.cnn.com/2016/11/09/politics/paul-ryan-says-trump-will-lead-unified-republican-government/index.html.

106 **he groused in a meeting with local conservative activists:** Murphy, Tim. "The Women Are in My Grill No Matter Where I Go." *Mother Jones* (blog). January 31, 2017. https://www.motherjones.com/politics/2017/01/dave-brat-women-obamacare-town-halls/.

106 **they'd go ahead without him if he refused to show up:** Remmers, Vanessa, and Patrick Wilson. "Meet the Women Who Are up in Dave Brat's Grill." *Richmond Times-Dispatch*. February 19, 2017. https://www.richmond.com/news/virginia/meet-the-women-who-are-up-in-dave-brat-s/article_c41b47cb-736a-58e4-9448-b99e8f7bac11.html.

106 **Coffman sneaked out a back door and fled the scene:** Stern, Mark Joseph. "GOP Congressman, Overwhelmed by Constituents Concerned About ACA Repeal, Sneaks out of Event Early." Slate. January 15, 2017. https://slate.com/news-and-politics/2017/01/rep-mike-coffman-sneaks-out-of-event-early-as-constituents-ask-about-aca-repeal.html.

107 **Duncan flatly refused their request for a town hall:** Dorman, Travis, and Rachel Ohm. "U.S. Rep. Duncan Rejects Town Hall Requests, Citing Extremists." *Knoxville News Sentinel*. February 6, 2017. https://www.knoxnews.com/story/news/politics/2017/02/06/us-rep-jimmy-duncan-rejects-town-hall-requests-citing-extremists-kooks/97525388/.

107 **"Duncan calling me a kook and a radical, I was heartbroken":** Bales-Sherrod, Lesli. "'Out of the Shadows': Indivisible East Tennessee Brings Together Like-Minded Progressives." *Daily Times*. February 12, 2018. https://www.thedailytimes.com/news/out-of-the-shadows-indivisible-east-tennessee-brings-together-like/article_8db64d13-f954-5751-b77e-55f35c7e96a7.html.

107 **staged a well-covered event outside his office, "Kookfest":** Ackerson, Leslie. "Duncan Protesters Collect Donation in Honor of Rep's Brother-in-Law." WBIR News. February 10, 2017. https://www.wbir.com/article/news/local/duncan-protesters-collect-donation-in-honor-of-reps-brother-in-law/51-406950584.

109 **Senator Gardner was trying to hide from his constituents:** Bush, Stan. "Sen. Gardner Moves Office to a Federal Courthouse." CBS Denver (blog). August 4, 2017. https://denver.cbslocal.com/2017/08/04/cory-gardner-office-federal-courthouse/.

111 **went ahead and put town halls on the books:** Lowry, Rich. "Town Hall Protests—Democrats Echo 2009 Tea Party Protests." National Review. February 14, 2017. https://www.nationalreview.com/2017/02/town-hall-protests-democrats-echo-2009-tea-party-protests/.

112 **with chants of "Do your job!":** Hanrahan, Mark. "'Do Your Job!': Oversight Chairman Faces Furious Crowd." NBC News. February 10, 2017. https://www.nbcnews.com/news/us-news/rep-jason-chaffetz-faces-angry-town-hall-crowd-utah-n719231.

113 **"I will die. That's not hyperbole":** Thompson, Doug. "'I Will Die,' Springdale Woman Tells Cotton." Arkansas Online. February 23, 2017. www.arkansasonline.com/news/2017/feb/23/i-will-die-springdale-woman-tells-cotto/.

116 **"a very paid, Astroturf-type movement":** Schor, Elana, and Rachael Bade. "Inside the Protest Movement That Has Republicans Reeling." Politico. February 10, 2017. http://politi.co/2AogOri.

116 **Brat urged the press to "Google 'Indivisible'":** Riddell, Kelly. "Meet 'Indivisible,' the Progressive Organization Behind the Raucous GOP Town-Halls." *Washington Times*. February 22, 2017. https://www.washingtontimes.com/news/2017/feb/22/meet-indivisible-progressive-organization-behind-r/.

117 **exposés "revealing" the secret playbook:** Gizzi, John. "Newsmax Exposes Group Behind Chaos at GOP Town Hall Meetings." Newsmax. February 24, 2017. https://www.newsmax.com/Newsfront/Town-Halls-GOP-Indivisible/2017/02/24/id/775464/.

117 **Got me!:** Lucas, Fred. "'Indivisible,' with George Soros Ties, Targets Republicans." Daily Signal. February 10, 2017. https://www.dailysignal.com/2017/02/10/indivisible-with-ties-to-george-soros-sows-division-against-trump-gop-lawmakers/.

119 **denouncing the moms as a "mob" of "unruly activists":** Kirkland, Allegra. "GOP Rep. Claims 'Assault' on Staffer By 'Mob' Staging Valentine's Day Protest." Talking Points Memo. February 15, 2017. https://talkingpointsmemo.com/dc/dana-rohrabacher-claims-staffer-assault-protesters-valentines-day.

119 **handwritten note Frelinghuysen had sent to a board member:** Sol-

omon, Nancy. "N.J. Activist Says GOP Congressman's Complaint Forced Her to Quit Her Job." NPR. May 16, 2017. https://www.npr .org/2017/05/16/528570746/n-j-activist-says-congressmans-complaint -forced-her-to-resign.

121 **to represent their no-show Republican congressman:** Wilson, Jennifer. "Angry Constituents Bring Chicken to Town Hall." FOX 47: Lansing & Jackson. February 24, 2017. https://www.fox47news.com/news/angry -constituents-bring-chicken-to-town-hall.

122 **The Sarasota group kayaked out to confront him:** Wise, Lindsay. "Activists Confront Republican Lawmakers Hundreds of Miles from Home." State. May 15, 2017. https://www.thestate.com/news/politics-government/article 150667762.html.

122 **"Laughter was our greatest weapon against the regime":** Popovic, Srdja, and Matthew I. Miller. 2015. *Blueprint for Revolution: How to Use Rice Pudding, Lego Men, and Other Nonviolent Techniques to Galvanize Communities, Overthrow Dictators, or Simply Change the World.* Spiegel & Grau.

126 **Trumpcare's approval ratings kept falling:** Pramuk, Jacob. "Rough Series of Polls Show Americans Broadly Disapprove of GOP Health-Care Plan." CNBC. June 28, 2017. https://www.cnbc.com/2017/06/28/senate-gop -health-care-bill-has-dismal-approval-rating-poll.html.

126 **A frustrated Ryan gave a speech:** Conway, Madeline. "Ryan: 'Obamacare Is the Law of the Land' for Foreseeable Future." Politico. March 24, 2017. https://www.politico.com/story/2017/03/obamacare-repeal-failed-paul -ryan-reaction-236478.

126 **Trumpcare had a staggeringly low 31 percent approval rating:** Kirzinger, Ashley, Bianca DiJulio, Liz Hamel, Elise Sugarman, and Mollyann Brodie. "Kaiser Health Tracking Poll—May 2017: The AHCA's Proposed Changes to Health Care." Henry J. Kaiser Family Foundation (blog). May 31, 2017. https://www.kff.org/health-costs/report/kaiser-health-tracking-poll -may-2017-the-ahcas-proposed-changes-to-health-care/.

126 **without time for most of the Republican caucus to even understand:** Cone, Allen. "Ryan: Claims House Rushed to Replace Obamacare a 'Bogus Attack.'" UPI. May 7, 2017. https://www.upi.com/Top_News /US/2017/05/07/Ryan-Claims-House-rushed-to-replace-Obamacare-a -bogus-attack/8591494175953/.

126 **with just two votes to spare:** "Final Vote Results for Roll Call 256." Clerk. House.gov. May 4, 2017. http://clerk.house.gov/evs/2017/roll256.xml.

127 ***"Na na na, na na na, hey hey, goodbye!"*:** Kaplan, Thomas, and Robert Pear.

"House Passes Measure to Repeal and Replace the Affordable Care Act." *New York Times*. May 4, 2017, sec. U.S. https://www.nytimes.com/2017/05/04/us/politics/health-care-bill-vote.html.

127 **we launched the Payback Project:** "Payback Project." Payback Project, n.d. Accessed July 18, 2019. https://www.paybackproject.org/.

127 **danced around a faux-casket:** "'The Wake': Political Theater." Indivisible Las Cruces. May 13, 2017. https://nmdistrict2.com/new-events/2017/5/13/5rrvvhc8i3qa8lwbcilvldslqmcpup.

139 **"Democrats will start objecting":** Haberkorn, Jennifer. "Democrats to Halt Senate Business over Obamacare Repeal." Politico. June 19, 2017. https://www.politico.com/story/2017/06/19/democrats-stop-senate-business-obamacare-239715.

140 **Disability activists stormed Republican offices:** Stein, Perry. "Disability Advocates Arrested during Health Care Protest at McConnell's Office." *Washington Post*. June 22, 2017, sec. Public Safety. https://www.washingtonpost.com/local/public-safety/disability-advocates-arrested-during-health-care-protest-at-mcconnells-office/2017/06/22/f5dd9992-576f-11e7-ba90-f5875b7d1876_story.html.

140 **the Senate wouldn't consider the Trumpcare bill:** Armour, Stephanie, and Kristina Peterson. "Short on Backers, GOP Delays Vote on Health Bill." *Wall Street Journal*. June 27, 2017, sec. Politics. https://www.wsj.com/articles/senate-health-bill-vote-delayed-until-after-congress-july-4-recess-1498586899.

142 **"residents were just surprised to see Mr. Heller there":** Robertson, Campbell, Dave Philipps, Jess Bidgood, and Emily Cochrane. "Senate Republicans Lie Low on the Fourth, or Face Single-Minded Pressure." *New York Times*. July 4, 2017, sec. U.S. https://www.nytimes.com/2017/07/04/us/politics/senate-republicans-lay-low-on-the-fourth-or-face-single-minded-pressure.html.

142 **people who came up were talking about health care:** Schoenfeld, Ed. "Murkowski Speaks with Constituents About Health Care During Senate Recess." Alaska Public Media (blog). July 10, 2017. https://www.alaskapublic.org/2017/07/10/murkowski-speaks-with-constituents-about-health-care-during-senate-recess/.

143 **Moran's own family pediatrician showed up:** Lerner, Kira. "Republican Senator Confronted by His Daughters' Pediatrician over Health Care Bill." Think Progress. July 6, 2017. https://thinkprogress.org/moran-town-hall-b2d31976774e/.

143 **Constituents flooded the venue:** Lowry, Bryan. "Packed Town Hall in Palco,

Kan., Urges Moran to Stand Firm Against GOP Health Bill." *Kansas City Star*. July 6, 2017. https://www.kansascity.com/news/politics-government /article159927569.html.

144 **In a bizarre press conference:** Pramuk, Jacob. "GOP Senators Shred 'Skinny' Obamacare Repeal—Then Say They'll Support It." CNBC. July 27, 2017. https://www.cnbc.com/2017/07/27/mccain-graham-johnson -lay-out-terms-for-supporting-obamacare-repeal.html.

145 **and then gave a thumbs-down:** "McCain Votes Against 'Skinny Repeal' Health-Care Bill." *Washington Post*. July 28, 2017. https://www.washington post.com/video/national/mccain-votes-against-skinny-repeal-health-care -bill/2017/07/28/206422e2-7356-11e7-8c17-533c52b2f014_video.html.

145 **Democrats in the chamber audibly gasped:** Stevenson, Peter W. "The Iconic Thumbs-down Vote That Summed Up John McCain's Career." *Washington Post*. August 27, 2018, sec. The Fix Analysis. https://www .washingtonpost.com/politics/2018/08/27/iconic-thumbs-down-vote-that -summed-up-john-mccains-career/.

146 **robbing millions of people of their health coverage:** Goldstein, Amy. " 'Skinny Repeal' of Obamacare Would Leave 16 Million More People Un-insured in a Decade." *Washington Post*. July 27, 2017, sec. Health & Science. https://www.washingtonpost.com/national/health-science/skinny-repeal -of-obamacare-would-leave-16-million-more-people-uninsured-in-a -decade/2017/07/27/8d0ab412-72dc-11e7-8f39-eeb7d3a2d304_story .html.

146 **outpouring of gratitude:** Kelly, Devin. "After Health Care Vote, Supporters Rally in Anchorage to Thank Murkowski." *Anchorage Daily News*. July 29, 2017. https://www.adn.com/slideshow/visual/photos/2017/07/29/after -healthcare-vote-alaskans-rally-around-their-senator/.

146 **spontaneous applause for Collins:** Manchester, Julia. "Collins Recounts 'Heartwarming' Welcome in Maine After Healthcare 'No' Vote." Hill. July 30, 2017. https://thehill.com/homenews/sunday-talk-shows/344527 -collins-reminisces-about-heart-warming-welcome-in-maine-after.

146 **signs thanking McCain along the road:** Johnston, Joy. "Cindy McCain Thanks Supporters Who Left Signs Along Road." *Dayton Daily News*. July 29, 2017. https://www.daytondailynews.com/news/national-govt--politics /cindy-mccain-thanks-supporters-who-left-signs-along-road/WZ4 QUzff9TJeUYQMuAOr3N/.

147 **"Another Round of Anger over Health Care":** Weigel, David. "At Raucous Town Halls, Republicans Have Faced Another Round of Anger over Health Care." *Washington Post*. August 11, 2017, sec. PowerPost. https://www

.washingtonpost.com/powerpost/at-raucous-town-halls-republicans-have
-faced-another-round-of-anger-over-health-care/2017/08/10/9d82cbbe
-7de9-11e7-83c7-5bd5460f0d7e_story.html.

147 **hundreds of attendees were angry about his vote:** Staff. "Rowdy Town Hall Crowds Greet Sen. Gardner. Health Care Vote Leads Concerns." Colorado Public Radio. August 15, 2017. https://www.cpr.org/2017/08 /15/rowdy-town-hall-crowds-greet-sen-gardner-health-care-vote-leads -concerns/.

148 **an op-ed by us and our policy director, Angel:** Levin, Ezra, Leah Greenberg, and Angel Padilla. "Who Saved Obamacare from the GOP? The American People." *Washington Post.* July 31, 2017, sec. PostEverything Perspective. https://www.washingtonpost.com/news/posteverything/wp/2017/07/31 /who-saved-obamacare-from-the-gop-the-american-people/.

CHAPTER 4: HOW TO BUILD POWER TOGETHER

153 **Research on new activists in the Trump era:** Fisher, Dana R. 2019. *American Resistance: From the Women's March to the Blue Wave.* Columbia University Press.

153 **middle- to upper-middle-class, and white:** Putnam, Lara, and Theda Skocpol. "Middle America Reboots Democracy." *Democracy: A Journal of Ideas.* Arguments. February 2018. http://d-scholarship.pitt.edu/33816/1 /Middle%20America%20Reboots%20Democracy%20_%20Democracy%20 Journal.pdf.

155 **multiracial, cross-class, intersectional progressive movement:** Coaston, Jane. "The Intersectionality Wars." Vox. May 28, 2019. https://www.vox .com/the-highlight/2019/5/20/18542843/intersectionality-conservatism -law-race-gender-discrimination.

155 **shape our experiences with systems of power and oppression:** Crenshaw, Kimberle. "Demarginalizing the Intersection of Race and Sex: A Black Feminist Critique of Antidiscrimination Doctrine, Feminist Theory and Antiracist Politics." *University of Chicago Legal Forum*, 1989, issue 1, Article 8: 31. https://chicagounbound.uchicago.edu/cgi/viewcontent.cgi?article =1052&context=uclf.

160 **tried to move compromises on immigration:** Valverde, Miriam. "Did Senate Pass Immigration Bills in 2006, 2013?" Politifact. January 26, 2018. https://www.politifact.com/punditfact/statements/2018/jan/26/ronald -brownstein/did-senators-pass-immigration-reform-bills-2006-20/.

160 **by painting him as soft on immigration:** Cantor had widely been seen as sympathetic to immigration reform, and, following his defeat, Politico

predicted that "Cantor loss kills immigration reform." See Kim, Seung Min. "Cantor Loss Kills Immigration Reform." Politico. Updated June 11, 2014. https://www.politico.com/story/2014/06/2014-virginia-primary-eric-cantor-loss-immigration-reform-107697.

160 **official election autopsy report released by the Republican National Committee:** Barbour, Henry, Sally Bradshaw, Ari Fleischer, Zori Fonalledas, and Glenn McCall. 2013. "Growth & Opportunity Project." Republican National Committee. http://s3.documentcloud.org/documents/623664/republican-national-committees-growth-and.pdf.

161 **it had a majority of *Republican* support:** Easley, Jonathan. "Poll: Two-Thirds of Republicans Back Citizenship for DACA Recipients." Hill. September 22, 2017. https://thehill.com/latino/351901-poll-two-thirds-of-republicans-back-citizenship-for-daca-recipients.

161 **Republican attorneys general threatened a lawsuit:** Kopan, Tal. "States Try to Force Trump's Hand on DACA." CNN. July 1, 2017. https://www.cnn.com/2017/06/30/politics/trump-daca-bind/index.html.

161 **demonstrations to pressure Trump not to rescind DACA:** Conley, Julia. "#DefendDACA: Nationwide Rallies Demand Protection for Young Immigrants." Common Dreams. August 15, 2017. https://www.commondreams.org/news/2017/08/15/defenddaca-nationwide-rallies-demand-protection-young-immigrants.

162 **Marielena Hincapié slammed Trump's move:** Shear, Michael D., and Julie Hirschfeld Davis. "Trump Moves to End DACA and Calls on Congress to Act." *New York Times.* September 5, 2017, sec. U.S. https://www.nytimes.com/2017/09/05/us/politics/trump-daca-dreamers-immigration.html.

162 **"We will not be thrown back into the shadows":** Ellis, Ralph. "Dreamers on DACA's End: 'We Will Not Be Thrown Back into the Shadows.'" CNN Politics. September 5, 2017. https://www.cnn.com/2017/09/05/politics/daca-dreamer-reaction/index.html.

167 **hunger strikes at Obama reelection campaign offices:** "DREAM Act Protesters Who Staged Sit-in at Obama's Denver Campaign Office, Call Off Hunger Strike, Vow More Actions to Come." HuffPost. June 13, 2012. https://www.huffpost.com/entry/dream-act-protesterswho-_n_1593739.

167 **Pelosi called the decision a "deeply shameful act":** "Pelosi Statement on DACA Termination." Speaker Nancy Pelosi. September 5, 2017. https://www.speaker.gov/newsroom/9517/.

167 **Obama described the attack on DACA as "wrong":** Johnson, Jenna. "Obama Calls President Trump's Decision to End DACA 'Wrong,' 'Self-

Defeating' and 'Cruel.'" *Washington Post*. September 5, 2017, sec. Politics. https://www.washingtonpost.com/news/post-politics/wp/2017/09/05 /obama-calls-trumps-decision-to-end-daca-wrong-self-defeating-and-cruel/.

168 **part of the chorus of national news organizations:** Gaudiano, Nicole. "Chuck Schumer Recounts the Art of Democrats' Deal with Donald Trump." *USA Today*. September 8, 2017. https://www.usatoday.com /story/news/politics/2017/09/08/chuck-schumer-recounts-art-democrats -deal-trump/643235001/.

168 **Indivisible joined with our partners:** "Immigrant Groups and Allies Call on Congressional Democrats to Force Vote on Dream Act." United We Dream. September 7, 2017. https://unitedwedream.org/2017/09/immigrant-groups -and-allies-call-on-congressional-democrats-to-force-vote-on-dream-act/.

173 **"My brother has DACA and my parents are undocumented":** Lee, Esther Yu Hsi. "Trump's Aides Urge Him to Keep DREAMers as He Deports Their Parents." Think Progress. August 22, 2017. https://thinkprogress.org /trump-aides-daca-bargain-immigration-9f42f0294585/.

175 **"we should've frankly been more assertive":** Caygle, Heather, and Elana Schor. "Dems Back Away from Brink on Dreamers." Politico. December 12, 2017. https://www.politico.com/story/2017/12/12/democrats-dreamers -immigrants-shutdown-293750.

176 **agrees, and he tells the advocate, "Make me do it":** Coates, Ta-Nehisi. "Evolving." *Atlantic*. June 24, 2011. https://www.theatlantic.com/national /archive/2011/06/evolving/240972/.

177 **Trump was up on the airwaves targeting Democratic senators:** Gibson, Ginger, and Doina Chiacu. "Trump Campaign Ad on Murder Raises Heat in Shutdown Fight." Reuters. January 20, 2018. https://www.reuters .com/article/us-usa-congress-shutdown-immigration/trump-campaign -ad-on-murder-raises-heat-in-shutdown-fight-idUSKBN1F914U.

177 **polls showed Democrats winning the messaging fight:** Rakich, Nathaniel. "The Public Blamed Trump for the Shutdown—but That May Be Changing." FiveThirtyEight. January 4, 2019. https://fivethirtyeight.com /features/the-public-blamed-trump-for-the-shutdown-but-that-may-be -changing/.

177 **millions of people, including Indivisibles, flooded the streets:** Lopez, German. "Women's March 2018: Millions Are Still Protesting Trump." Vox. January 23, 2018. https://www.vox.com/policy-and-politics/2018/1 /23/16922884/womens-march-attendance.

177 **By Monday it was over:** Stolberg, Sheryl Gay, and Thomas Kaplan. "Gov-

ernment Shutdown Ends After 3 Days of Recriminations." *New York Times*. January 22, 2018. https://www.nytimes.com/2018/01/22/us/politics/congress-votes-to-end-government-shutdown.html.

177 **"Democrats cave on Shutdown," tweeted President Trump:** Stolberg, Sheryl Gay, and Thomas Kaplan. "Government Shutdown Ends After 3 Days of Recriminations." *New York Times*. January 22, 2018. https://www.nytimes.com/2018/01/22/us/politics/congress-votes-to-end-government-shutdown.html.

178 **Supreme Court declined Trump's request:** Lind, Dara. "The Supreme Court May Have Just Kept DACA on Life Support for Several More Months." Vox. February 26, 2018. https://www.vox.com/2018/2/26/17053202/daca-supreme-court-ruling-trump.

179 **message to communities under threat is almost always "Wait":** "Immigrant Groups and Allies Call on Congressional Democrats to Force Vote on Dream Act." United We Dream. September 7, 2017. https://unitedwedream.org/2017/09/immigrant-groups-and-allies-call-on-congressional-democrats-to-force-vote-on-dream-act/.

179 *the white moderate who is more devoted to "order" than to justice*: King, Martin Luther, Jr. "Letter from a Birmingham Jail [King, Jr.]." African Studies Center, University of Pennsylvania. April 16, 1963. https://www.africa.upenn.edu/Articles_Gen/Letter_Birmingham.html.

180 **"Well, what the hell's the presidency for?":** Caro, Robert A. 1982. *The Passage of Power: The Years of Lyndon Johnson*. Knopf. 428.

181 *"the power that we hold to transform our conditions"*: Garza, Alicia, and Jesenia Santana. "Ally or Co-conspirator?: What It Means to Act #InSolidarity." Move to End Violence. September 7, 2016. http://www.movetoendviolence.org/blog/ally-co-conspirator-means-act-insolidarity/.

183 **"We showed the country that it is possible":** Gomez, Alan, and Ledyard King. "House Passes Bill to Protect 'Dreamers,' but Faces Long Odds in Republican-Led Senate." *USA Today*. June 4, 2019. https://www.usatoday.com/story/news/politics/2019/06/04/house-passes-bill-dreamers-tps-but-senate-unlikely/1337753001/.

183 **even the Republican propaganda network Fox News refused to run it:** Stelter, Brian, and Oliver Darcy. "NBC and Fox Finally Stop Running Trump's Racist Ad After It Was Viewed by Millions." CNN Business. November 5, 2018. https://www.cnn.com/2018/11/05/media/nbc-trump-immigration-ad/index.html.

184 **Democratic leadership embraced a funding bill giving Trump billions:**

Davis, Julie Hirschfeld, and Emily Cochrane. "House Passes Senate Border Bill in Striking Defeat for Pelosi." *New York Times*. June 27, 2019. https://www .nytimes.com/2019/06/27/us/politics/border-funding-immigration.html.

184 **agents to carry out sexual assault and abuse on a wide scale:** "Report Reveals Widespread Sexual Assault In Immigration Detention." HuffPost. May 7, 2017. https://www.huffpost.com/entry/report-reveals-widespread-sexual -assault-in-immigration_b_590fc4d2e4b0f71180724604.

184 **but far too little public outrage or oversight:** Ali, Safia Samee. "Sexual Assaults in Immigration Detention Centers Rarely Get Investigated, Advocacy Group Charges." NBC News. April 12, 2017. https://www .nbcnews.com/news/us-news/sexual-assaults-immigration-detention-centers -don-t-get-investigated-says-n745616.

CHAPTER 5: HOW TO MAKE WAVES

189 **where there were active Tea Party protests:** Madestam, Andreas, Daniel Shoag, Stan Veuger, and David Yanagizawa-Drott. "Do Political Protests Matter? Evidence from the Tea Party Movement*." *Quarterly Journal of Economics* 128, no. 4 (November 2013): 1633–85. https://doi.org/10.1093/qje /qjt021.

190 **A study of Women's March mobilizations:** Pinckney, Jonathan. "Did the Women's March Work? Re-Evaluating the Political Efficacy of Protest." Submission to 2019 Mobilization Conference, n.d., 22. https://static1 .squarespace.com/static/57fbfb81e3df28f99496b5a0/t/5ccf2541f9619a23 bcf11999/1557079363726/Pinckney+Women%27s+March+Paper.pdf.

200 **called attention to his unwillingness to appear in public:** Smith, Rich. "Where's Congressman Dave Reichert? His Constituents Can't Seem to Find Him." *Stranger*. February 22, 2017. https://www.thestranger .com/slog/2017/02/22/24884014/wheres-congressman-dave-reichert-his -constituents-cant-seem-to-find-him.

200 **Jayapal joined them for an "Adopt a District" town hall:** Hsieh, Steven. "Pramila Jayapal to Attend Town Hall in No-Show Dave Reichert's District." *Stranger*. July 14, 2017. https://www.thestranger.com /slog/2017/07/14/25289919/pramila-jayapal-is-attending-a-town-hall-in -dave-reicharts-district-where-he-has-been-a-ghost.

200 **The star of the ad? The empty chair:** Smith, Rich. "Another New Challenger Enters the Race for Reichert's District: Dr. Kim Schrier." *Stranger*. August 8, 2017. https://www.thestranger.com/slog/2017/08/07/25333922/another -new-challenger-enters-the-race-for-reicherts-district-dr-kim-schrier.

202 **they deal with Indivisible people outside their office every week:**

Golshan, Tara. "The Simple Explanation for All the Republican Retirements: Congress Sucks." Vox. February 2, 2018. https://www.vox
.com/2018/2/2/16879086/republican-retirements-congress-explained.

202 **Costello himself announced his retirement:** Golshan, Tara. "Republican
Rep. Ryan Costello Isn't Running for Reelection. That's Big for Democrats."
Vox. March 26, 2018. https://www.vox.com/2018/3/26/17164586/republi
can-pennsylvania-ryan-costello-retire-2018.

203 **incumbents win reelection around 90 percent of the time:** "Reelection
Rates over the Years." n.d. OpenSecrets.org, Center for Responsive Politics.
Accessed July 25, 2019. https://www.opensecrets.org/overview/reelect
.php.

204 **cause that rarely stirs people's blood:** the U.S. tax code. We chatted with
Katie Farnan of Indivisible Front Range Resistance fame about these events,
and relied on journalist Jacob Weindling's accounting of the event for some
of the details: https://www.pastemagazine.com/articles/2017/11/what-i
-saw-at-a-protest-against-the-republican-tax.html.

204 **benefits of the tax cut to the rich and corporations:** Staff. "A Prelimi-
nary Analysis of the Unified Framework." Tax Policy Center. September 27,
2017. https://www.taxpolicycenter.org/publications/preliminary-analysis
-unified-framework.

204 **Trump and his congressional supporters downplayed that part:** Long,
Heather. "The Average American Family Will Get $4,000 from Tax Cuts,
Trump Team Claims." *Washington Post*. October 16, 2017, sec. Economic
Policy. https://www.washingtonpost.com/news/wonk/wp/2017/10/16
/the-average-american-family-will-get-4000-from-tax-cuts-trump-team
-claims/.

206 **Indivisible dressed up as billionaires in mock support:** Lyons, Jarrett.
"GOP's Senate Tax Bill Met with Protests Across Country." Salon. November 29, 2017. https://www.salon.com/2017/11/29/gops-senate-tax-bill
-met-with-protests-across-country/.

208 **48 percent of Americans approved of the prospective bill:** Shepard, Steven. "Poll: 48 Percent Approve of Trump's Tax Proposal." Politico. October
4, 2017. https://www.politico.com/story/2017/10/04/trump-tax-proposal
-polling-243426.

208 **its popularity was down to 26 percent:** "Half The Public Say Their Taxes
Will Go Up Under GOP Plan." Monmouth University Polling Institute
(blog). December 18, 2017. https://www.monmouth.edu/polling-institute
/reports/monmouthpoll_us_121817/.

209 **Republican had pressured his mistress to have an abortion:** Seyler,

Matt. "Anti-Abortion Rep. Tim Murphy Resigns After Report He Asked Lover to End Pregnancy." ABC News. October 5, 2017. https://abcnews .go.com/Politics/anti-abortion-rep-tim-murphy-asked-mistress-terminate /story?id=50274843.

210 **February, 65 percent of Republican ads:** Robillard, Kevin. "Republicans Abandon Tax Cut Message in Pa. Special Election." Politico. March 13, 2018. https://www.politico.com/story/2018/03/13/pennsylvania-special-elec tion-preview-tax-republicans-458276.

210 **"Rick Saccone fights hard for working families":** Kamisar, Ben. "New GOP Ad Attacks Dem in Pa. Special Election over Pelosi." Hill. January 31, 2018. https://thehill.com/homenews/campaign/371488-new-gop-ad -attacks-dem-in-pa-special-election-over-pelosi.

210 **voters agreed that the bill "benefited large corporations":** Kapur, Sahil, and Joshua Green. "Internal GOP Poll: 'We've Lost the Messaging Battle' on Tax Cuts." Bloomberg. September 20, 2018. https://www.bloomberg .com/news/articles/2018-09-20/internal-gop-poll-we-ve-lost-the-messaging -battle-on-tax-cuts.

210 **support for Trump's tax bill continuing to fall:** Stewart, Emily. "The Republican Tax Law Is Becoming Less Popular, Not More." Vox. June 22, 2018. https://www.vox.com/policy-and-politics/2018/6/22/17492468/republi can-tax-cut-law-poll.

214 **driving down his approval ratings:** Cadei, Emily. "Tied to Trump, These Two California Republican Congressmen Lag in Poll." *Sacramento Bee*. February 6, 2018. https://www.sacbee.com/news/politics-government/capitol -alert/article198560324.html.

214 **Rohrabacher was known in D.C. as:** Arnsdorf, Isaac, and Benjamin Oreskes. "Putin's Favorite Congressman." Politico. November 23, 2016. https://politi.co/2EbppEv.

216 **"a booming bat signal to Democrats":** Krieg, Gregory. "Indivisible Backs Rohrabacher Challenger as Progressives Vie to Unseat Old Democratic King-makers." CNN. May 2, 2018. https://www.cnn.com/2018/05/02/politics /grassroots-groups-endorsements-democratic-primaries/index.html.

220 **Dana Rohrabacher, for instance:** Sanger-Katz, Margot. "Republicans Are Suddenly Running Ads on Pre-existing Conditions. But How Accurate Are They?" *New York Times*. October 16, 2018. https://www.nytimes .com/2018/10/16/upshot/republicans-health-care-ads-midterms.html.

221 **Democrats unleashed a devastating ad:** Bowman, Bridget. "New York Race Spotlights National Clash over Health Care." Roll Call. October 3,

2018. https://www.rollcall.com/news/politics/one-house-race-spotlights
-national-clash-over-health-care.

221 **ad featuring an actor dressed as Bigfoot:** Kessler, Pat. "Reality Check: Phillips Ad Finds Bigfoot Looking for Rep. Paulsen." WCCO: CBS Minnesota. September 19, 2018. https://minnesota.cbslocal.com/2018/09/19/reality-check-bigfoot-ad/.

221 **countered by running a series of wildly racist ads:** Murphy, Tim. "Republicans Are Deploying Staggeringly Racist Ads in Upstate New York." *Mother Jones* (blog). September 28, 2018. https://www.motherjones.com/politics/2018/09/republicans-anthony-delgado-big-city-rapper/.

CHAPTER 6: A DAY ONE DEMOCRACY AGENDA

233 **Agnew had been forced to resign:** For a gripping history of Agnew's rise and downfall, check out Rachel Maddow's "Bag Man" podcast.

234 **Trust in government was at an all-time low:** "Public Trust in Government: 1958–2019." *Pew Research Center. U.S. Politics & Policy* (blog). April 11, 2019. https://www.people-press.org/2019/04/11/public-trust-in-government-1958-2019/.

234 **Instead he looked optimistically to the future:** "Inaugural Addresses of the Presidents of the United States: Jimmy Carter." Avalon Project. Yale Law School. January 20, 1977. https://avalon.law.yale.edu/20th_century/carter.asp.

234 **"one of the broadest political reform packages ever":** Weaver, Warren, Jr. "Carter Proposes End of Electoral College in Presidential Votes." *New York Times*. March 23, 1977, sec. Archives. https://www.nytimes.com/1977/03/23/archives/carter-proposes-end-of-electoral-college-in-presidential-votes.html.

235 **Heritage Foundation declared it a mistake:** R., Milton. "Carter's Election Reform Proposal." Heritage Foundation. April 20, 1977. https://www.heritage.org/election-integrity/report/carters-election-reform-proposal.

235 **Republican National Committee denounced the package:** Perlstein, Rick. "Jimmy Carter Got It Right: Race, Ronald Reagan, and How the Right Gutted His Visionary Electoral Reform." Salon. September 5, 2015. https://www.salon.com/2015/09/05/jimmy_carter_got_it_right_race_ronald_reagan_and_how_the_right_gutted_his_visionary_electoral_reform/.

235 **The die was cast:** "Public Financing, Campaign Spending Bills." CQ Almanac Online Edition. 1978. https://library.cqpress.com/cqalmanac/document.php?id=cqal78-1237181.

235 **Democracy reform in the post-Nixon era was dead:** Watergate and Nix-on's resignation did lead to a whole host of reforms, just none of the pro-democracy reforms included in Carter's big package of proposals. Sam Berger and Alex Tausanovitch at the Center for American Progress provide a good overview of the good that did come out of this dark period: https://www .americanprogress.org/issues/democracy/reports/2018/07/30/454058 /lessons-from-watergate/.

236 **"a sweeping anti-corruption proposal":** Nilsen, Ella. "House Demo-crats Officially Unveil Their First Bill in the Majority: A Sweeping Anti-Corruption Proposal." Vox. November 30, 2018. https://www.vox.com /policy-and-politics/2018/11/30/18118158/house-democrats-anti-corruption -bill-hr-1-pelosi.

236 **"a broad political overhaul":** DeBonis, Mike. "House Democrats to Unveil Political Reform Legislation as 'H.R. 1.'" *Washington Post*. November 30, 2018, sec. PowerPost. https://www.washingtonpost.com/politics/2018/11/30 /house-democrats-unveil-political-reform-legislation-hr/.

236 **"Biggest Voting-Rights Bill to Appear in Congress Since the Civil Rights":** Pierce, Charles P. "This Is the Biggest Voting-Rights Bill to Ap-pear in Congress Since the Civil Rights Movement." *Esquire*. January 7, 2019. https://www.esquire.com/news-politics/politics/a25778915/democrats -anti-corruption-bill-voting-rights/.

236 **arguing that the proposed legislation was "unnecessary":** "The Facts About H.R. 1—the For the People Act of 2019." Heritage Foundation. Febru-ary 1, 2019. https://www.heritage.org/election-integrity/report/the-facts -about-hr-1-the-the-people-act-2019.

236 **wrote an op-ed picking apart the proposal:** McConnell, Mitch. "Mitch McConnell: Behold the Democrat Politician Protection Act." *Washing-ton Post*. January 17, 2019, sec. Opinions. https://www.washingtonpost .com/opinions/call-hr-1-what-it-is-the-democrat-politician-protection-act /2019/01/17/dcc957be-19cb-11e9-9ebf-c5fed1b7a081_story.html.

236 **"vociferous in their condemnation":** Cochrane, Emily. "Judiciary Hearing on Democrats' Election Bill Turns into Partisan Brawl." *New York Times*. January 29, 2019. https://www.nytimes.com/2019/01/29/us/politics /house-democrats-election-ethics-bill.html.

236 **block the bill from even getting a vote:** Nilsen, Ella. "Senate Dem-ocrats Unveiled an Anti-Corruption Companion Bill. Mitch McCon-nell Is Already Blocking It." Vox. March 27, 2019. https://www.vox .com/2019/3/27/18284171/senate-democrats-anti-corruption-hr1-schumer -mcconnell.

245 **historical, international lesson on how democracies, well, die:** Levitsky, Steven, and Daniel Ziblatt. 2018. *How Democracies Die*. Broadway Books.

248 **thirty years after the filibuster first came into existence:** Binder, Sarah A. "The History of the Filibuster." Brookings (blog). April 22, 2010. https:// www.brookings.edu/testimonies/the-history-of-the-filibuster/.

249 **Lodge proposed a bill to establish federal oversight:** Waldman, Michael. 2016. *The Fight to Vote*. Simon & Schuster, 83.

249 **there were seven motions to end a filibuster:** "U.S. Senate: Cloture Motions." United States Senate, n.d. Accessed July 25, 2019. https://www.senate .gov/legislative/cloture/clotureCounts.htm.

250 **McConnell amended it to give Trump two new justices:** Davis, Susan. "Senate Pulls 'Nuclear' Trigger to Ease Gorsuch Confirmation." NPR. April 6, 2017. https://www.npr.org/2017/04/06/522847700/senate-pulls-nuclear -trigger-to-ease-gorsuch-confirmation.

250 **conservative states, can prevent a vote from ever taking place:** Seitz-Wald, Alex. "5 Reasons to Kill the Filibuster." Salon. November 28, 2012. https://www.salon.com/2012/11/28/five_reasons_to_kill_the_filibuster/.

251 **take it from Barack Obama:** Axelrod, Tal. "Obama: Filibuster Makes It 'Almost Impossible' to Govern." Hill. November 20, 2018. https://thehill.com /homenews/senate/417736-obama-filibuster-makes-it-almost-impossible -to-govern-abolish-it.

254 **Alexander Hamilton wrote grumpily:** Hamilton, Alexander. "The Federalist Papers." Congress.gov. December 14, 1787. https://www.congress .gov/resources/display/content/The+Federalist+Papers#TheFederalist Papers-22.

255 **"corrupt and immoral price in order to get a barely acceptable deal":** Hertzberg, Hendrik. "Alexander Hamilton Speaks Out (III): Two Senators per State, Regardless of Population?" *New Yorker*. January 8, 2011. https:// www.newyorker.com/news/hendrik-hertzberg/alexander-hamilton-speaks -out-iii-two-senators-per-state-regardless-of-population.

255 **residents of those other states get *forty-two* senators:** Faris, David. "A Ferocious Plan for Democrats to Reconquer America." Week. January 5, 2017. https://theweek.com/articles/670638/ferocious-plan-democrats-reconquer -america.

255 **there are more Republican-leaning states:** "2020 Electoral College Rating." Cook Political Report. January 9, 2019. https://www.cookpolitical .com/sites/default/files/2019-01/EC.pdf.

255 **In 2040, half the population will live in just eight states:** "National Population Projections." Weldon Cooper Center for Public Service, n.d. Accessed

July 25, 2019. https://demographics.coopercenter.org/national-population
-projections.

255 **"Republicans are on the verge of a durable structural advantage":** Bouie,
Jamelle. "The Senate Is as Much of a Problem as Trump." *New York Times*.
May 10, 2019, sec. Opinion. https://www.nytimes.com/2019/05/10/opinion
/sunday/senate-democrats-trump.html.

256 **pay more in federal taxes than residents in twenty-two other states:**
"SOI Tax Stats Gross Collections by Type of Tax and State IRS Data Book
Table 5." IRS, n.d. Accessed July 25, 2019. https://www.irs.gov/statistics
/soi-tax-stats-gross-collections-by-type-of-tax-and-state-irs-data-book
-table-5.

256 **The history of Washington, D.C., is instructive:** For a great political history
of D.C., check out *Dream City: Race, Power, and the Decline of Washington
D.C.* by Harry Jaffe and Tom Sherwood (20th edition, 2014).

256 **federal government revoked the city's ability to govern itself:** Masur, Kate.
"Capital Injustice: Why the District of Columbia Still Lacks Voting Rights."
New York Times. March 28, 2011, sec. Opinion. https://www.nytimes
.com/2011/03/29/opinion/29masur.html.

257 **John Dingell, the longest-serving member of Congress:** Matthews,
Dylan. "John Dingell: To Fix Congress, Abolish the Senate." Vox. December 4, 2018. https://www.vox.com/2018/12/4/18125539/john-dingell
-abolish-senate.

257 **One option for admitting new states is to split up existing states:** Egelko,
Bob. "Splitting up California: State Supreme Court Takes Initiative off Ballot." *San Francisco Chronicle*. July 18, 2018. https://www.sfchronicle.com
/politics/article/Splitting-up-Calif-State-Supreme-Court-takes-13085880
.php.

258 **heavily tied up with the fight over maintaining segregationist power:**
Stebenne, David. "The Political Dealmaking That Finally Brought Hawaii
Statehood." *Smithsonian*. June 15, 2017. https://www.smithsonianmag.com
/history/what-puerto-rico-learn-hawaii-180963690/.

258 **passed with an overwhelming 79 percent support:** Hersher, Rebecca.
"D.C. Votes Overwhelmingly to Become 51st State." NPR. November 9, 2016.
https://www.npr.org/sections/thetwo-way/2016/11/09/501412360/d-c
-votes-overwhelmingly-to-become-51st-state.

259 **Yes, snowplows:** McCartney, Robert. "Why Can't D.C. Become a State?
Opponents Cite Grave Snowplow Threat as One of Several Specious Ob-
jections." *Washington Post*. September 14, 2014, sec. Local. https://www
.washingtonpost.com/local/critics-of-dc-statehood-cite-specious-objections

-such-as-grave-snowplow-threat/2014/09/17/c258ff62-3e9a-11e4-b0ea
-8141703bbf6f_story.html.

259 **gave the game away when he explained why he opposes D.C. statehood:**
Stein, Perry. "Kasich on D.C. Voting Rights: 'That's Just More Votes in the
Democratic Party.'" *Washington Post*. April 21, 2016, sec. Local. https://
www.washingtonpost.com/news/local/wp/2016/04/21/kasich-on-d-c
-voting-rights-thats-just-more-votes-in-the-democratic-party/.

259 **given its status as the country's capital:** R., Hewitt. 1993. "D.C. Statehood:
Not Without a Constitutional Amendment." Heritage Foundation. August
27, 1993. https://www.heritage.org/political-process/report/dc-statehood
-not-without-constitutional-amendment.

259 **openly describing the idea of D.C. and Puerto Rican statehood:** Nichols, John. "Mitch McConnell Calls Puerto Rican Statehood 'Full-Bore
Socialism.'" *Nation*. June 18, 2019. https://www.thenation.com/article
/mitch-mcconnell-puerto-rico-full-bore-socialism/.

260 **The story of Nevada statehood is fascinating:** "Nevada Statehood." n.d.
Online Nevada Encyclopedia. Nevada Humanities. Accessed July 25, 2019.
http://www.onlinenevada.org/articles/nevada-statehood.

261 **Take the Pennsylvania House elections of 1794:** "U.S. Congressional
Election 14 October 1794." Wilkes.edu, n.d. Accessed August 4, 2019. http://
staffweb.wilkes.edu/harold.cox/rep/Congress%201794.pdf.

262 **academic research finds that it *matters*:** Drutman, Lee. "To Fix Congress,
Make It Bigger. Much Bigger." *Washington Monthly*. December 2018. https://
washingtonmonthly.com/magazine/november-december-2018/to-fix
-congress-make-it-bigger-much-bigger/.

263 **most people don't feel represented by either party:** Drutman, Lee, William A. Galston, and Tod Lindberg. "Spoiler Alert: Why Americans' Desires
for a Third Party Are Unlikely to Come True." Democracy Fund Voter Study
Group. September 2018. https://www.voterstudygroup.org/publication
/spoiler-alert.

263 **vast majority of Americans live in "safe" House districts:** Fraga, Bernard
L., and Eitan D. Hersh. "Are Americans Stuck in Uncompetitive Enclaves? An
Appraisal of U.S. Electoral Competition." *Quarterly Journal of Political Science*
13, no. 3 (August 2018): 291–311. https://doi.org/10.1561/100.00017161.

263 **the number of competitive House districts had declined:** Wasserman,
David, and Ally Flinn. "Introducing the 2017 Cook Political Report Partisan Voter Index." Cook Political Report. April 7, 2017. https://cookpolitical
.com/introducing-2017-cook-political-report-partisan-voter-index.

264 **fewer ten years ago than there were fifty years ago:** Ferejohn, John A. "On

the Decline of Competition in Congressional Elections*." *American Political Science Review* 71, no. 1 (March 1977): 166–76. https://doi.org/10.1017/S0003055400259364.

264 **"more and more areas come, in essence, pre-gerrymandered":** Enten, Harry. "Ending Gerrymandering Won't Fix What Ails America." FiveThirtyEight (blog). January 26, 2018. https://fivethirtyeight.com/features/ending-gerrymandering-wont-fix-what-ails-america/.

264 **One political scientist sums it up:** Masket, Seth. "The Convenient Scapegoat of Gerrymandering." Vox. March 29, 2017. https://www.vox.com/mischiefs-of-faction/2017/3/29/15109082/gerrymandering-convenient-scapegoat.

264 **Gerrymandering of state legislature districts:** Willis, Jay. "Republican Gerrymandering Has Basically Destroyed Representative Democracy in Wisconsin." *GQ*. December 5, 2018. https://www.gq.com/story/republican-gerrymandering-wisconsin.

265 **"There are dictators who win by less":** Enten, Harry. "Ending Gerrymandering Won't Fix What Ails America." FiveThirtyEight (blog). January 26, 2018. https://fivethirtyeight.com/features/ending-gerrymandering-wont-fix-what-ails-america/.

266 **worried about the increase of "foreigners":** Conley, Dalton, and Jacqueline Stevens. "Build a Bigger House." *New York Times*. January 23, 2011. https://www.nytimes.com/2011/01/24/opinion/24conley.html.

266 **"There is absolutely no reason, philosophy, or common sense":** Drutman, Lee. "To Fix Congress, Make It Bigger. Much Bigger." *Washington Monthly*. December 2018. https://washingtonmonthly.com/magazine/november-december-2018/to-fix-congress-make-it-bigger-much-bigger/.

266 **If we were to expand the House:** Editorial Board. "America Needs a Bigger House." *New York Times*. November 9, 2018, sec. Opinion. https://www.nytimes.com/interactive/2018/11/09/opinion/expanded-house-representatives-size.html.

266 **Congressional Apportionment Amendment:** Drutman, Lee. "To Fix Congress, Make It Bigger. Much Bigger." *Washington Monthly*. December 2018. https://washingtonmonthly.com/magazine/november-december-2018/to-fix-congress-make-it-bigger-much-bigger/.

268 **As recently as the mid-twentieth century:** Schaller, Thomas F. "Multi-Member Districts: Just a Thing of the Past?" Larry J. Sabato's Crystal Ball. March 21, 2013. http://www.centerforpolitics.org/crystalball/articles/multi-member-legislative-districts-just-a-thing-of-the-past/.

268 **Multimember districts are still used at the state level:** "State Legislative

Chambers That Use Multi-Member Districts." Ballotpedia: The Encyclopedia of American Politics, n.d. Accessed July 25, 2019. https://ballotpedia .org/State_legislative_chambers_that_use_multi-member_districts.

269 **"voters and candidates say they're happier with it"**: Editorial Board. "Vote for Me! For Second Place, at Least?" *New York Times*. June 9, 2018, sec. Opinion. https://www.nytimes.com/2018/06/09/opinion/ranked-choice -voting-maine-san-francisco.html.

269 **growing number of major American cities:** "Ranked Choice Voting/ Instant Runoff." FairVote, n.d. Accessed July 25, 2019. https://www.fair vote.org/rcv#where_is_ranked_choice_voting_used.

269 **Manhattan has four overwhelmingly Democratic districts:** This example comes from political scientist Lee Drutman, source: https://www.nytimes .com/2018/06/19/opinion/gerrymandering-districts-multimember.html.

269 **he ended up winning the seat with second-choice votes:** "November 2018 Elections." FairVote, n.d. Accessed July 25, 2019. https://www.fairvote .org/november_2018_maine_elections.

270 **"no other reforms are likely to be effective without it":** Page, Benjamin I., and Martin Gilens. 2017. *Democracy in America?: What Has Gone Wrong and What We Can Do About It.* University of Chicago Press, 226.

271 **Opinion polls back up this knee-jerk reaction:** "5. The Electoral College, Congress and Representation." Pew Research Center. U.S. Politics & Policy (blog). April 26, 2018. https://www.people-press.org/2018/04/26/5-the -electoral-college-congress-and-representation/.

271 **"Whatever idealized deliberation and bonhomie":** Drutman, Lee. "To Fix Congress, Make It Bigger. Much Bigger." *Washington Monthly*. December 2018. https://washingtonmonthly.com/magazine/november-december -2018/to-fix-congress-make-it-bigger-much-bigger/.

271 **more districts would mean more opportunity for gerrymandering:** Thanks to Ian Milhiser at ThinkProgress for raising this point with us in conversation.

272 **groups behind improving the fairness of our political institutions:** "The Fair Representation Act: Racial Minority Voting Rights FAQ." FairVote, n.d. Accessed July 25, 2019. https://fairvote.app.box.com/s/6d11x wnf9ykavj8ib5201p9ne0kl4q0t.

272 **significantly lower proportion of representatives of color:** Richie, Robert, and Steven Hill. "The Case for Proportional Representation." Boston Review. March 1998. http://bostonreview.net/archives/BR23.1/richie .html.

272 **the *most common* voting system was proportional representation:**

"Electoral Systems Around the World." FairVote, n.d. Accessed July 25, 2019. https://www.fairvote.org/research_electoralsystems_world.

273 **Supporters of these reforms include:** "The Fair Representation Act." Fair-Vote, n.d. Accessed July 25, 2019. https://www.fairvote.org/fair_rep_in _congress.

273 **"one reform to save America":** Brooks, David. " One Reform to Save America." *New York Times*. May 31, 2018, sec. Opinion. https://www.nytimes .com/2018/05/31/opinion/voting-reform-partisanship-congress.html.

273 **"the only way a democracy can survive":** Editorial Board. " A Congress for Every American." *New York Times*. November 10, 2018, sec. Opinion. https:// www.nytimes.com/interactive/2018/11/10/opinion/house-representa tives-size-multi-member.html.

273 **so far as to label them a "quixotic fantasy":** Levitz, Eric. "America's Po-litical System Is Rigged Against the Left (and Always Has Been)." *New York Magazine*. Intelligencer. July 10, 2019. http://nymag.com/intelligencer /2019/07/aoc-pelosi-feud-gerrymandering-why-cities-lose.html.

274 **Cruz dismissed the idea that the Court needed nine justices:** Totenberg, Nina. "If Clinton Wins, Republicans Suggest Shrinking Size of Supreme Court." NPR. November 3, 2016. https://www.npr .org/2016/11/03/500560120/senate-republicans-could-block-potential -clinton-supreme-court-nominees.

275 **In his first two years as president:** Gramlich, John. "With Another Su-preme Court Pick, Trump Is Leaving His Mark on Higher Federal Courts." Pew Research Center (blog). July 16, 2018. https://www.pewresearch.org /fact-tank/2018/07/16/with-another-supreme-court-pick-trump-is-leaving -his-mark-on-higher-federal-courts/.

275 **"Obama judges" and "Trump judges":** Durkin, Erin, and Ben Jacobs. "Trump Hits Back at John Roberts: 'You Do Indeed Have Obama Judges'— as It Happened." *Guardian*. November 21, 2018, sec. U.S. News. https://www .theguardian.com/us-news/live/2018/nov/21/us-politics-donald-trump -nancy-pelosi-democrats-republicans.

276 **"carry out elections, but the results will be preordained":** Millhiser, Ian. "Let's Think About Court-Packing." *Democracy Journal*. Winter 2019. https://democracyjournal.org/magazine/51/lets-think-about-court -packing-2/.

277 **commit to automatic expansions of the Court going forward:** Tucker, Todd. "Off-Balance: Five Strategies for a Judiciary That Supports Democ-racy." Roosevelt Institute (blog). November 13, 2018. https://rooseveltinsti tute.org/off-balance-five-strategies-judiciary-supports-democracy/.

278 **Congress could also impose term limits for Supreme Court justices:** This idea came to us from Brian Fallon, head of the national progressive court reform nonprofit Demand Justice, and Tyler Cooper, with another national nonprofit, Fix the Court. https://news.bloomberglaw.com/ip-law/insight -fixed-terms-for-supreme-court-justices-checks-constitutionality-boxes.

278 **senior status excluded Supreme Court justices:** Stras, David R., and Ryan W. Scott. "Are Senior Judges Unconstitutional?" *Cornell Law Review* 92, no. 453 (2007): 70. http://cornelllawreview.org/files/2013/02/Stras _Scott_92-3.pdf.

278 **taken senior status and continue to issue opinions:** Barnes, Robert. "Retired Supreme Court Justices Still Judge—and Get Judged." *Washington Post.* March 10, 2013, sec. Politics. https://www.washingtonpost.com/politics /retired-supreme-court-justices-still-judge-and-get-judged/2013/03/10 /1b22943c-897f-11e2-8d72-dc76641cb8d4_story.html.

279 **battle over the judiciary could become "a full-out war":** Millhiser, Ian. "Let's Think About Court-Packing." *Democracy Journal.* Winter 2019. https://democracyjournal.org/magazine/51/lets-think-about-court-pack ing-2/.

282 **9 million of these people are lawful permanent residents:** "Population Estimates: Lawful Permanent Resident Population in the United States: January 2015." Homeland Security: Office of Immigration Statistics. May 2019, 6. https://www.dhs.gov/sites/default/files/publications/lpr_population _estimates_january_2015.pdf.

282 **majority of the roughly 11 million undocumented Americans:** "Profile of the Unauthorized Population—US." Migrationpolicy.org, n.d. Accessed July 25, 2019. https://www.migrationpolicy.org/data/unauthorized-immigrant -population/state/US.

282 **he wanted fewer immigrants from "shithole countries":** Kirby, Jen. "Trump Wants Fewer Immigrants from 'Shithole Countries' and More from Places like Norway." Vox. January 11, 2018. https://www.vox .com/2018/1/11/16880750/trump-immigrants-shithole-countries-norway.

283 **Scotland and Austria have extended voting to sixteen-year-olds.:** Dahlgaard, Jens Olav. "The Surprising Consequence of Lowering the Voting Age." *Washington Post.* March 1, 2018, sec. Monkey Cage (Analysis). https://www.washingtonpost.com/news/monkey-cage/wp/2018/02/28 /the-surprising-consequence-of-lowering-the-voting-age/.

283 **6 million American citizens are deprived of the right to vote:** Uggen, Christopher, Ryan Larson, and Sarah Shannon. "6 Million Lost Voters: State-Level Estimates of Felony Disenfranchisement, 2016." Sentencing Project.

October 6, 2016. https://www.sentencingproject.org/publications/6-million-lost-voters-state-level-estimates-felony-disenfranchisement-2016/.

283 **In many other democracies:** Lemon, Jason. "Can Prisoners Vote In Other Countries? Bernie Sanders Wants Felons to Cast Ballots While Incarcerated." *Newsweek*. April 24, 2019. https://www.newsweek.com/which-countries-felons-vote-1405142.

283 **vary widely among the states:** Chung, Jean. "Felony Disenfranchisement: A Primer." Sentencing Project. June 27, 2019. https://www.sentencingproject.org/publications/felony-disenfranchisement-a-primer/.

284 **a legacy that stretches back to the era of slavery:** For a powerful overview of the links between the nineteenth century slave state and today's state of mass incarceration, check out Ava DuVernay's 2016 documentary *13th*.

284 **20 percent of all potential Black voters in the country are disenfranchised:** Chung, Jean. "Felony Disenfranchisement: A Primer." Sentencing Project. June 27, 2019. https://www.sentencingproject.org/publications/felony-disenfranchisement-a-primer/.

284 **If this feels uncannily like the Three-Fifths Compromise:** Rivers, Christina R. "'Felon Power': Prison Gerrymanders, the ⅗ Clause, and the Incarceration of Democracy." SSRN Scholarly Paper ID 2675381. Rochester, NY: Social Science Research Network. https://papers.ssrn.com/abstract=2675381.

285 **Reagan signed the single largest immigration reform law:** Staff. "A Reagan Legacy: Amnesty for Illegal Immigrants." NPR. July 4, 2010. https://www.npr.org/templates/story/story.php?storyId=128303672.

286 **This could also have a "trickle-up" effect:** Dahlgaard, Jens Olav. "Trickle-up Political Socialization: The Causal Effect on Turnout of Parenting a Newly Enfranchised Voter." *American Political Science Review* 112, no. 3 (August 2018): 698–705. https://doi.org/10.1017/S0003055418000059.

286 **publicly embraced lowering the voting age:** Kay, Jazmin. "Nancy Pelosi Proposes Lowering the Voting Age to 16 or 17." Generation Progress (blog). August 6, 2015. https://genprogress.org/nancy-pelosi-proposes-lowering-the-voting-age-to-16-or-17/.

286 **Pelosi reiterated her support for the idea:** Bowden, John. "Pelosi Says She Backs Lowering Voting Age to 16." Hill. March 14, 2019. https://thehill.com/homenews/house/434115-pelosi-says-she-backs-lowering-voting-age-to-16.

288 **"skills necessary to make informed decisions are firmly in place":** Steinberg, Laurence. "Why We Should Lower the Voting Age to 16." *New York Times*. March 2, 2018. https://www.nytimes.com/2018/03/02/opinion/sunday/voting-age-school-shootings.html.

288 **according to some studies, *more* knowledgeable:** Hart, Daniel, and Robert Atkins. "American Sixteen- and Seventeen-Year-Olds Are Ready to Vote." *Annals of the American Academy of Political and Social Science* 633, no. 1 (2011): 201–22.

288 **their voting rates are far higher:** Douglas, Joshua. 2017. "The Right to Vote Under Local Law." SSRN Scholarly Paper ID 2816972. Rochester, NY: Social Science Research Network. https://papers.ssrn.com/abstract=2816972.

288 **"I don't think felons oughta be allowed to vote":** Perry, Mitch. "Tampa Attorney Argues Against Proposed Voter Restoration Amendment." Florida Politics (blog). November 3, 2017. https://floridapolitics.com/archives/248704-tampa-attorney-argues-proposed-voter-restoration-amendment.

289 **legislature and governor gutted the initiative:** Rozsa, Lori. "Florida Governor Signs Bill Making It Harder for Felons to Regain Voting Rights." *Washington Post.* June 28, 2019, sec. Politics. https://www.washingtonpost.com/politics/florida-governor-signs-bill-making-it-harder-for-felons-to-regain-voting-rights/2019/06/28/5e446828-9a0b-11e9-916d-9c61607d8190_story.html.

290 **"could leave a dramatically diminished version of democracy in its wake":** Nichols, John, and Robert W. McChesney. "The Death and Life of Great American Newspapers." *Nation.* March 18, 2009. https://www.thenation.com/article/death-and-life-great-american-newspapers/.

290 **got it from the three big networks:** ABC, CBS, and NBC: Hindman, Douglas Blanks, and Kenneth Wiegand. 2008. "The Big Three's Prime-Time Decline: A Technological and Social Context." *Journal of Broadcasting & Electronic Media* 52, no. 1 (2008): 119–35. https://doi.org/10.1080/08838150701820924.

290 **well-known and well-liked by broad swaths of Americans:** Bowman, Karlyn. "The Decline of the Major Networks." *Forbes.* July 27, 2009. https://www.forbes.com/2009/07/25/media-network-news-audience-opinions-columnists-walter-cronkite.html#af5c17147a5f.

291 **Newspaper circulation has declined literally every year:** "Town by Town, Local Journalism Is Dying in Plain Sight." CNBC. March 10, 2019. https://www.cnbc.com/2019/03/10/town-by-town-local-journalism-is-dying-in-plain-sight.html.

291 **nearly 47 percent of newspaper jobs disappeared:** Grieco, Elizabeth. "U.S. Newsroom Employment Has Dropped a Quarter since 2008, with Greatest Decline at Newspapers." Pew Research Center (blog). July 9, 2019. https://www.pewresearch.org/fact-tank/2019/07/09/u-s-newsroom-employment-has-dropped-by-a-quarter-since-2008/.

291 **The economic model for local news has collapsed:** Madrigal, Alexis C.

"Local News Is Dying, and Americans Have No Idea." *Atlantic*. March 26, 2019. https://www.theatlantic.com/technology/archive/2019/03/local-news -is-dying-and-americans-have-no-idea/585772/.

291 **"local news deserts" across the country:** "The Expanding News Desert: The Loss of Local News." University of North Carolina at Chapel Hill, School of Media and Journalism, Center for Innovation and Sustainability in Local Media. Expanding News Desert (blog), n.d. Accessed July 25, 2019. https://www.usnewsdeserts.com/reports/expanding-news-desert/.

293 **nearly 80 percent of Democrats trust the media:** "For Americans, Trusting the Media Has Become a Partisan Issue—Daily Chart." 2019. Economist. April 3, 2019. https://www.economist.com/graphic-detail/2019/04/03 /for-americans-trusting-the-media-has-become-a-partisan-issue.

293 **a full-fledged propaganda operation:** Mayer, Jane. "The Making of the Fox News White House." *New Yorker*. March 4, 2019. https://www.new yorker.com/magazine/2019/03/11/the-making-of-the-fox-news-white -house?utm_medium=social&utm_source=twitter&mbid=social_twitter &utm_brand=tny&utm_social-type=owned.

293 **drive the entire American electorate to the right:** Arceneaux, Kevin, Martin Johnson, Rene Lindstadt, and Ryan Vander Wielen. "Fox News Pushes Democrats and Republicans to Be More Conservative, Especially around Election Time." London School of Economics US Centre. United States Politics and Policy (blog). April 2, 2015. https://blogs.lse .ac.uk/usappblog/2015/04/02/fox-news-pushes-democrats-and-republicans -to-be-more-conservative-especially-around-election-time/.

293 **Fox News is responsible for a significant vote swing:** Martin, Gregory J., and Ali Yurukoglu. "Bias in Cable News: Persuasion and Polarization." *American Economic Review* 107, no. 9 (2017): 2565–99. https://pubs.aeaweb .org/doi/pdf/10.1257/aer.20160812.

293 **non–news watchers were more informed than Fox News watchers:** Rayfield, Jillian. "Study: Watching Fox News Actually Makes You Stupid." *Rolling Stone*. May 24, 2012. https://www.rollingstone.com/politics/politics -news/study-watching-fox-news-actually-makes-you-stupid-235770/.

294 **reach about 40 percent of U.S. households:** Chang, Alvin. "Sinclair's Takeover of Local News, in One Striking Map." Vox. April 6, 2018. https:// www.vox.com/2018/4/6/17202824/sinclair-tribune-map.

294 **as much of a conservative bullhorn as Fox News.:** For a good overview of Sinclair Broadcast Group's reach and conservatism, take a look at the *New Yorker* long-form piece by Sheelah Kolhatkar, "The Growth of Sinclair's Conservative Media Empire" (October 15, 2018): https://www.newyorker

.com/magazine/2018/10/22/the-growth-of-sinclairs-conservative-media
-empire. Wil S. Hylton, though, identified the growing behemoth more than a
decade ago in a long-form piece for *GQ*, "Not Necessarily the News" (December 2005): http://reprints.longform.org/not-necessarily-the-news-hylton.

294 **believes that "99.9 percent of the media is left of center":** Wofford, Ben. "Sinclair Broadcast Group Hostile Takeover." *Rolling Stone*. April 24, 2018. https://www.rollingstone.com/politics/politics-features/sinclair-broad castings-hostile-takeover-629299/.

294 **required to read the exact same script:** Kolhatkar, Sheelah. "The Growth of Sinclair's Conservative Media Empire." *New Yorker*. October 15, 2018. https://www.newyorker.com/magazine/2018/10/22/the-growth-of-sinclairs-con servative-media-empire.

294 **Trump campaign struck a deal with the media giant:** Dawsey, Josh, and Hadas Gold. "Kushner: We Struck Deal with Sinclair for Straighter Coverage." Politico. December 16, 2016. https://politi.co/2IodmRi.

294 **"unfair that the FCC wouldn't approve the Sinclair Broadcast merger":** Gold, Hadas. "Trump Slams His Own Administration's Actions on Sinclair-Tribune Deal." CNN Business. July 25, 2018. https://money.cnn .com/2018/07/25/media/trump-tweet-sinclair-tribune-fcc/index.html.

295 **"Net Neutrality is the First Amendment of the Internet":** Cyril, Malkia. "FCC's Plan to Repeal Net Neutrality Will Silence Black Voices." Root. November 22, 2017. https://www.theroot.com/fcc-s-plan-to-repeal-net-neutrality -will-silence-black-1820676304.

296 **driven dramatic surges—or collapses—in entire sectors of the media:** Hazard Owen, Laura. "One Year in, Facebook's Big Algorithm Change Has Spurred an Angry, Fox News-Dominated—and Very Engaged!— News Feed." Nieman Lab (blog). March 15, 2019. https://www.niemanlab .org/2019/03/one-year-in-facebooks-big-algorithm-change-has-spurred -an-angry-fox-news-dominated-and-very-engaged-news-feed/.

296 **Facebook has instead divided us into warring camps:** Karr, Timothy, and Craig Aaron. "Beyond Fixing Facebook: How the Multibillion-Dollar Business Behind Online Advertising Could Reinvent Public Media, Revitalize Journalism and Strengthen Democracy." Free Press. February 2019. https://www.freepress.net/sites/default/files/2019-02/Beyond-Fixing-Facebook -Final_0.pdf.

296 **Facebook accepted ads from Putin-linked sources:** Shane, Scott. "These Are the Ads Russia Bought on Facebook in 2016." *New York Times*. November 1, 2017, sec. U.S. https://www.nytimes.com/2017/11/01/us/politics /russia-2016-election-facebook.html.

297 **70 percent of all web traffic on the Internet flows through:** Cuthbertson, Anthony. "Who Controls the Internet? Facebook and Google Dominance Could Cause the 'Death of the Web.'" *Newsweek*. November 2, 2017. https:// www.newsweek.com/facebook-google-internet-traffic-net-neutrality -monopoly-699286.

297 **Facebook had just shy of $56 billion in revenue in 2018:** "FB—Facebook Inc Financial Results." CNN Business, n.d. Accessed July 25, 2019. https:// money.cnn.com/quote/financials/financials.html?symb=FB.

297 **Google had about $137 billion:** "Alphabet Announces Fourth Quarter and Fiscal Year 2018 Results." Alphabet, Inc. February 4, 2019. https://abc.xyz /investor/static/pdf/2018Q4_alphabet_earnings_release.pdf.

297 **just behind California in terms of revenue:** "2017 State Tax Revenue." Federation of Tax Administrators, n.d. Accessed July 25, 2019. https://www .taxadmin.org/2017-state-tax-revenue.

297 **it has plans to expand even further:** Fischer, Sara. "Sinclair Plots National Expansion." Axios. April 23, 2019. https://www.axios.com/sinclair-plots -national-broadcasting-expansion-sports-news-514cdaa0-87a7-4ed0-9061 -294d0f8b4b43.html.

299 **an early Facebook investor and mentor to founder:** McNamee, Roger. "I Mentored Mark Zuckerberg. But I Can't Stay Silent About What's Happen- ing." *Time*. January 17, 2019. https://time.com/5505441/mark-zuckerberg -mentor-facebook-downfall/.

299 **"Mark's power is unprecedented and un-American":** Hughes, Chris. "It's Time to Break Up Facebook." *New York Times*. May 14, 2019, sec. Opinion. https://www.nytimes.com/2019/05/09/opinion/sunday/chris-hughes -facebook-zuckerberg.html.

300 **the United States drastically underinvests in media:** Coren, Michael J. "Americans Could Barely Buy a Coffee with What They Spend per Year on Public Media." Quartz. September 9, 2018. https://qz.com/1383503/amer icans-could-barely-buy-a-coffee-with-what-they-spend-per-year-on-public -media/.

301 **proposes a big new "Public Interest Media Endowment":** Karr, Timothy, and Craig Aaron. "Beyond Fixing Facebook: How the Multibillion-Dollar Business Behind Online Advertising Could Reinvent Public Media, Revi- talize Journalism and Strengthen Democracy." Free Press. February 2019. https://www.freepress.net/sites/default/files/2019-02/Beyond-Fixing -Facebook-Final_0.pdf.

301 **which cost about $230 billion per year:** Rogers, David. "Politico Analysis: At $2.3 Trillion Cost, Trump Tax Cuts Leave Big Gap." Politico. February

28, 2018. https://www.politico.com/story/2018/02/28/tax-cuts-trump-gop
-analysis-430781.

301 **Free Press recommends adding a small tax:** Karr, Timothy, and Craig
Aaron. "Beyond Fixing Facebook: How the Multibillion-Dollar Business Behind Online Advertising Could Reinvent Public Media, Revitalize Journalism
and Strengthen Democracy." Free Press. February 2019. https://www.free
press.net/sites/default/files/2019-02/Beyond-Fixing-Facebook-Final_0.pdf.

302 **to fund public media "sinful and tyrannical":** Gonzalez, Mike. " 'Is There
Any Justification for Continuing to Ask Taxpayers to Fund NPR and PBS?' "
Knight Foundation, n.d. Accessed July 25, 2019. https://www.knightfoundation
.org/public-media-white-paper-2017-gonzalez.

303 **carefully guarded from government or from party control:** Califano, Joseph, Jr. "How President Johnson Set the Stage for Passage of the Public
Broadcasting Act." Current. May 5, 2017. https://current.org/2017/05/how
-president-johnson-set-the-stage-for-passage-of-the-public-broadcasting
-act/.

303 **Americans trusted PBS and NPR news more than any other:** "Perceived Accuracy and Bias in the News Media." Gallup, Inc. & Knight Foundation. 2018. https://kf-site-production.s3.amazonaws.com/publications
/pdfs/000/000/255/original/KnightFoundation_AccuracyandBias_Report
_FINAL.pdf.

303 **Even GOP voters oppose cutting funding:** "New National Survey Shows
73 Percent of Voters—Including Most Republicans—Oppose Eliminating
Federal Funding for Public Television." PBS. February 16, 2017. http://
www.pbs.org/about/blogs/news/survey-shows-voters-oppose-eliminating
-federal-funding.